D0575381

BEARS

BEARS

Monarchs of the Northern Wilderness

WAYNE LYNCH

Foreword by Gary Alt   c. 1

The Mountaineers
Seattle, Washington

93 94 95 96 5 4 3 2 1

Published in the U.S.A. in 1993 by The Mountaineers
Founded 1906 "...to explore, study, preserve and
enjoy the natural beauty of the outdoors..."
1011 S.W. Klickitat Way, Seattle, WA 98134

Published simultaneously in Canada by
Greystone Books
Douglas & McIntyre Ltd.
1615 Venables Street
Vancouver, British Columbia
V5L 2H1

Library of Congress Cataloguing-in-Publication Data

Lynch, Wayne.
  Bears : monarchs of the northern wilderness
  / Wayne Lynch,
    p.   cm.
  Includes bibliographical references and
  index.
  ISBN 0-89886-372-4
  1. Bears.   I. Title.
QL737.C27L95   1993
599.74'446-dc20   93-666
                      CIP

The following publishers have given permission to use
quoted material:
From *Polar Bears* by Ian Stirling. Copyright © 1988 by The
University of Michigan. Reprinted by permission of Ian
Stirling and the University of Michigan Press. From
California Grizzly by Tracy I. Storer and Lloyd P. Tevis, Jr.
Copyright © 1955 by the Regents of the University of
California. Reprinted by permission of the University of
California. From *The Giant Pandas of Wolong* by George B.
Schaller, Hu Jinchu, Pan Wenshi and Zhu Jing. Copyright
© 1985 by the University of Chicago. Reprinted by
permission of the University of Chicago. From *The Status and
Conservation of Bears of the World* by Christopher Servheen.
Copyright © 1990 by the International Association for Bear
Research and Management. Reprinted by permission of the
International Association for Bear Research and
Management. From "Piranhas of the Frozen Seas" by Jon
Percy in *Nature Canada*, May 1989. Copyright © 1989 by
Nature Canada. Reprinted by permission of Jon Percy and
Nature Canada.

Editing by Nancy Flight
Text design by Alex Hass
Cover design by Rose Cowles
Maps by Lisa Ireton
Typeset by The Typeworks
Printed and bound in Singapore

To Aubrey,

who shared the vision and the champagne

CONTENTS

PREFACE

When I was a boy, bears were the demons in all of my nightmares. During the day, they lurked in the dark recesses of my imagination, and at night they skulked from the shadows to stalk and chase me. I stopped having those frightening dreams thirty years ago, but I have never stopped thinking about bears. ¶ I first thought about writing a book on bears in September 1982. At the time, I was finishing a book on the ecology of the prairie grasslands, entitled *Married to the Wind*, and I wondered what book project I should tackle next. The prairie book had taken five years to research and write, and I had decided that I wanted my next book to take less time to complete. ¶ I got the idea to write about bears one night as I read Paul Schullery's fine book, *The Bears of Yellowstone*. I thought, "What if I wrote about the bears of the Northern Hemisphere?" Such a book had not been written, and I reasoned that since there were only four species of bears, surely there couldn't be more than a few hundred key references to read and I could finish the book in three years, easily. Aside from my naivete about the amount of technical material published on bears, I didn't count on the seductiveness of the animals themselves. Once I was immersed in the project, I became obsessed with these remarkable animals. ¶ Eventually the book would take nine years to complete. I would review almost ten thousand technical papers and attend dozens of scientific meetings. Over the years, I would take more than thirty thousand photographs, travel over 225 000 kilometres (140,000 miles) visiting all of the major bear habitats in North America and spend hundreds of hours observing bears in the wild. And when it was over, I would lie in bed and wish I could start again. I would become a bear groupie. In fact, I can never imagine a time in my life when I will not be fascinated by bears. ¶ For thousands of years, bears have captivated the human imagination and have become woven into a rich fabric of myths, legends and anecdotes. Such stories are frequently embellished and modified around campfires, where entertainment ranks above accuracy. In addition, the bear has been variously seen as circus clown, roadside beggar, hunting trophy, agricultural pest, zoo entertainer and symbol of the wilderness. Nearly everyone has experienced bears in at least one of these contexts, and yet none of these labels really captures the essence of the bear. My intention in this book is to remove many of the stereotypes and untruths and some of the mystery but none of the magic that surrounds these magnificent carnivores.

Although I hope biologists and bear researchers will find value in this book, I have written it for those who live in bear country and who want a better understanding of the bears with which they live. It is also written for those who visit bear country and want greater knowledge with which to interpret their wilderness ex-

perience. And it is written for those who may never see a bear but who nonetheless want these animals to survive because they fuel the human spirit.

In *Bears: Monarchs of the Northern Wilderness*, you will accompany me on a journey that I never planned. As we delve into the lives of the northern bears, you will discover surprising similarities with our own lives. Bears can be tender and gentle, frightened and angered, and idle and busy. I hope that after reading *Bears* you will understand what it means to be a bear and you will never look at this animal in the same way again. I also hope that the book will influence how you view every other creature with which we share this Earth.

ACKNOWLEDGEMENTS

No one spends nine years chasing after bears without receiving considerable help along the way. The Canada Council, the Alberta Foundation for the Literary Arts, and Alberta Culture awarded me generous grants, and my success in obtaining these grants was due, in part, to the respected recommendations of magazine editors Ian Darragh and Ross Smith, publisher Michael Burch and biologist Dr. David Henry. ¶ Others who helped were David Krygier, general manager of Calberta Manufacturing, who supplied me with a custom parka that always kept me warm, Bob Schimpf, who provided me with uncountable photocopies, and Joe Van Os of Joseph Van Os Photo Safaris, who indirectly funded some of my field work when he hired me as a naturalist on numerous tours to the Arctic. ¶ Ranchers Francis and Myrna Walker had nothing to do with the bear project but everything to do with my life as a freelancer. They supported me in the early years of my career, and I will never forget their generosity. ¶ One of the greatest rewards of working as a science writer is to work with scientists. Over the years I contacted dozens of scientists. They listened patiently to my questions, returned my frequent telephone calls, answered my letters and often invited me to their field camps. More than this, they were always gracious, always understanding and always unselfish in sharing their time, experience and knowledge. Space does not allow me to mention everyone, but I would especially like to thank Steve Amstrup, Tom Barry, Ken Elowe, Steve Emslie, Andy Derocher, Dave Garshelis, John Hechtel, Anne Holcroft, Howard Hunt, Charles Jonkel, Kate Kendall, Wayne McCrory, Ralph Nelson, Peter Oeltgen, Malcolm Ramsay, Don Reid, Joe Rieffenberger, Chris Servheen, Ole Jakob Sorensen, Alasdair Veitch and John Wooding. To all of them I am greatly indebted. ¶ Four scientists deserve special thanks. Dr. Gary Alt, a black bear biologist with the Pennsylvania Game Commission, discussed bears with me for hours, included me often in his field research and gave me confidence to write this book. Biologist Larry Aumiller of the McNeil River Brown Bear Sanctuary believed in me and helped in many ways to bring this book to fruition. Peter Clarkson, the wolf/grizzly biologist for the Northwest Territories, invited me into his home, loaned me his office, took me tagging grizzlies and taught me the difference between bears and pigs. And finally, Dr. Ian Stirling, a polar bear biologist with the Canadian Wildlife Service, and one of the foremost bear biologists in the world, offered me rare opportunities to observe polar bears in the wild and sent me numerous technical papers. All of these men introduced me to the secret world of the bear, and they helped me to understand and appreciate the animal better.

Once I had written the book, I surrendered the text to four respected authorities for technical review: Drs. Gary Alt, Barrie Gilbert, David Henry and Ian Stirl-

ing. To my relief, they were gentle in their criticisms and constructive in their suggestions, and I thank them for their attention to detail.

In fifteen years as a writer, I have never worked with a finer editor than Nancy Flight. She was methodical and professional, and she showed a rare understanding of science. Above all, she was good, and I thank her for improving the text immensely.

Most of all, I am indebted to my wife, Aubrey Lang, to whom this book is dedicated. After seventeen years of marriage, she is still the most interesting and exciting person I know. She was a constant help in the field and in the office, and her unselfish enthusiasm was a continual source of strength and encouragement.

FOREWORD

Evolution endowed bears with a high level of curiosity and an opportunistic feeding strategy that served them well for many thousands of years. But as humans became the dominant force in the bears' environment, this formerly successful strategy often led to their demise. Bears who investigated homesteads did not last long. Perceiving these bears as a threat to their meagre resources and considering them incompatible with human habitation, settlers killed them in defence of their crops and livestock. Bears were also killed for their meat, for their fat, which could be used in cooking, and for their skin, which was marketed or used for clothing. ¶ As many of the forested regions of eastern North America were cleared for farming, black bears became restricted to a shrinking range. In a matter of decades, the massive grasslands of central North America were swallowed up by the settlers, and the plains grizzly went the way of the bison. In western North America, cattle and sheep farmers indiscriminately trapped, shot, and poisoned predators, and as a result the brown bears were quickly exterminated from nearly all their range in the western United States and Mexico. Unfortunately, the frontier mentality persisted long after the frontier was gone. ¶ The settlers had triumphed over the bear. But not everyone celebrated. Some, like Adolph Murie and Aldo Leopold, whose environmental philosophies were not based on economics, began to speak out against the deplorable rape and pillage of natural resources. People gradually started to take more interest in the future of animals like bears, and that interest gave birth to change. National parks were formed to preserve at least some of the remaining natural resources, and laws were enacted and enforced to protect bears and other animals from over-exploitation. During the 1960s, in an extraordinary act of international cooperation, the five polar countries—Canada, Greenland, Norway, the former Soviet Union and the United States—met and jointly agreed to strictly control hunting throughout the Arctic in response to decreasing polar bear populations. As a result, polar bear numbers have increased dramatically since then.

Nevertheless, human activities such as agriculture, deforestation, mining and exploration for oil continue to destroy bear habitat throughout the world. When habitat is lost, there is little we can do to bring back the bears.

But the problem goes far beyond habitat loss. Bears are often needlessly killed, not for what they have done, but for what people think they might do. Many people unjustifiably fear bears and still believe they cannot survive where humans exist. That is a fallacy.

In Pennsylvania, for example, we have learned that if given a chance, black bears can not only survive but actually thrive in the confines of large human developments. For this to happen, however, people have to learn to live with bears and respect them. In many areas it is not the lack of food or cover that limits how many bears can survive—it is human attitudes.

The coexistence of bears and people largely depends on public education. When education replaces fallacies with facts, and fear with respect, humans will become more tolerant and allow bear populations and ranges to expand. The more people learn about bears, the more likely they are to care about the survival of the bears. To that end, *Bears: Monarchs of the Northern Wilderness* makes a valuable contribution not only to the future of the northern bears but to the future of human beings as well, helping to ensure that our children will also enjoy a world with bears.

Dr. Gary Alt
Director of Bear Research,
Pennsylvania Game Commission

INTRODUCTION

The Carnivores

Bears belong to the carnivore group of mammals, and carnivores have always fascinated humankind. When we think of carnivores, we think of large, powerful predators equipped with deadly canine teeth and long, sharp claws. We imagine carnivores to have senses far superior to our own, hunting with stealth, speed and coordination, and dispatching their victims with surgical precision. These attributes, whether real or imagined, have always filled humans with awe and envy. Because of this, we have often used the images of carnivores to adorn our flags, emblems and armour, and killing a large carnivore is still an implied act of bravery and a manifestation of manhood, even when the animal is completely outranked by sophisticated modern weaponry. ¶ Today, out of a total of about 4500 mammals, there are only 231 species of carnivores throughout the world. Carnivores vary in size from the 50-gram (1¾-ounce) least weasel (*Mustela nivalis*) to the 750-kilogram (1653-pound) polar bear, which is fifteen thousand times the weight of the least weasel (Nowak and Paradiso 1983). ¶ A carnivore is not simply a mammal that eats meat. Many mammals that are *not* carnivores include flesh in their diet when the opportunity arises. For example, Franklin ground squirrels (*Spermophilus franklinii*) will eat young birds, arctic hares (*Lepus arcticus*) will scavenge from carcasses, and even caribou (*Rangifer tarandus*) will sometimes eat lemmings. All of the mammals that are classified as carnivores arose from the same ancestors, the miacids, which lived 60 to 70 million years ago (Savage 1977). ¶ The modern carnivores consist of seven families: the dog family, the raccoon family, the weasel family, the mongoose family, the hyena family, the cat family and the bear family. Following is a brief outline of the six families of carnivores related to the bears.

The Dog Family—Family Canidae

There are thirty-five species of canids, including the fox, wolf, coyote and jackal. The canids are medium-sized carnivores adapted to swift running in relatively open terrain. Canids are extremely adaptable and range from solitary hunters to members of highly integrated packs.

The Raccoon Family—Family Procyonidae

The raccoon family includes the ringtail, kinkajou and coati, as well as the raccoon. There are sixteen species of procyonids, and all are small, long-bodied carnivores with long tails. Many have distinctive facial markings, such as masks or spots, and most are nocturnal. Except for the red panda, which lives in the foothills of the Himalayas, all of the procyonids live in the temperate and tropical forests of the Americas.

The Weasel Family—Family Mustelidae

The weasel family, which includes sixty-seven species, is the largest family of carnivores. The mustelids are small to medium-sized carnivores with long bodies and relatively short legs. From the arboreal martens to the burrowing badgers and the aquatic otters, they display a diversity of hunting strategies. All of the mustelids have well-developed anal glands, which produce a thick, strong-smelling fluid called musk. These glands are most developed in the skunks, a subgroup of thirteen mustelids, which have evolved the ability to spray musk to defend themselves. All skunks advertise their weaponry with conspicuous black and white fur.

The Mongoose Family—Family Viverridae

The mongoose family, which contains sixty-six species, is almost as large as the weasel family, and together the two families comprise two-thirds of all living carnivores. Members of the mongoose family, or viverrids, are small carnivores that survive on a general diet of fruit, insects, eggs, reptiles, birds and small mammals. The viverrids closely resemble the miacids, the ancient ancestors of all carnivores, and include not only mongooses but also the civets, genets and meercats. If these animals are unfamiliar to you, it is not surprising, since the viverrids are found only in Africa and southern Asia.

The Hyena Family—Family Hyaenidae

This is the smallest family of carnivores, with only four species. Hyenas are generally large carnivores with strong teeth and jaw muscles, which they use to crush bones. Although hyenas frequently scavenge on the kills of other carnivores, they are capable predators in their own right and prey on many large animals. Today hyenas are restricted to the dry grasslands of Africa and southern Asia, but at one time there were hyenas in North America as well.

The Cat Family—Family Felidae

The felids, all thirty-five species, are the most carnivorous of all the carnivores; plant foods play a very minor role in their diet. All of the felids are efficient predators. They have short jaws and sharp canine teeth to deliver a quick, lethal bite. The felids are widely distributed and are found in every type of habitat from dense forests to deserts.

THE BEAR FAMILY— FAMILY URSIDAE

Bears are large, heavy-bodied carnivores with thick, powerful limbs. They are the largest of the carnivores, and even though the African lion is often touted as the King of Beasts, a lion would be no match for most adult brown bears or polar bears. In the arenas of ancient Rome, where lions were sometimes pitted against brown bears, the lions were invariably killed by the burly bruins. Appendix A discusses this role and other roles of the bear throughout history.

Bears walk on the soles of their feet, as we do, not on their toes, as most other carnivores do. A bear's feet are flat and broad and armed with five heavy, curved claws. When a bear walks, its front feet toe-in, and this rotational mobility enables bears to climb and dig better.

All bears have large heads with small eyes and rounded ears. Their coats are usually long, with very few markings, although many species have a white or

The eyes in all bears face forward, endowing them with binocular vision. Such vision enhances depth perception—an important requirement for a predator.

cream-coloured chest patch, and the giant panda, of course, has very distinctive markings. The shaggy coat of many bears hides their very short tail, which is rarely over 12 centimetres (4¾ inches) long.

Except for the polar bear, bears are predominantly plant eaters, although a number of species will hunt periodically, and all of them will eat meat if the opportunity arises.

The Naming Business

Scientists have always strived to put order into everything they do. Several hundred years ago, the science of taxonomy—the business of assigning a technical name to every living creature—arose. An animal's scientific name not only identifies it to scientists of all nationalities and languages but also identifies an animal's relatedness to other similar animals. For example, con-

sider three different species of bears: the brown bear, the polar bear and the spectacled bear. The scientific name for the brown bear is *Ursus arctos*, for the polar bear it is *Ursus maritimus*, and for the spectacled bear it is *Tremarctos ornatus*. The fact that the brown bear and the polar bear share the same genus, *Ursus*, shows that they are more closely related to each other than either is to the spectacled bear, which belongs to a different genus, *Tremarctos*.

Early in the business of taxonomy, bears, and all other mammals, were assigned their scientific names based primarily on characteristics of their skeletons, as well as certain behavioural traits that they shared with presumably closely related species. What early taxonomists failed to recognize was that the behaviour *and* the skeleton of an animal species may vary tremendously, depending on where the animal lives. Thus, taxonomists often assigned a new scientific name to a member of a known species when it came from a different geographical location. They assumed that because there were minor differences it must be a new species, when in fact it was just a local variant of a single wide-ranging species.

In 1918, C. H. Merriam identified eighty-six kinds of grizzlies and brown bears in North America alone (Merriam 1918). We now recognize only *one* species of brown bear, which ranges from the Cantabrian Mountains of Spain across the breadth of the former Soviet Union into Alaska and down through western Canada into the northern United States. Today, in different parts of North America, the brown bear is called the coastal brown bear, the Alaskan brown bear, the Kodiak bear or the grizzly bear, but whichever common name you assign to the animal there is still only one species of brown bear in the world—*Ursus arctos*.

The methods used in taxonomy today are much more sophisticated than they were in the days of Merriam. Now scientists use complex molecular techniques to compare blood proteins and analyze the chromosomes to determine the relatedness between species (Nash and O'Brien 1987). Still, many bear biologists do not completely agree with the scientific names chosen for some of the bears, in particular, two of the tropical bears—the sun bear and the sloth bear. Nonetheless, in view of the findings of recent molecular studies (Golden, Giri and O'Brien 1989), I have included these two tropical bears in the common genus *Ursus*.

Bear Species

Although there is disagreement about what to call some of the tropical bears, everyone at least recognizes that there are eight species of bears in the world:

Northern Bears
- the polar bear, *Ursus maritimus*
- the brown bear, *Ursus arctos*
- the Asiatic black bear, *Ursus thibetanus*
- the American black bear, *Ursus americanus*

Tropical Bears
- the sloth bear, *Ursus ursinus*
- the sun bear, *Ursus malayanus*
- the spectacled bear, *Tremarctos ornatus*
- the giant panda, *Ailuropoda melanoleuca*

It is natural to discuss the four northern species together for a number of reasons. First, only the northern bears have been studied to any degree, and there is a wealth of information available on the polar bear, the brown bear and the American black bear. Research is only beginning on the fourth northern bear, the Asiatic black bear, but I have included the Asiatic black bear in the text because it seems to fill the same niche in Asia as the American black bear fills in North America, and the two species lend themselves readily to comparisons.

A second reason to group the northern bears together is that they are closely related to each other and they share a common scientific group, the genus *Ursus*. The tropical bears are a more diversely related group, since three distinct genera are represented.

A third link among the northern bears is that they share similar northern environments, and the ranges of the different species often overlap.

Finally, only the northern bears hibernate; this fascinating metabolic adaptation to winter is not seen in any of the tropical bears.

Scientists know very little about any of the four species of tropical bears, with the possible exception of the giant panda, which has been studied somewhat in the last ten to fifteen years. Appendix B contains a summary of our current knowledge of these four species of bears.

Following is a brief description of each of the four species of northern bears and where they are found.

The polar bear has the smallest ears of any of the northern bears— an adaptation to minimize the loss of body heat.

THE POLAR BEAR

The magnificent polar bear is arguably the largest of all of the bears, although some coastal brown bears can reach the size of the largest polar bears. Adult male polar bears weigh between 300 and 800 kilograms (between about 660 and 1765 pounds). Standing on all fours, a large male polar bear may be 1.5 metres (5 feet) at the shoulder and stretch 3 metres (10 feet) from the tip of its nose to the tip of its tail. If a huge male polar bear were to suddenly rear up on its hind legs immediately in front of you, the animal's massive size and its 3.5-metre (11-foot) height would instantly concentrate your thoughts on the afterlife. Female northern bears are usually half to three-quarters the size of males, and female polar bears average between 150 and 350 kilograms (between about 330 and 772 pounds) (DeMaster and Stirling 1981).

Polar bears range in colour from silvery white to a light yellow or straw colour. Cubs are always pure white, but some bears, especially adult males, turn yellow as they get older. Some researchers have suggested that the colour of a polar bear's fur changes with the seasons and that the fur is whitest when the bears molt in the summer and then gradually yellows afterwards from oxidation by the sun.

The only other noticeable colour on a polar bear is black, which is the colour of the animal's nose, lips, tongue and claws. A polar bear's claws, which are often hidden by the long fur on its feet, are thick and slightly curved and may be up to 6.5 centimetres (2 inches) long. The claws on a bear's foot, unlike the claws of most cats, are not retractable, so they rub against the ground when the animal walks. Nonetheless, polar bear claws are surprisingly sharp.

The scientific name for the polar bear is *Ursus maritimus*, which means "sea bear," and polar bears are found in the northern marine areas of Alaska, the Commonwealth of Independent States, Norway's Svalbard Archipelago, Greenland and Canada (Figure I.I).

The silvery-white coat of these two young polar bear cubs contrasts with the yellowish-white fur of their adult mother.

The polar bear occupies more of its original range than any of the other species. Scientists estimate that there are 25,000 to 40,000 polar bears throughout the world, divided into approximately six or more core populations. Polar bears within each core population stay roughly within their own area of the Arctic and generally do not mingle with bears of other populations. These core populations are often centred on traditional denning and seal-hunting areas.

In the 1960s, the world's polar bear population was estimated to be half of what it is today. Strict controls on hunting and remarkable international cooperation among the five polar nations where the bears are found have permitted the population to increase to its present size.

Today the world polar bear population is thought to be reasonably stable, and bears are hunted by native people in Greenland, Alaska and Canada. The average annual harvest of polar bears in these three areas is over a thousand animals, seven hundred of which are shot in Canada.

THE BROWN BEAR

In 1814, Governor DeWitt Clinton spoke to the Philosophical Society of New York about grizzly bears in the frontier regions along the Missouri River, calling them "the terror of the savages, the tyrant of all other animals, devouring alike man and beast and defying the attack of whole tribes of Indians." What Clinton failed to tell his urban audience was that the grizzly bear was usually only ferocious when defending itself

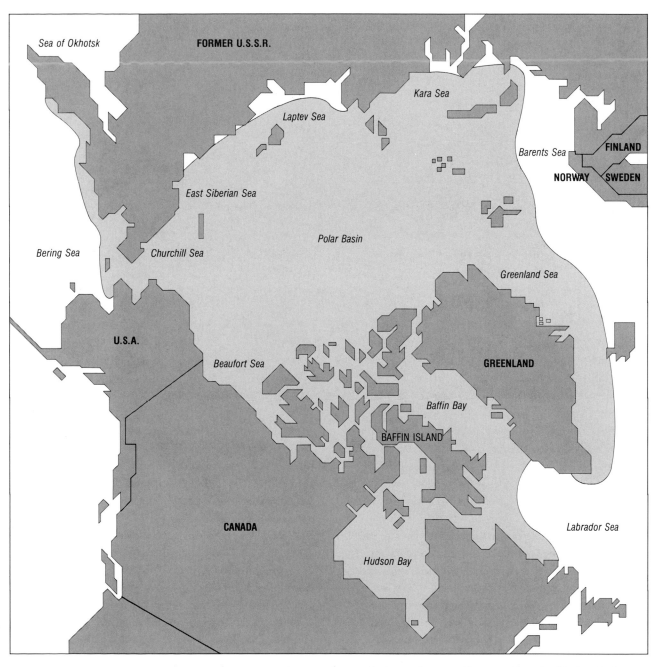

Figure I.1 *The estimated distribution of the polar bear,* Ursus maritimus, *in the arctic seas adjacent to Canada, Alaska, the former Soviet Union, Greenland and Norway (Stirling and Guravich 1988).*

This 1½-year-old brown bear was photographed in June. The bear's coat will bleach during the summer months, and it will be even more blond by the time the bear dens in the fall.

and its offspring, and only after they had been chased and wounded with arrows and rifle balls. Humans have always maligned wild animals that could ably defend themselves, and the grizzly bear, along with brown bears everywhere, has long been mistreated and misunderstood.

The brown bear's present range may cover a greater area of land than even that of the polar bear. From edge to edge, extending from northern Spain eastward to Yellowstone National Park the brown bear's global range is nearly 29 000 kilometres (18,020 miles) wide.

Within its vast range, the brown bear exhibits tremendous variation in colour. Brown bears may be bleached blonds or brunet, auburn or almost black. Often the colour is not uniform, and the legs on many a brown bear may be markedly darker than the animal's

back or flanks. Within a single population, brown bears may display an entire spectrum of colours and tones. On Kodiak Island, in Alaska, for example, 6 per cent of the brown bears were blond, 15 per cent were light brown, 36 per cent were medium brown, and 43 per cent were dark brown (Troyer and Hensel 1969).

Brown bear cubs often have a distinctive white, tan or cream-coloured collar partially or completely encircling their necks. The band of light fur usually disappears by the time the young bears are two years old. In Russia and North America, the fur on some brown bears has a frosted appearance. The long guard hairs in the coats of these bears is tipped with white or tan, giving the animal a grizzled appearance. This is the derivation of the common name grizzly bear, or silvertip.

The front claws of a brown bear vary in colour from ivory to black, with dark brown being the most common shade. Pale-coloured claws, such as those pictured, are usually seen in older bears.

Henry Kelsey, a Hudson Bay Company employee in the late 1600s, was the first European to describe the appearance of the North American grizzly, or brown bear. Kelsey kept an extensive journal of his travels on the Canadian prairies, and he first mentions the grizzly bear in his journal entry for 20 August 1691: "this plain affords nothing but short Round sticky grass & Buffilo & a great sort of a Bear that is neither White nor Black But silver hair'd like our English Rabbit."

Whichever colour the bear is, and wherever it lives in Eurasia or North America, the acceptable common name for *Ursus arctos* is the brown bear. To distinguish interior brown bears in North America from coastal brown bears, however, the interior bears are often called grizzly bears, whether they have grizzled fur or not. Throughout the text, I have commonly used the name brown bear, but occasionally I use "grizzly" when referring to interior brown bears. The important point to remember is that grizzlies and brown bears are the same animal.

Brown bears occupy a great many different habitats, from rich coastal areas to sparsely vegetated arctic tundra. A bear's adult size depends greatly on where the bear lives and what it eats. The average male brown bear—if there is such a beast—weighs between 150 and 380 kilograms (between 330 and 838 pounds), stands a little over a metre (3¼ feet) tall at the shoulder, and is slightly over 2 metres (6 feet) in body length (Craighead and Mitchell 1982).

Brown bears that fish for salmon in rich coastal regions skew the weight curves upwards. These bears are the largest of their kind, and males commonly weigh over 0.5 metric tons (½ ton), with some exceptional individuals exceeding 680 kilograms (1500 pounds). The largest of these bears stands 1.5 metres (5 feet) tall at the shoulder and is 2.5 metres (8¼ feet) long.

You will likely see the tracks of a brown bear more often than the animal itself, and you may wonder whether you can determine the size of a bear from the size of its tracks. The rear track of a large male brown

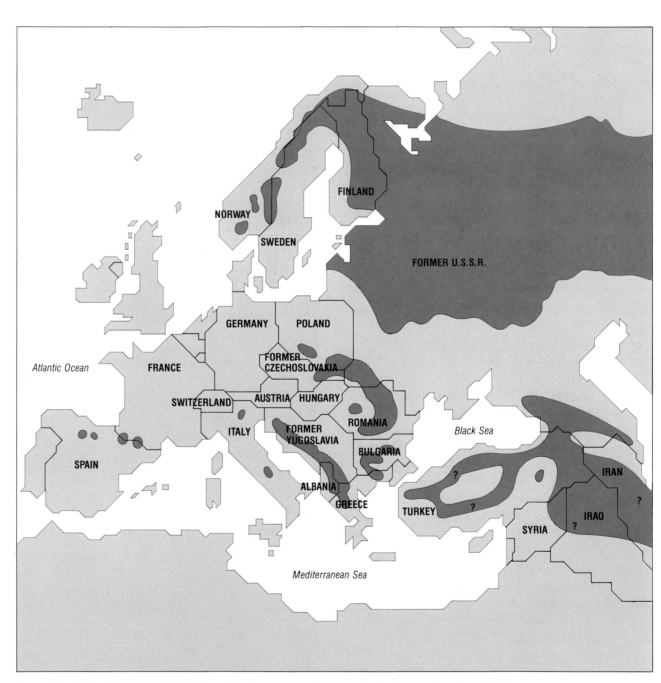

Figure I.2 Estimated current distribution of the brown bear, Ursus arctos, **in Europe (Servheen 1990).**

A young brown bear has all of its permanent teeth except its canines by the time it is ten months of age. The canine teeth finish growing in the bear's fifth summer.

bear may be truly immense, measuring as much as 35 centimetres (14 inches) in length and 20 centimetres (8 inches) in width. Unfortunately, the size of a bear's track does not increase at the same rate as its body weight, and some heavy bears have relatively small feet. About all you can tell from the tracks is whether they belong to a cub, juvenile or adult bear. Beyond that point, a tracker cannot distinguish between the tracks of an adult female and those of an adult male unless the tracks are exceptionally large; it may then be safe to assume they were made by a large adult male.

Every popular writer mentions the immense claws of the brown bear, and I keep a record of some of the more colourful descriptions I have read. I am particularly entertained by writers who pad their prose with melodrama such as "the bear wielded its claws like weapons of wanton destruction," and "the hunter was doomed under the assault of the grizzly's claws which the animal flailed like ripping rapiers of death." The claws of the brown bear are certainly a noticeable feature of the bear's anatomy, but they evolved as digging tools, not as "weapons of wanton destruction." The claws vary in colour from black to ivory, with dark brown being the most common colour. The claws are large, strong and slightly curved, and the front claws are about 1¾ times longer than the rear claws. The front claws on many brown bears may be 9 centimetres (3 inches) long, and I have measured claws that were over 12 centimetres (4¾ inches) long.

Today it is estimated that the world population of brown bears is between 125,000 and 150,000 animals. In Spain, France and Italy, small remnant populations of 100 bears or less still manage to survive in the locations shown in Figure I.2 (Servheen 1990).

In the former Soviet Union, there are an estimated 100,000 brown bears, the lion's share of the total world population. The bears occupy a range of habitats from temperate forest to tundra, but the greatest number of bears are found in the vast expanse of coniferous forest that covers the breadth of that nation (Figure I.3).

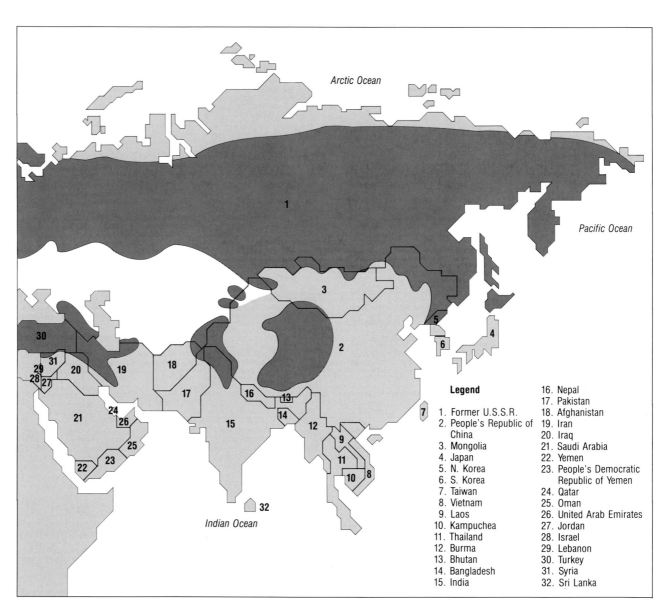

Legend

1. Former U.S.S.R.
2. People's Republic of China
3. Mongolia
4. Japan
5. N. Korea
6. S. Korea
7. Taiwan
8. Vietnam
9. Laos
10. Kampuchea
11. Thailand
12. Burma
13. Bhutan
14. Bangladesh
15. India
16. Nepal
17. Pakistan
18. Afghanistan
19. Iran
20. Iraq
21. Saudi Arabia
22. Yemen
23. People's Democratic Republic of Yemen
24. Qatar
25. Oman
26. United Arab Emirates
27. Jordan
28. Israel
29. Lebanon
30. Turkey
31. Syria
32. Sri Lanka

Figure I.3 Estimated current distribution of the brown bear, Ursus arctos, in Eurasia (Servheen 1990).

In North America in 1800, the brown bear ranged from northern Alaska to northern Mexico, and the continent was home to an estimated 100,000 brown bears (Figure I.4). The decline of the brown bear on this continent has been almost as drastic as it was in Europe (Brown 1985). In North America today, there are

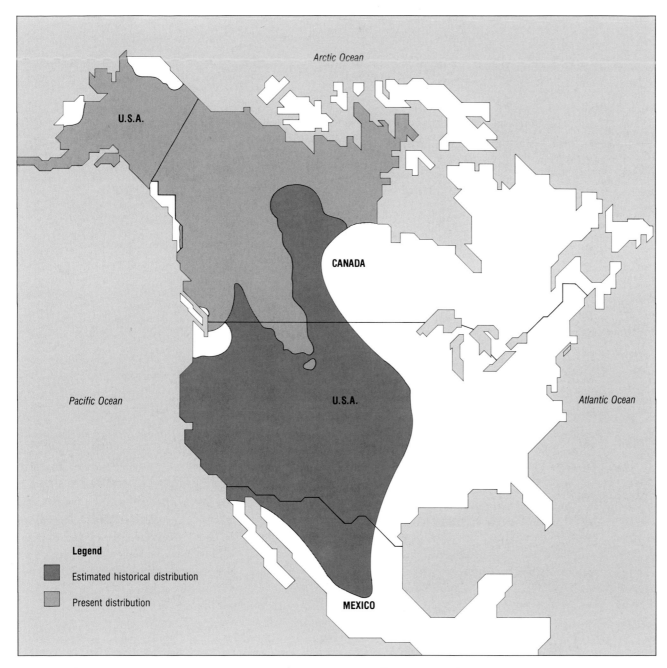

Figure I.4 Distribution of the brown bear, Ursus arctos, *in North America (Servheen 1990).*

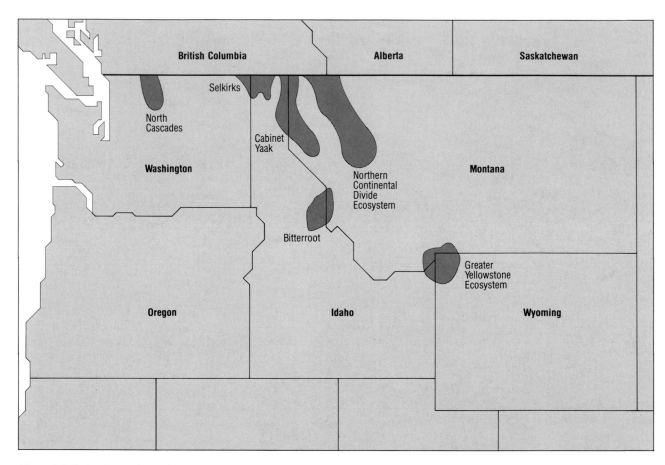

Figure I.5 *Today fewer than a thousand brown bears are found within the six remnant populations that occur in the lower forty-eight states. Most of the bears are in two areas, the Northern Continental Divide Ecosystem and the Greater Yellowstone Ecosystem (Servheen 1990).*

about 40,000 to 50,000 brown bears, which are evenly divided between Canada and the United States (Servheen 1990; Banci 1991). Most of the brown bears in the United States are found in Alaska. In the lower forty-eight states, there are fewer than 1000 brown bears left, and the bears occupy less than 1 per cent of their original range (Figure I.5).

THE ASIATIC BLACK BEAR

The Asiatic black bear, also called the Himalayan black bear, lives in moist, broadleafed forests through-

out much of southern Asia. Its range extends from Pakistan, and possibly Afghanistan, eastward over northern India into China and Southeast Asia. Separate populations also occur in eastern Russia and Korea, in Taiwan and in Japan (Figure I.6). It is not known how many Asiatic black bears live in each area.

The Asiatic black bear is smaller than the brown bear, with which it shares part of its range. Male black bears weigh between 110 and 150 kilograms (between 243 and 331 pounds), but in autumn large individuals sometimes reach 180 kilograms (397 pounds). The

The head of an Asiatic black bear is framed by a thick mane of fur, making the animal's head appear much larger than it is.

adult females, as usual, are smaller and weigh between 65 and 90 kilograms (between 143 and 198 pounds), but some may weigh as little as 47 kilograms (104 pounds). When walking on all fours, a large adult male bear may be a metre (3¼ feet) tall at the shoulder and 1.5 to 2 metres (5 to 6 feet) long from from its nose to its tail (Nowak and Paradiso 1983; Prater 1971).

The Asiatic black bear is similar in size and habits to the American black bear, although the black bear in North America sometimes gets much larger when it lives in an area offering a rich diet. Paleontologists believe that the Asiatic and the American black bears shared a common ancestor, *Ursus abstrusus*, as recently as three to four million years ago. At that time, this small, primitive black bear occurred in both Asia and North America. During the Ice Age that followed, *Ursus abstrusus* gradually evolved into today's American and Asiatic black bears (Kurtén and Anderson 1980).

Asiatic black bears have a dense coat of shiny black fur, though on rare occasions their coat may be a dark reddish-brown. The bear's head is framed by a thick mane of fur. The fringe of fur is longest on the sides of the animal's neck, where the hair can be over 15 centimetres (6 inches) long, making the bear's head appear much larger than it is.

Other names for the Asiatic black bear are moon bear and white-breasted bear. These names originate from the large patch of cream-coloured or yellowish-white fur on the bear's chest. The patch of fur is often crescent-shaped, like a moon—hence the name moon bear. The bear also has white or cream-coloured fur on its chin and along its lower lip. The bear's mane and the white fur on its chin readily distinguish the Asiatic black bear from its close American relative.

Like the American black bear, the Asiatic black bear climbs well, and both species often forage and rest in the tops of trees. Both species have strong, sharply curved claws that are relatively short, about 4 to 5 centimetres (1 to 2 inches) long. In addition, both black bears have very little fur on the underside of their feet.

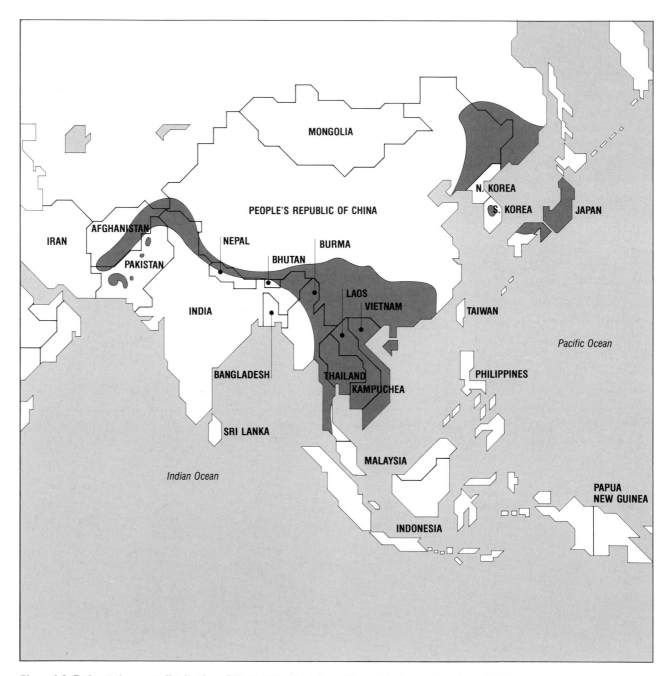

Figure I.6 Estimated current distribution of the Asiatic black bear, Ursus thibetanus *(Servheen 1990).*

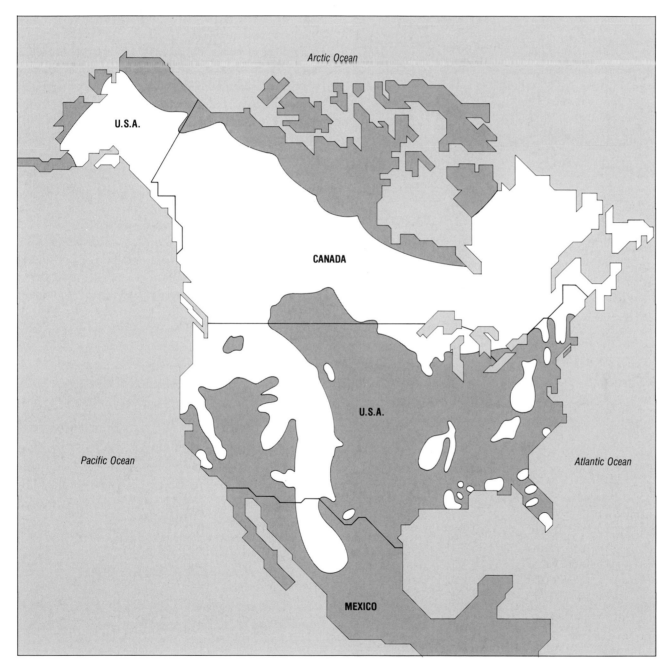

Figure I.7 Estimated current distribution of the American black bear, Ursus americanus *(Servheen 1990).*

It is commonly believed that a standing bear is an aggressive bear about to charge. Actually, when a bear stands on its hind legs, as this American black bear is doing, it is simply trying to see better so that it can decide what to do next.

The sharply curved claws and the furless soles are adaptations to climbing.

In the mid-1980s, the Asiatic black bear became the source of great excitement among bear biologists. For years, villagers from the Barun Valley in Nepal, 24 kilometres (15 miles) southeast of Mount Everest, had said there was another kind of bear besides the Asiatic black bear living in their secluded mountain valley. When scientists trekked into the valley in 1983, they hoped to discover a new species of bear, the Nepali tree bear. The two bears were believed to have different habits and to occupy different ecological niches.

The tree bear was the same colour and had markings similar to those of the Asiatic black bear, but the tree bear had a thicker mane around the collar. A fully grown tree bear was believed to weigh only half as much as an adult Asiatic black bear. Furthermore, local knowledge had it that the black bear was primarily terrestrial, whereas the tree bear spent most of its time aloft, where it constructed complex nests of branches on which it ate and slept (Taylor-Ide 1984).

Science is a heartless, impartial judge, and it soon brought down those who thought they might have discovered something new high in the trees of Nepal. Indeed, the Nepali tree bear *did* spend most of its time in trees. It *did* build elaborate nests, and it even turned out to be much smaller than the Asiatic black bear. What it did *not* turn out to be was a new species. The Nepali tree bears were simply juvenile Asiatic black bears, probably occupying a different niche to avoid conflict and competition with larger adult bears.

THE AMERICAN BLACK BEAR

The American black bear, *Ursus americanus*, outnumbers all of the other northern bears bears combined, with a total population of somewhere around 450,000 animals (Servheen 1990). In many areas, the number of black bears is increasing. In the northeastern United States, one reason for the increase in

About a quarter of all American black bears have a white chest blaze, which is present from the time the animal is a month old.

bears is that abandoned farms, formerly cleared by the early settlers, have begun to revert to forests, creating ideal habitat for black bears. Another factor contributing to the increase in black bears is the change in the animal's status from vermin to valued big-game animal. This change has led to better management of bear populations everywhere. Furthermore, the widespread use of poisons has been banned from most public lands, and as a consequence, fewer bears are now indiscriminately killed.

Probably the factor that has contributed most to the black bear's success is the animal's adaptable nature and its ability to coexist with humans. Black bears can, and do, live in association with people if they are given the chance. A good example of this is seen in a housing development in northeastern Pennsylvania. There are over two thousand homes in this forested housing development, called Hemlock Farms, covering an area of less than 20 square kilometres (8 square miles). As Pennsylvania bear biologist Dr. Gary Alt says, "If you showed this area to most of the bear experts in the world they would likely say that it is impossible for any bear to exist in a place like this. Yet, more than 20 black bears live in this housing development. In fact, one female bear raised 29 cubs in 10 years, a world's record, without losing a single cub." Alt concludes: "It isn't the bears that lack the ability to adapt, it's the people. And the problem is, it isn't what the bears *do* that frightens people as much as what the people *think* they might do."

The adaptable black bear is found throughout the forested regions of North America, and as shown in Figure I.7, the black bear is found in a large portion of northern Mexico, in all of Canada's provinces and territories except Prince Edward Island, and in thirty-two of the fifty American states (Servheen 1990). The black bear also thrives in a greater variety of habitats than any other bear. Black bears are found in the temperate rain forests of the Pacific coast, in the boreal forest that stretches across the breadth of the continent from

Alaska to Newfoundland, beyond the treeline in the Ungava Peninsula of northern Quebec and even out onto the sea ice along the coast of Labrador, an area that seems more suited to polar bears than black bears. The versatile black bear also flourishes in the desert scrub of Arizona, in the hardwood forests of the eastern states, in the cypress swamps of Georgia and Florida, and in the gigantic redwood forests of California.

The diet of the black bear varies from one region to another, and over time, the different diets have helped produce different-sized bears. Average weights range from 40 to 70 kilograms (88 to 154 pounds) for adult females and from 60 to 140 kilograms (132 to 309 pounds) for adult males. The dimensions of the bears are similar to those of the Asiatic black bear (Pelton 1982).

Despite these average values, male black bears weighing over 272 kilograms (600 pounds) are reported in many areas of eastern North America, and there is even a report of a 364-kilogram (802-pound) male bear from Riding Mountain National Park in southern Manitoba. A black bear of that size is larger than most interior brown bears in North America.

American black bears, unlike their Asiatic counterparts, are not always black, and the bears occur in a number of different colour phases. Many carnivores, especially some canids, occur in a range of colours. Wolves (*Canis lupus*) may be grey, black or white. The arctic fox (*Alopex lagopus*), in its winter coat, may be either all white or a dull slate grey, and the red fox (*Vulpes vulpes*), especially those animals that live in cold regions, can be red, black (the so-called "silver" fox) or a beautiful grey and red combination referred to as a "cross" fox. The American black bear, however, shows the greatest colour variation of any of the carnivores.

Nearly all of the black bears in Alaska, northern Canada and the eastern third of the continent from Newfoundland to Florida are black. Like all black bears, the muzzle on these bears is often tan or brown, and some of them have a small white or cream-coloured chest blaze. As you move west and south, the black bears occur in a variety of shades of brown, including cinnamon, honey, light brown and dark chocolate. In Minnesota, 6 per cent of the black bears are brown; in central British Columbia, 40 per cent are brown; and in Idaho 63 per cent are brown. In some areas of Arizona more than 95 per cent of the black bears are shades of brown (Cowan 1938; Rounds 1987). Danvir, Lindzey and Chapman (1983) reported that of the black bears in Utah, 28 per cent were black, 43 per cent were brown, 17 per cent were cinnamon, and 12 per cent were blond.

In general, brown-coloured black bears are more common in open areas. Black livestock are known to absorb greater quantities of solar energy and are more likely to suffer from heat stress than lighter-coloured livestock. The same may apply to bears, and the light brown coats of many animals in the warm areas of the American Southwest may be a strategy to reduce heat stress (Alt 1981; Rogers 1980).

In the Pinaleño Mountains of Arizona, Waddell and Brown (1984) found that there was a tendency for the darker bears to be found on the cooler and wetter northern side of the mountain. Most of the paler brown-coloured bears, and all the blond bears, were found on the drier and warmer south slopes.

The rarest colour phase of the black bear is seen in the so-called glacier bear. I have only seen this bear in captivity, and although its fur is often described as blue, I would describe the colour as grey. The glacier bear is only found in a small area of northwestern British Columbia and southeastern Alaska. Most of the black bears in this heavily forested coastal region are actually black, and the blue colour phase is quite rare.

For me, the most beautiful colour phase of the black bear is seen in the white Kermode bear, which is found in west-central British Columbia. It is most abundant in several offshore islands along the coast. The yellowish-white Kermode bear with its ivory-coloured claws is not an albino. It has brown eyes and a black

The Tshimshian-speaking people of coastal British Columbia believed that the Kermode bear, a rare white colour phase of the American black bear, had great spiritual power.

nose like most black bears. I have seen a photograph of a white Kermode bear with two black cubs, and another picture of a black mother bear with one black cub and one white cub.

The rest of the book discusses the four northern bear species simultaneously, following them through the months of the year. You will find out how each bear is adapted to its own environment and how its environment, in turn, has influenced the individual bear's behaviour. You will also learn what each species of bear is doing at different times of the year and discover the differences and similarities that exist between the species.

When all the dangerous cliffs are fenced off, all of the trees that might fall on people are cut down, all of the insects that bite have been poisoned . . . and all of the grizzlies are dead because they are occasionally dangerous, the wilderness will not be made safe. Rather, the safety will have destroyed the wilderness.

—R. Yorke Edwards,
Canadian
environmentalist

The first time I handled a bear cub was on a picture-perfect afternoon in March 1986. I had struggled up a mountain in western Alberta with the late biologist Orvall Pall to a thick stand of lodgepole pine where a mother black bear and her two cubs were denned. ¶ As we approached the bear den, I could clearly hear the squeal of cubs from 10 metres (33 feet) away. The bear family was home. The sound of the cubs made my heart race. I prepared myself for the mother bear to erupt from her den, eyes ablaze, roaring and drooling, and with flailing claws to tear Orvall and me to shreds. But the mother bear had never read a hunting magazine and didn't know the proper way to react to our intrusion. Instead, she remained placidly inside her den after she was darted, as I have seen many other bears do since then. ¶ Once the mother bear was anesthetized, we pulled the bear family out of its den. The cubs whined like babies and clung to my chest like Velcro. The young bears were less than two months old and weighed only 2 to 3 kilograms (4½ to 6½ pounds) each. When I stuck the smallest one inside my coat to keep it warm, it squirmed to the top of my shoulder, nestled its nose against the base of my neck and fell asleep. ¶ It is exhilarating to touch a wild creature, and I savoured the moment as I squatted beside the mother bear. I ran my fingers slowly through her fur, buried my nose in her pelt to inhale the scent of wildness, and examined her body with medical precision. I wanted to know bears as well as I could. When I examined the curve of her claws and the points on her teeth, I didn't see instruments of injury but tools of survival. On that afternoon in March, I discovered another side of the bear, the side that is never publicized, the vulnerable side. ¶ For bear biologists,

March is the month for "den work"—relocating radio-collared bears in their dens to examine the new litters of cubs. At this time of the year, bears are near the end of their winter hibernation. When bears hibernate, they do not eat, drink, urinate, or defecate for months at a time, a metabolic feat unmatched in the animal world. Scientists have unravelled many of the secrets of bear hibernation, some of which are relevant to human medicine.

A BEAR IN HIBERNATION— DOWN BUT NOT OUT

Black bears and brown bears den for the same reason that most other mammals den—to conserve energy at a time of the year when weather conditions are severe and food is scarce. For polar bears, denning is primarily a reproductive strategy. A den is a sheltered environment in which to have cubs, and normally only pregnant female polar bears den in the winter. All of the other polar bears in a population spend the winter hunting on the sea ice.

Most brown bears and black bears den for 4 to 6 months every year—a third to half of their lives. Denning consumes more time in a bear's life than any other activity. Black bears from southern Alaska, near the northern extreme of the species' range, spend the longest recorded times in dens; they routinely den for 6 to 7 months. The record is held by an adult female bear that denned for 247 days—8¼ months (Schwartz, Miller and Franzmann 1987).

While in their winter dens, bears, like most other mammals, are dormant, a phenomenon commonly called hibernation. Although many mammals—including such unrelated species as tenrecs, echidnas, dwarf lemurs, bats, rodents and bears—are said to hibernate, the details of how these different animals undergo their dormancy often vary considerably (Lyman et al. 1982; French 1988).

Hibernation has been studied most thoroughly in ro-dents, especially in North American ground squirrels. When a ground squirrel slips into hibernation, most of its bodily functions slow down drastically. Over the course of a day or two, the animal's heart rate will plunge from a blurring five hundred to six hundred beats per minute to a modest twenty-five beats or less, its metabolism will drop to 1/25 of its normal level, and its body temperature will chill to within freezing. The body temperature of the arctic ground squirrel (*Spermophilus parryii*), the most northerly ranging ground squirrel, may even dip below the freezing point, to −2.9° C (26° F) (Barnes 1989).

Once a ground squirrel is deep in hibernation, it appears dead. The animal is curled into a tight little ball, with its head tucked between its legs and its long, bushy tail wrapped around its body for insulation. With a body temperature hovering around the freezing point, it is not surprising that the hibernating ground squirrel is unresponsive and feels cold to the touch.

Hibernation is a method to conserve energy, so once a ground squirrel has reached this depth of torpidity, the best strategy would be for the animal to remain like that until spring, burning as little energy as possible. However, this is not what happens. Ground squirrels, and all other hibernators, wake up periodically throughout the winter and rev their heart rates and body temperatures back up to normal.

The front half of the ground squirrel's body "wakes up" first as the temperature inside its chest and head begins to rise. It is unclear how the animal generates all of the heat necessary to raise its body temperature, but some of the heat probably comes from the animal's heart. At body temperatures near freezing, the squirrel's blood is thick and the flow through its blood vessels is sluggish. These factors force the heart to pump harder than normal, and the extra work generates added heat. Once the ground squirrel's body temperature begins to rise, the animal starts to shiver violently, and these involuntary muscle contractions generate the additional heat needed to raise its temperature completely back up to normal.

It takes a tremendous amount of energy for a ground squirrel to arouse itself from deep hibernation. It has been estimated that the energetic cost of one arousal is the same as for ten days of hibernation, and a ground squirrel arouses itself many times throughout the winter, usually once every week or two.

It is clear that ground squirrels *must* arouse themselves from hibernation, but it is not so clear *why* they must. There are probably numerous metabolic reasons, one of which is the need to periodically urinate and eliminate waste products from their bodies. After a denning ground squirrel has relieved itself, it usually slips back into hibernation within twenty-four hours.

For a long time, most people assumed that since bears disappear in the winter, they probably hibernate in the same way as ground squirrels. It was not until 1958 that "hiberniks" (the nickname that hibernation researchers give themselves) began to examine winter dormancy in bears. They soon learned that although the bodily functions of denning bears slow down in winter, the reductions are much less dramatic than in deep hibernators such as the ground squirrel (Folk 1967; Watts et al 1981; Watts and Jonkel 1988).

A hibernating bear's heart rate drops from forty to seventy beats per minute to about eight to twelve beats per minute, its metabolism slows down by a half, and its body temperature drops only slightly, by 3 to 7C° (5 to 9F°). In fact, if a bear's body temperature falls below 20°C (68°F), the animal has a cardiac arrest.

In milder regions, such as North Carolina, Florida and Louisiana, a hibernating black bear, unlike a hibernating ground squirrel, is often completely awake. If you look inside a bear den, the animal may lift its head and look back at you, and if the bear feels in danger it may get up and run away. In more northern areas, however, the bears appear to slump into a deeper hibernation. Researchers found that denning black bears in Minnesota commonly did not awaken until after several minutes of prodding and handling,

During hibernation, the body temperature of an arctic ground squirrel may drop below freezing. By a process of supercooling, the squirrel is able to prevent ice crystals from forming in its tissues.

Most adult black bears, including mother bears, hibernate during the winter, but newborn cubs do not; they remain alert and active.

and if the animals tried to run away, their movements were initially slow and stiff. Similarly, in Pennsylvania biologists reported that some hibernating bears did not even raise their heads until they were poked two or three times. In Tennessee, bears that fled from their dens often moved away very slowly. Recent research has revealed that blood flow to the muscles of hibernating bears is restricted and may explain why the movements of some bears are slow and awkward when they first awaken from hibernation (Rogers 1987; Rogers and Durst 1987).

Most denning studies are of American black bears, not Asiatic black bears, brown bears or polar bears, though it is likely that the details are the same in all four species. American black bears are less aggressive towards researchers and more apt to stay inside their dens or, at worst, run away. Polar bears and brown bears, in contrast, may charge any person who ventures too near their dens; this predisposition naturally tends to stifle scientific curiosity.

Some researchers refer to bear hibernation as winter sleep, winter dormancy, or carnivorean lethargy to differentiate it from the deep hibernation of ground squirrels, which they call true hibernation. Regardless of what you call the process, all hibernating mammals are attempting to achieve the same thing: to conserve energy and lessen the drain on their fat reserves, which they rely on to fuel them through the winter months.

Since the bodily functions of a hibernating bear do not slow down nearly as much as those of the ground squirrel, you might conclude that the bear is a less capable hibernator. You would be right if it were not for the fact that the ground squirrel must arouse itself repeatedly throughout the denning period to urinate and sometimes to defecate. The bear, however, will not urinate or defecate for five to six months or more, and once it slips into hibernation, it remains in this energy-conserving state for the entire denning period. This is a remarkable feat of physiology, unique to the hibernating bear.

While hibernating, bears live off their thick layer of fat and may lose a quarter to a third of their body weight. Brown bears on Kodiak Island, Alaska, lose 45 kilograms (100 pounds) or more during the winter.

Normally, when mammals starve themselves, they burn a small amount of muscle protein as well as fat. The metabolic wastes from the breakdown of the protein, chiefly urea, are dangerous and must be eliminated in the urine or else the animal will eventually die from urea poisoning. Because bears do not urinate while they are hibernating, they have evolved a unique method to deal with the buildup of urea. They simply recycle it, using the constituents of urea to manufacture new proteins.

Sometimes the most esoteric discoveries in science have far-reaching implications. Urea metabolism in hibernating bears is an example of this phenomenon. An understanding of how the black bear controls urea levels in its body when it is not drinking or eating has recently allowed physicians to better manage patients with severe kidney disease. Since these patients are unable to filter the urea from their own blood, this task must be done by a kidney machine. Discoveries made in the study of hibernation in bears has helped doctors develop a special diet that reduces the frequency with which these patients need dialysis (Nelson et al 1973; Nelson and Beck 1984).

DEN MOTHERS

The metabolic marvel of bear hibernation allows these animals to survive, sometimes for half a year or more, without eating or drinking and without eliminating any bodily wastes. If we tried to do the same, we would die within seven to ten days. Even more amazing, female bears give birth at this time and nurse a litter of cubs for several months afterwards, while they are still in hibernation.

Bear cubs are born during the coldest months of the year. Young brown bears and black bears are born in

Young bear cubs, such as this eight-week-old American black bear, have surprisingly long, sharp claws, which they use to crawl through their mothers' thick fur.

January and February, whereas young polar bears are born from late November to January.

Brown and black bears usually have litters of two or three cubs, but rare litters of six have been reported in both species (Rowan 1947; Wilk et al. 1988). Polar bears have smaller litters than the other northern bears, usually one or two cubs. Triplets are uncommon, and a litter of four cubs has been reported only once (Stirling, Calvert and Andriashek 1984).

The age of the mother bear influences the size of her litter. In general, older bears are heavier and have larger litters. This trend is seen in polar bears and brown bears, but the best documentation comes from American black bears. In Pennsylvania black bears, the average age of a female with a single cub was 4 years old. If the litter contained two cubs, the mother's average age jumped to 5.5 years. In three-cub litters, the mother's average age was 6.2 years, and the largest litters, those containing four and five cubs, were produced by the oldest females, which had an average age of 7.8 years (Alt 1989).

It appears that as a mother bear ages, she matures reproductively and is then able to produce larger litters. Older females are also more experienced at finding food, and their improved nutritional condition may further contribute to their ability to have larger litters. The habitat also influences the size of litters, and female bears that live in food-rich habitats produce more cubs than females that live in habitats where food is scarce and poor in quality. This last point is discussed in greater detail in Chapter 3.

Like many mammals, the mother bear licks her newborns thoroughly to clean away the embryonic membranes. The licking dries the cubs' fur, thus improving the pelt's insulation. In many carnivores, as the mother licks her offspring, she learns to recognize the young animal's individual odour as well as coating her youngster with the odour of her own saliva. For a mother bear, however, individual recognition of her cubs while she is in hibernation is probably not important, since

At birth, an American black bear cub has grey-blue eyes. Usually the colour changes to brown by the time the cub is six to eight months old.

she never leaves them. In fact, a hibernating bear's sense of smell may be impaired.

The discovery that hibernating bears may be unable to recognize the odour of their own offspring was made accidentally when biologists tried to introduce young orphaned cubs to foster mother black bears that were still in their winter dens. When an orphan bear cub was tossed into an occupied den or left just outside the den entrance, almost invariably the foster mother would first sniff at the cub and then scoop it into the den and adopt it. Apparently, the bear could not identify the orphan by its odour and assumed that the cub was one of her own (Clarke, O'Pezio and Hackford 1980; Alt and Beecham 1984).

The researchers tried a similar tactic with mother bears after they had left their winter dens and come out of hibernation. This time the adoption attempts failed. As soon as the mother bears smelled the foreign cubs, they recognized that the orphans were not their own and immediately killed them (Alt 1984a).

Besides licking the birth fluids from her cubs and consuming the embryonic membranes, a mother bear also eats the afterbirth. This practice keeps the winter den clean and eliminates any odours that might attract predators. In those carnivores that do not hibernate, the mother may eat the afterbirth for its nutritional value. It is speculated that by consuming the afterbirth, the mother does not need to leave her young so quickly after their birth in order to hunt.

The Baby Bruin

It is hard to think of a more photogenic animal than a two-month-old bear cub, but "homely" is the word that best describes a newborn cub. Newborn bear cubs are extremely small—the size of chubby chipmunks. Although they are covered with very short hair, they look almost naked. They are toothless, their eyes are sealed shut, and their ears are just fleshy tabs on the sides of their head. What they lack in looks, they make

A newborn bear cub keeps warm by snuggling into the curl of its mother's body.

up for in voice; these little bruins can scream like banshees.

Newborn brown bear and polar bear cubs weigh around 600 to 700 grams (21 to 25 ounces). Black bear cubs are smaller yet, and in the northeastern United States the average cub is 23 centimetres (9 inches) long and weighs a mere 360 grams (12 ounces) (Alt 1989). In general, a newborn bear cub weighs about 1/300 to 1/500 as much as its mother. The young of most other carnivores weigh between 1/25 and 1/70 as much as their mothers, and a human infant weighs around 1/15 as much as its mother (Oftedal and Gittleman 1989; Gittleman and Oftedal 1987).

Bear cubs are not the smallest newborn mammals in comparison with the size of their mothers; that distinction belongs to the marsupials. For example, the entire litter of six to nine young of a Virginia opossum (*Didelphis virginiana*), a marsupial that shares much of its range with the American black bear, would fit into a tablespoon and weigh less than a quarter. A newborn opossum weighs only 1/15,000 as much as its mother!

Still, when compared with the young of other carnivores, newborn bear cubs are surprisingly small, and it is the hibernating condition of the mother that explains their tiny size. No other mammal gives birth to its young while hibernating. Because of the contraints imposed upon the mother bear by hibernation, she cannot sustain the metabolic needs of her unborn cubs beyond a certain size and must halt the pregnancy early, when the cubs are still quite premature. Once the cubs are born, she can sustain them on her milk and still continue to hibernate (Ramsay and Dunbrack 1986).

Bear Milk and Nursing

A bear cub's eyes do not open completely until the animal is six weeks old. So how do newborn cubs locate their mother's nipples? The answer is that they migrate towards heat. When bear researchers trained a heat-sensitive, infrared camera on a hibernating mother bear, they discovered that she radiated body heat from two main areas—her muzzle and her nipples. Thus, newborn bear cubs find their meals by homing in on the hottest spots on their mother's body (Alt 1989).

Mother black bears and brown bears have six nipples—two pairs on their chest, and another pair in their groin. There seems to be no rationale for the placement of the nipples until you consider the body position in which a bear commonly hibernates.

When a mother bear is in her den, she frequently curls up with her nose pointed towards her tail. In this posture, Dr. Gary Alt believes the six nipples are brought close together in a pocket formed by the mother's body. If she had nipples on her abdomen, they would be lost in the folds of her belly and the cubs could not reach them. Since the mother bear also breathes into this small space, it is a warm, comfortable place for the cubs to nurse.

In carnivores, if not all mammals, the number of nipples that a female has is related to the number of young that she regularly produces. Thus, female polar bears, which have smaller litters than the other northern bears, have four nipples on the chest and none in the groin (Derocher 1990).

Milk production is a characteristic of all mammals, but the composition of milk differs tremendously among mammals, closely reflecting the biology of the animal and the urgency with which the mother must transfer energy to her offspring. Marine mammals, like the hooded seal (*Cystophora cristata*), produce very rich milk, containing 50 per cent fat (whipping cream is usually 30 per cent fat). The hooded seal pup nurses for only four days, the shortest nursing period known for any mammal, and in that time the pup doubles its birth weight and gains an astonishing 20 kilograms (44 pounds) (Bowen, Oftedal and Boness 1985). At the other end of the spectrum are humans, who may nurse for as long as two or three years. Human milk is relatively low in fat, containing less than 4 per cent fat. The calorically weak composition of human milk reflects the long period of infant dependency.

Bear milk is between these two extremes, containing between 20 and 40 per cent fat. Of all bears, polar bears have the fattiest milk. I once tasted some from a female bear that had just come out of her den in early March. The milk was quite creamy in texture, but it had very little taste. Another writer observed that polar bear milk "smells somewhat like seal and tastes like cod-liver oil." The writer had sampled the milk at a time when the bears were on the sea ice hunting seals, and this activity undoubtedly influenced the flavour of the milk (Jenness, Erickson and Craighead 1972).

The mother's rich milk fattens up her tiny cubs so that they become large and strong enough to follow her when she eventually leaves the family's winter den. As is discussed in the next section, this is especially important for young polar bear cubs, which leave the den when weather conditions may be extremely harsh and the family may travel long distances to reach the sea ice, where they must go to hunt seals.

Interestingly, the sun bear (*Ursus malayanus*), which lives in the Asian tropics, produces milk that has a relatively low fat content—only about 10 per cent. The cubs of these tropical bears are not subjected to the same post-denning rigours as are the cubs of northern bears, and the low fat content of the sun bear's milk may be a reflection of this fact.

When kittens or puppies nurse, they tread rhythmically with their front paws against their mother's body as they suck. This behaviour, called a milk tread, is widespread in the cat family and is also seen in weasels, foxes and hyenas, but it is not seen in bears. The milk tread is thought to stimulate the mother and encourage the release of her milk. I think it is quite possible that

the function of the milk tread has been replaced in bears by a vocal nursing signal, which is unique among the carnivores.

When all species of bear cubs nurse, they produce a loud, continuous humming noise while they are sucking. The characteristic noise, which is sometimes called a nursing chuckle, is loud enough to be heard outside a bear's den. I have heard it a number of times. Like the milk tread, the nursing chuckle may facilitate milk release and signal the lethargic mother bear to retain her body position while her cubs are feeding.

Nursing sessions usually last less than ten minutes, and the cubs nurse every two or three hours. When there is more than one cub in a litter, each cub may assume ownership of one or more nipples and always suck from these nipples. A large, aggressive cub may bully its smaller siblings and nurse from all of the nipples. When this happens, the cubs may fight with each other over nursing rights. The mother bear rarely interferes in these squabbles, and the cubs must resolve their own disputes.

One March along the western coast of Hudson Bay, I examined a litter of polar bear cubs that illustrated some of the consequences of nursing rivalry. There were three cubs in the litter. Although they had been born on the same day, their weights three months later were vastly different. The runt of the litter weighed 7 kilograms (15½ pounds), the middle cub weighed 11 kilograms (24 pounds), and the bully weighed a chunky 16 kilograms (35 pounds)—2½ times more than the runt. I knew the largest cub was a bully because I watched him dominate the other two cubs and because he was the only cub without scars on his nose. The two smaller cubs had multiple thin scars on their noses and muzzles, probably acquired in fights with the largest cub. The runt of the litter was most heavily scarred and also had a fresh wound on its upper lip. Polar bear cubs similar in size to the runt often do not survive. Clearly, in the struggle for survival and the competition for milk, the meek inherit nothing.

Milk is not a bear cub's only source of fluid. On two different occasions I watched black bear cubs lap saliva from the edge of their mother's mouth. At the time that I saw this happen, a female black bear with two cubs was hibernating in a surface nest and I was seated on the ground only 5 metres (16½ feet) away from the family of bears. I recorded their behaviour in my field notes: "The licking lasted several minutes each time, and the mother bear was quite tolerant of her cubs. The behaviour looked practised and familiar to her. Each time, she kept her mouth slightly agape while the cubs licked repeatedly at the sides of her mouth."

Licking saliva is a widespread behaviour in nursing rodents, and it has also been reported in several carnivores, namely, the long-tailed weasel (*Mustela frenata*), the genet (*Genetta spp.*) and the civet (*Viverra civetta*), but it has never been described in bears before (Ewer 1973). Saliva may simply be an additional source of fluid for cubs, or it may serve a greater function. If, like human saliva, bear saliva contains digestive enzymes, it might contribute to digestion in the cubs when their own systems are just beginning to function.

In the first winter of their life, newborn bear cubs do not hibernate, even though their mother is hibernating when she gives birth to them. Consequently, like all baby mammals, bear cubs urinate and defecate after they eat. The mother bear eats her cubs' droppings and drinks their urine, thus keeping the winter den clean and also recovering some of the fluids she loses through nursing. Because a hibernating bear never drinks and its only source of water during this time is from the metabolism of its fat reserves, a nursing mother bear is on a tight fluid ration.

Normally, bear cubs will not void unless induced by their mother, who licks them around the anal area. This behaviour permits the mother bear to recover as much water as possible from her offspring. I learned about this adaptation first hand when I cared for an orphan black bear cub. The cub would not urinate until I

A newborn bear cub has a relatively large tongue. This probably allows it to form a tighter seal around its mother's nipple and makes nursing easier.

wiped its bottom with a warm, wet paper towel. If that had not worked, I was not prepared to carry my maternal responsibilities any further.

Abandoning the Den

By the time a mother bear and her cubs leave their winter den, the cubs are between three and four months of age. At this age, young black bears weigh about 3 or 4 kilograms (6 to 9 pounds), and young polar bears weigh between 9 and 11 kilograms (20 to 25 pounds). Brown bear cubs weigh somewhat less than polar bears but are heavier than blacks. The cubs have grown from near-naked, homely little creatures to bright-eyed, inquisitive little balls of fur. (I promised one bear biologist that I would resist the temptation to use the word "cute" to describe bears, but no other word describes a young bear cub better.)

Researchers believe that most bear cubs survive the first few months of life and live to greet the wide-open wilderness when the family first leaves the winter den. Beyond that moment, however, many bear cubs die. Starvation, predators and disease will claim a third of all black bear cubs in their first year of life. Most of these will die before they are six months old (Elowe 1987; LeCount 1987). Brown bears cubs fare worse than young black bears; up to 40 per cent of brown bear cubs never reach their first birthday (Bunnell and Tait 1985). Less is known about the survival of polar bear cubs, but Andy Derocher, a reseacher in Hudson Bay, found that between 1987 and 1990, 51 per cent of the cubs in that area died by their first autumn.

Most polar bear mothers leave their winter dens a month or two earlier than either brown bear or black bear mothers. Female polar bears in the southern part of their range, namely in Hudson Bay and James Bay, leave their winter dens between late February and mid-March. Bears from more northern populations in Canada, and in Alaska and the former Soviet Union, leave a little bit later, from mid-March to mid-April. In the next section, we will follow a family of polar bears as they journey out onto the ice.

JOURNEY TO THE ICE

Most female polar bears that have denned have been cramped inside for four or five months, and they need time to become mobile again. When the mother bear finally squeezes out of her den for the first time, her outing may be a brief one. She rolls in the snow and stretches her thick limbs, which have been folded for months. With relish, she buries her face in powder snow and licks the flakes from her lips, much as you or I might stand in the spray of a shower to flush away our morning grogginess.

After a day or two, when the female has made several short outings, the tiny white heads of her cubs appear at the opening to the den for the first time. The cubs implore their mother to return to them with repeated calls of "maa, maa." In response, the female ambles back to the den, and her presence finally coaxes the cubs to venture outside.

Most polar bear families stay in the vicinity of their winter dens for a week or two (Jonkel et al. 1972; Uspenski and Belikov 1980). During this time the mother bear is still quite lethargic. In one study in Norway's Svalbard Archipelago, the mother bears were inactive 94 per cent of the time (Hansson and Thomassen 1983). It is quite likely that the mother bears are still hibernating, metabolically, when they first emerge from their winter dens, and the days they spend near their den may give them time to accelerate their metabolism back to normal.

In western Hudson Bay, most of the female bears have not eaten since the previous August, when the ice disappeared from the bay, obligating them to a seven-month fast. It is not surprising, then, that when the bears first emerge from their winter dens, they often dig under the snow to eat vegetation. In some areas of Hudson Bay, the bears commonly eat grasses, sedges and sphagnum moss. Less frequently they eat labrador tea (*Ledum groenlandicum*) and even strip lichens from the trees. The bears eat only small amounts of vegetation, however, and at this time of the year they probably derive very little nutrition from the plants (Kolenosky and Prevett 1983).

When a mother polar bear and her cubs finally leave the area of their winter den, they may need to travel far to reach the sea and the seals that they will hunt. The maternity dens in Hudson Bay are farthest from the sea, typically more than 50 kilometres (31 miles) inland. The distances are less in the Canadian High Arctic, where most maternity dens are situated within 16 kilometres (10 miles) of the coast. Mother bears on Wrangel Island off the northeastern coast of Siberia den within 8 kilometres (5 miles) of the sea, and in Svalbard the dens are usually less than a kilometre (a half mile) from the coast.

As the mother bears lead their families to the sea, their progress is slow. A study conducted in Jones Sound in the Canadian High Arctic found that bears travelled only 2 to 5 kilometres (1¼ to 3 miles) a day, with frequent stops to rest and nurse along the way (Killiaan, Stirling and Jonkel 1978).

In Hudson Bay, where the bears travel farthest to reach the sea, the course of the family is not meandering but amazingly straight. Biologist George Kolenosky wrote that "the ability of females to travel direct routes over featureless terrain was remarkable and indicated a highly developed system of navigation. Near the sea, the odor of open water may assist orientation, but inland there appeared to be few navigational aids" (Kilenosky and Prevett 1983).

When a mother polar bear with newborn cubs journeys to the sea ice from her winter den, she stops frequently to nurse and rest her cubs.

It is not known how polar bears navigate, but if they are like other animals, they may use a number of methods. It is possible that bears could use the angle of the sun and make adjustments for the season and the time of day as birds do to travel accurately in one direction. Bears might also be able to detect the weak magnetic field of the Earth. Many birds can do this, as can some species of fish and some species of reptiles, but this ability has not yet been proven to exist in mammals.

Regardless of *how* bears navigate, it is clear that they can do so quite accurately. Analyzing over 1000 kilometres (621 miles) of polar bear tracks made by female bears leaving maternity dens along Hudson Bay, Ramsay and Andriashek (1986) found that all of the mother bears walked in a northeast direction to reach the ice. This direction would guarantee that the bears always

intercepted an area of the bay where there would be seals to hunt.

Along southern Hudson Bay, mother bears and their cubs journey to the ice more or less in a straight line, but the mother bear will frequently follow streams if they course in the same general direction in which she wishes to travel. Even in areas of tundra, trees and bushes frequently grow along the banks of streams, and the bears may follow these streams to shelter from the wind. The vegetation along streams also traps blowing snow into drifts in which the mother bear can dig a temporary den if the weather becomes too severe for travel.

The average daytime temperatures during March, when the bears leave their dens along Hudson Bay, are −20°C to −30°C (−4°F to −22°F). One year when I was

Polar bears frequently follow each other's tracks. By doing so, an animal may find a partially eaten seal carcass that it can either steal or scavenge.

observing bears at that time, there was a three-day cold spell with record temperatures of −42°C (−43°F). A brisk northwest wind drove the windchill down to −70°C (−94°F). Polar bear cubs cannot withstand such extreme temperatures, and it is likely that during such weather a mother bear would dig a temporary den in which to shelter her family until the conditions for travel improved.

Young polar bear cubs cannot withstand temperatures below −30°C (−22°F) (Blix and Lentfer 1979). Although their pelts are well developed when the bear family leaves its winter den, the young cubs still have no subcutaneous fat and lose body heat more readily than adult bears. To compensate, cubs have a higher metabolic rate. This is like turning up the thermostat on the furnace inside a house that is poorly insulated. The house is kept warm, but it consumes more fuel. The high metabolic rate of polar bear cubs is sustained by the calorie-rich fuel that they get from their mothers in the form of rich, fatty milk.

When bear families cross small areas of open water in their winter travels, the cubs often ride on their mother's back. Cubs get soaked to the skin when they are immersed in water, and they chill rapidly because they have no fat layer to insulate them. It has been estimated that a polar bear cub immersed in ice water could last only ten minutes before its body temperature would cool to the point of no return (Blix and Lentfer 1979).

Once the bears reach the coast, they may still need to journey another 100 kilometres (62 miles) offshore to reach the seals. The surface of the sea ice is often littered with large slabs of broken ice, and these blocks of ice may pile up into immense pressure ridges that make travel difficult for small young cubs. Sometimes in travelling over such rough ice, a mother bear may lift a cub over an obstacle by grabbing it by the scruff of its neck and hoisting it up and over. If one of the cubs in a litter, usually the runt, lags behind the others, the mother bear displays great patience and will

A single cub, with no competition from littermates, may grow very fast. This four-month-old polar bear cub weighed 20.5 kilograms (45 pounds).

repeatedly walk back to it to coax the youngster along. In rare cases, a cub may even ride on its mother's back, especially when the cub is cold or weak. In James Bay, a female was seen giving the smallest of her three cubs a ride for a considerable distance (Jonkel et al. 1972).

Once the bear family is on the sea ice, the mother bear must stay alert for adult male bears that can pose a threat to her offspring. I saw one female bear with two small cubs in a jumble of rough ice several kilometres (about a mile) offshore from the western coast of Hudson Bay. The mother had stationed herself and her cubs on the highest ice hummock in the area. It appeared that she had chosen the lofty perch because it provided her with a good view of the surrounding ice and any approaching bears.

Now the mother bear is ready to begin her hunt for seals and other marine animals. Although the ice may appear to be an unvarying frigid platform, the mother bear knows that within the vast expanse of the sea ice there are rich oases where life abounds and there are wastelands in which nothing stirs but the wind. The last section of this chapter discusses the many complexities of arctic ice, and how polar bears successfully exploit the different areas.

ON THE SEA ICE

When you stand on the sea ice in the High Arctic, the world around you has great beauty, but it appears to have no life. The blinding glare from the snow, the pen-

PREVIOUS PAGE: *A pressure ridge may reach a height of 10 metres (33 feet). Often the ridge extends beneath the ice to a depth three times greater than its height.*

etrating cold and the probing bite of the wind tell you that you are in a landscape carved by extremes. I have always been fascinated by arctic wildlife because of the raw tenacity the animals display in thriving where few other creatures, including myself, could. If the Arctic were nothing more than this, it would have held my fascination. But as I studied polar bears and the world in which they live, I discovered an ecosystem with unimagined depth, complexity and variation. There are entire food chains within the ice, and the sea ice is as variable as the forest in a mountain valley. When you understand this, you can better understand how a large carnivore such as the polar bear can glean a livelihood from this seemingly barren, hostile environment.

Life beneath the Ice

The Arctic imposes severe limitations on the existence of life, for there are many months of darkness and paralyzing cold. Yet even when the sea ice is 2 metres (roughly 6 feet) thick, an entire community of plants and animals thrives on its undersurface.

Algae begins to bloom in the cracks and crevices on the underside of the sea ice in late winter, as soon as the sun returns to the Arctic. The algae forms a thick green-brown layer in the lower few centimetres of the ice. At times, the algae detaches from the ice and hangs in green, mucuslike strands. Single-celled protozoans graze on the algae, and they in turn are hunted by turbellarians (flatworms), nematodes (roundworms) and amphipods (Horner 1976).

Amphipods, also called sea lice, are shrimplike creatures, a few centimetres (an inch or two) long. Amphipods have been referred to as the "piranhas of the frozen seas," for not only do they graze on algae, but, lured by the scent of blood, they will also converge in swarms on injured victims, such as netted fish, and reduce them to skeletons. Dewey Soper, a Canadian arctic researcher in the 1920s, relied on amphipods to clean caribou skulls he had collected for the National Museum. He simply suspended the skulls in the sea

and the amphipods stripped off all the fat and meat.

For at least one arctic expedition of the last century, amphipods meant the difference between life and death. Writer Jon Percy (1989) recalled the event:

Lt. Adolphus Greely and 25 men were stranded during the winter of 1883 in the Canadian Arctic. His journal is punctuated with references to a continuing dependence on amphipods to alleviate their desperate hunger. Early on he observed that 'the minute animals have opened up to us a new avenue of escape.' With pieces of sealskin clothing as bait, the stranded men sometimes managed to catch 10-15 kilograms [22 to 33 pounds] of the lifesaving amphipods daily. Seven survivors, largely sustained by their crustacean harvest, were mercifully rescued the following summer.

Amphipods, roundworms and flatworms are eaten by arctic cod (*Boreogadus saida*) and polar cod (*Arctogadus glacialis*). The 15- to 30-centimetre (6- to 12-inch) cod are in turn hunted by seabirds and seals; the seals are then stalked by polar bears.

The undersurface of the arctic sea ice has been compared with a tropical coral reef because of its high productivity. The ice algae begins to bloom on the undersurface of the sea ice many months before summer conditions return to the Arctic. This early algal growth expands the season during which the arctic waters are productive, enabling a greater profusion of life to abound in the Arctic. Ultimately, the extended period of algal growth is the foundation on which polar bears depend for their survival.

Types of Ice

Authorities recognize as many as seven different types of sea ice. For our purposes, we will only consider the types of ice where polar bears commonly hunt. In a study in the Beaufort Sea of northwestern Canada, for example, polar bears were most often sighted on three types of sea ice (Stirling et al. 1975).

The greatest number of bears were sighted on shift-

The Baillie-Hamilton Polynya in the Canadian High Arctic—a body of persistent open water despite the −20°C (−4°F) temperatures.

ing pack ice. This offshore ice is continually assaulted by winds and ocean currents, which cause it to repeatedly fracture and refreeze. This process produces a diverse ice habitat with a myriad of cracks, small leads of open water and patches of thin, young ice through which ringed seals can easily scratch breathing holes.

Bears were also spotted on shorefast ice. This type of ice adheres to coastlines and is typically quite stable. Shorefast ice may extend many kilometres offshore, and at its outer edge it merges with the shifting pack ice. Pressure ridges often form across the surface of the shorefast ice, and snowdrifts may accumulate along the length of these ridges. Ringed seals (*Phoca hispida*) dig caves in the snowdrifts from below and haul out into these to rest and give birth to their pups in March and April. Shorefast ice is hunted least by adult male polar

bears and most by female polar bears with cubs. The females may prefer to hunt in shorefast ice because there are fewer other bears, especially adult males, to threaten their cubs.

In the Beaufort Sea, when polar bears were not hunting in the shifting pack ice zone, they were most commonly found along a floe edge, an area of ice adjacent to an expanse of open water.

Leads and Polynyas

It was a big surprise to me to discover that some arctic seas never freeze. Scattered throughout the Arctic there are numerous areas of open water that stay free of ice even when air temperatures plummet to subzero levels for months at a time. When this open water is linear, it is called a lead. Leads may be many kilo-

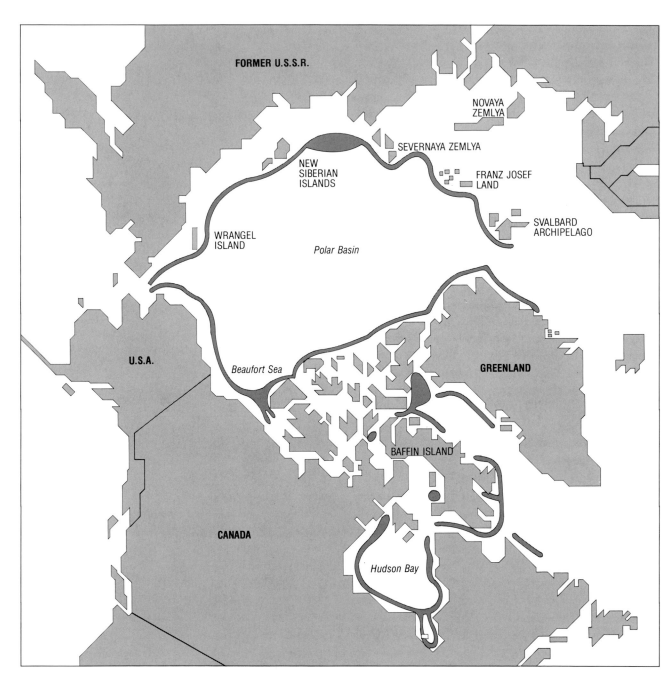

Figure 1.1 The location of major leads and polynyas in the Arctic (Stirling and Guravich 1988).

The flamboyant king eider (Somateria spectabilis) *drake is a diving duck that feeds on crustaceans, starfish and insects. It and many other ducks, geese and seabirds rely on the open water of polynyas to enable them to return to their breeding grounds early.*

metres wide and hundreds of kilometres long. Leads often run parallel to coastlines, and they frequently form at the junction between the stable shorefast ice and the shifting pack ice. There is an immense lead system, for example, around the entire perimeter of Hudson Bay. An even larger lead completely rings the polar basin. This lead has been called the Arctic Ring of Life, emphasizing its importance to northern wildlife (Figure 1.1).

Areas of ice-free water that are not linear are called polynyas. Polynyas vary in size from those that are 100 metres (100 yards) in diameter to those that cover hundreds of square kilometres. There are major polynyas in the Beaufort Sea, in northwestern Hudson Bay, off the northern coast of Siberia, and in Cumberland Sound in southeastern Baffin Island (Figure 1.1). The largest polynya in Canada, called North Water, is located at the upper end of Baffin Bay. North Water may get as large as 85 000 square kilometres (33,000 square miles), an area larger than Lake Superior (Stirling and Cleator 1981).

Polynyas can vary considerably in size from year to year, but they invariably recur in the same location every year. It is somewhat of a mystery how polynyas are able to stay free of ice despite the cold winter conditions, but it is believed that winds, currents, tides and upwellings combine to keep the water open.

Whalers and indigenous arctic peoples have known for a long time that polynyas attract wildlife. Even though these areas of open water cover only about 3 or 4 per cent of the total ice surface in the Arctic, they are the biological hot spots of the region. Biologist David

The thick-billed murre (Uria lom-via) is one of the most abundant seabirds in the Northern Hemi-sphere, with an estimated world population of 56 million.

Nettleship has found only one major seabird colony in the entire Canadian Arctic that was *not* associated with a polynya. Seabirds such as northern fulmars (*Fulmarus glacialis*), black-legged kittiwakes (*Rissa tridactyla*) and thick-billed murres (*Uria lomvia*) swarm to polynyas to feed in the early spring. The open water enables the birds to return to their nesting cliffs and get started while most of the sea is still covered in ice.

In late April one year, on the southern coast of Devon Island, I counted thousands of northern fulmars crowding the snow-covered ledges of Cape Liddon when temperatures were well below freezing and ice covered the ocean for as far as I could see. A helicopter pilot that flew into camp told me that there was a polynya 50 kilometres (31 miles) away where the birds were likely flying to feed.

Polynyas lure more than seabirds. All marine mammals, of course, must breathe, and polynyas are important overwintering sites for ringed and bearded seals, walruses (*Odobenus rosmarus*) and whales. Belugas (*Delphinapterus leucas*) are the most common whales found in polynyas, but these areas of open water sometimes also attract that cetacean unicorn the narwhal (*Monodon monoceros*) and the burly 100-metric-ton (118-ton) bowhead whale (*Balaena mysticetus*). The concentration of marine mammals is a powerful attractant to polar bears.

Polynyas may attract wildlife not only because they are areas of open water in an otherwise frozen landscape but also because they may be areas of greater productivity. Upwellings, which I suggested earlier as one of the possible explanations of polynyas, pull rich organic materials (silicates, phosphates and nitrates) up from the ocean floor to the sunlit surface, where they can again be used by algae and plankton. Since these minute plants and animals comprise the base of the arctic food chain, when they proliferate they sustain a greater number of seabirds, seals and bears.

On rare occasions, leads and polynyas become covered with ice, or just fail to develop at all, with dire con-

The lumps on the neck of an adult bull walrus are thickenings of the skin that protect the animal from injury from an opponent's tusks when the bulls jab each other during squabbles.

sequences for the wildlife. When the Cape Bathurst Polynya in the Beaufort Sea failed to open one spring, 100,000 migrating common and king eiders (*Somateria mollissima* and *S. spectabilis*, respectively) died. There was no open water when the ducks arrived after their long migration flight, and the birds starved to death (Barry 1968).

One winter heavy ice conditions had a disastrous impact on the seals and the polar bears in the Beaufort Sea. Within a year the number of ringed and bearded seals dropped by a half, and they produced only 1/10 the normal number of offspring. In about two years the number of polar bears dropped by a third, and they produced only half as many cubs as usual. It took over five years for the polar bear population to recover (Stirling, Calvert and Andriashek 1984).

Polynyas that ice over in the winter do not always spell disaster for the polar bears in an area. At times, when the weather changes abruptly for the worse, the amount of open water in a polynya may shrink. If the whales and walruses using the polynya are unable to flee to another area of open water, the animals gradually become packed into a smaller and smaller space. Unlike ringed seals, which can maintain breathing holes in ice 2 metres (6½ feet) thick, whales and walruses have only a limited ability to break through ice. Walruses can ram through ice that is 20 centimetres (8 inches) thick, as can the brawny bowhead whales. The smaller beluga and narwhal are limited to much thinner ice, usually no thicker than 10 centimetres (4 inches) (Fay 1982). When the ice in a polynya becomes too thick for whales and walruses to break through, the animals withdraw to the last pools of open water. In these circumstances, they are like goldfish trapped in a bowl.

In one incident in the Chukchi Sea off the western coast of Alaska, polar bears killed forty belugas when a group of the them accidentally became trapped in a small lead surrounded by thick pack ice. Observers did not know how many bears had done the killing, but an

Young polar bears in their first year of life rarely stray far from their mother, even when she is hunting.

estimated thirty polar bears scavenged from the carcasses that were scattered around the opening in the ice (Lowry, Burns and Nelson 1987). An eyewitness account of a polar bear killing a beluga in Novaya Zemlya in Russia reported that the bear lay on the ice with its paws outstretched and killed the beluga with a crushing blow to the animal's head when it surfaced within range (Freeman 1973).

The Polar Bear's Diet

The walrus is the largest of the polar bear's possible prey. Adult walruses are 3 to 3½ metres (10 to 11½ feet) long and weigh a strapping 800 to 1200 kilograms (1764 to 2646 pounds), and they can ably defend themselves with their pointed tusks. Not surprisingly, then, it is always reported that polar bears prey most often on

calves and subadult animals. A recent study at Dundas Polynya in the Canadian High Arctic took a closer look at how walruses and polar bears interacted in late winter and early spring.

In Dundas Polynya, female walruses with calves typically hauled out in groups of four or more animals. The calves always rested closer to the water than the adults, and though the calves often slept, the females remained alert. The males, in contrast, were less vigilant and were more reluctant to enter the water. Researchers Calvert and Stirling (1990) wrote: "A polar bear could approach a male walrus to within a few meters. When a bear approached that closely, the walrus would back into the water slowly, ready to fight with its tusks if necessary."

Between 1981 and 1989, Calvert and Stirling (1990)

found evidence of ten walruses that they believed were wounded or killed by polar bears. The study concluded that polar bears may kill more walruses than has been previously reported, and furthermore, although calves and subadult animals are most vulnerable, large male polar bears are also capable of killing adult male walruses.

Marine mammals are the mainstay of a polar bear's diet, from the standard fare of ringed seals to the less frequent dietary delights of bearded seals to the uncommon pleasures of whales and walruses. But polar bears have been known to eat more unusual fare on occasion.

In midwinter, a herd of muskoxen (*Oribos moschatus*) may leave their range on any of Canada's High Arctic Islands and travel across the sea ice to another island. Helicopter pilot Steve Miller sighted a group of nine or ten muskoxen in the middle of M'Clintock Channel, 45 kilometres (28 miles) from shore, headed for Prince of Wales Island. Out on the ice, the shaggy beasts might easily run into a polar bear. It is not known how muskoxen respond to polar bears in this situation, but it is safe to assume that the animals likely huddle together in the defensive circle that works so well for them against wolves.

When muskoxen are alone, they may be more vulnerable and more likely to be attacked. An Inuit hunter from Grise Fiord watched a polar bear attack a solitary muskox on the ice between Ellesmere Island and Devon Island, and in northeastern Greenland there are several reports of polar bears attacking and killing muskoxen, most often lone adult bulls (Thing, Henrichsen and Lassen 1984). It didn't take a great stretch of my imagination to picture polar bears hunting muskoxen, especially once I learned that muskoxen sometimes venture far from land onto the sea ice.

A more unusual polar bear food is kelp, which I still can't quite believe. Arctic researcher Ian Stirling (Stirling and Cleator 1981) wrote that "in some polynya areas where the water is shallow, such as along the coast of southeast Baffin Island, the kelp fronds lie against the underside of the ice and up into seal breathing holes. Polar bears feed on these plants extensively throughout the winter."

In Norway's Svalbard Archipelago, kelp is commonly found in the stomachs of polar bears. The stomach of one bear contained 8.5 kilograms (19 pounds) of the plants. Norwegian writer Lono (1970) observed "a female bear, together with a year-old cub, diving between ice floes to a depth of 3 to 4 metres [10 to 13 feet] to get seaweed. They both came up with large tangles of seaweed which they laid on the ice. They selected the best, ate that, and dived again for more. When I left after half an hour they were still doing it."

Humans eat kelp for the iodine and other trace minerals contained in the plant, and perhaps polar bears eat it for similar reasons. Whatever we finally discover, it is unlikely that we will ever completely understand the life of the polar bear, and it is fitting that there will always be some mystery surrounding the habits of this magnificent carnivore.

In the end we will conserve only what we love. We will love only what we understand. We will understand only what we are taught.

— Baba Dioum,
Senegal

I left the bears at nightfall. For seven hours, I had watched a female black bear and her two cubs loll in the sunshine, recovering from the confinement of months in a winter den. Days earlier, the mother bear had squeezed her black bulk through a narrow cleft to exit the jumble of rocks that was her winter den. Once she was out in the open, she had cautiously moved her cubs to a dense thicket of scrub oak, only 50 metres (164 feet) away. She raked grasses and leaves into a pile with her paw and built a nest on the ground. Here in the dense thicket, her family was safe from other bears, and she could let her lethargy lift. ¶ In the hours that I watched this family of bears, I shot twelve rolls of film, but not a single photograph captured the magic of those moments. The cubs climbed up their mother like a mountain to be conquered, perched on her head, then slid down her back. Sometimes they would slip and land with a thud in the nest, squeal in alarm, and totter back to their mother's side. Frequently a twig or an errant leaf became a rival to wrestle, and in the skirmish a cub might stray from the security of the nest. The mother would then slowly scoop the young bear back with a gentle sweep of her great paw. Afterwards she would nuzzle the cub and attempt to restrain its wanderings, but the cubs were charged with the energy of newborn life and could not be subdued so easily. ¶ Finally, overtaken by fatigue, the young bears slept, hidden within the shaggy curl of their mother's body. When they awoke, they nursed in unison, and then with their bellies full they again began their assault on life.

DEN EMERGENCE

Most brown and black bears vacate their winter dens over a one- to two-month period during April and May. Physiological factors, such as the bear's age and sex, its fat reserves and its reproductive status, affect the timing of den emergence. So do environmental factors, such as latitude and altitude. As might be predicted, the duration of the den emergence period is longest in northern areas, such as Canada, Alaska and northern Russia, where winter conditions are the harshest. In general, bears that live in northern regions come out of their dens later than bears that live farther south, and in mountainous regions, the bears that den at high elevations emerge later than bears that den lower down. Other environmental factors that influence the time of den emergence are temperature, snow cover, photoperiod and the availability of food. Each of these variables affects why a bear leaves its den when it does.

Physiological Factors

The sequence of den emergence is roughly the same in American and Asiatic black bears and in brown bears. Adult male bears leave their winter dens first, and adult females with newborn cubs leave last—as much as four to six weeks after the adult males. The other members of the population, namely, subadult males and females, and adult females with yearlings or two-year-old offspring, leave sometime in between. Although the precise reason why this occurs has not been worked out, it may be related to the different energy reserves and energy requirements that exist among adult males, subadults and females with cubs.

By the time a male bear reaches adulthood, he has a well-established home range on which he has learned to forage efficiently. Thus, every winter he begins the denning period with an ample reserve of fat. Because of these fat reserves, the adult male bear can leave his den early in the spring even if there is no food available. In addition, an adult male bear can be twice the size of an adult female, and his size enables him to range over large areas and thus to capitalize on widely scattered sources of food, such as carrion, which are sometimes available in early spring. His size also enables the bear to prey more easily on animals such as deer, elk and moose that have been weakened by the hardships of winter. Finally, it may be advantageous for adult males to leave their dens to scout their home range and locate potential mates before the spring breeding season begins.

A female bear with cubs has many reasons for not leaving her winter den early. Early in the spring there is very little food around, and the search for food would drain a mother bear's fat reserves, which are already taxed by her nursing cubs. In a fascinating study of a grizzly family in the Brooks Range of Alaska, Gebhard (1982) estimated that a grizzly mother will burn as many as 4000 kilocalories a day nursing her cubs, and she may lose as much as 10 to 15 kilograms (22 to 33 pounds) of body fat in the early nursing period. Moreover, the colder weather conditions that normally prevail in early spring would require the young bear cubs to burn extra calories to maintain their body temperature; naturally these calories would come from nursing, further depleting the mother bear's fat reserves. Premature den emergence would also expose young cubs to a number of risks. Small cubs might have trouble keeping up with their mother, and since they cannot climb to safety or run fast at this age, they could fall prey to predators, in particular other bears, which sometimes try to kill them.

A subadult bear leaves its den somewhere between the early-bird adult males and the tardy females with newborn cubs. The subadult is the teenager of the bear world, inexperienced and generally less skilled at finding food than an adult. The subadult is in a vulnerable age class in any population of bears and often enters its den with marginal fat reserves. If it left its den at the same time as adult males, the added energy drain of be-

ing active in the freezing cold of early spring would quickly use up its remaining fat reserves, which it needs to survive the lean times that are typical of the early weeks after denning. Even when a subadult bear does find a good source of food, such as carrion, it is often driven off by the first adult bear that wanders along. If the subadult is a young male, there is the added problem that he may have recently left his mother's home range and must struggle to eke out an existence in the unfamiliar surroundings of a new area. As well, since a subadult bear is sexually immature, there is not the lure of breeding to entice it out early.

However, a subadult bear gains nothing by staying in its den as long as mothers with cubs since, it has no offspring to protect and sequester in the security of a den. Although it may continue to lose weight after it leaves its winter den, a subadult can probably scrounge enough food to justify being out and moving around.

If any bear fails to accumulate enough fat to fuel it through the winter, it may prematurely abandon its den and become active during the winter. Such desperate attempts to stave off starvation may be fatal.

Reports of bears roaming the woods in the middle of winter are not uncommon. Although sometimes these animals are sick or old, quite often they are subadults who did not have enough fat reserves to last the denning period. This occurs often enough that hunters in southeastern Russia have a special name for these animals: "shatuns." The name applies to both brown bears and Asiatic black bears caught in this perilous circumstance (Bromlei 1965).

Environmental Factors

Snow cover and temperature are two environmental factors that may also influence the timing of den emergence. A number of studies have looked at the effects of these two factors, but the results are inconclusive.

Since snow cover hampers movement and makes any activity more laborious, bears that leave their dens when the snow is deep expend more energy. In two studies of Alaskan brown bears, heavy spring snowfall led to late den emergence. But in the mountains of the Yukon, Pearson (1975) found that male grizzlies that denned at high elevations dug themselves out of their dens and plowed through deep snow fields to reach valley bottoms.

In Alaskan black bears, biologists (Schwartz, Miller and Franzmann 1987) found that when snow lasted longer than usual in the spring, bears left their dens later. In other years when the snow disappeared early, the biologists expected the bears to leave early as well, but the bears surprised them and did not leave right away. It seemed the bears were not waiting for the snow to melt as their cue to depart.

The relationship between temperature and den emergence is just as unclear as it is for snow cover. Logically, warm spring temperatures should induce bears to get up and moving, and indeed in black bears in Ontario (Northcott and Elsey 1971), Idaho (Beecham, Reynolds and Hornocker 1983), and Washington (Lindzey and Meslow 1976), warm temperatures seemed to do just that, and bears left their dens soon after the mercury started to climb. In Minnesota, veteran bear researcher Dr. Lynn Rogers (1987) found that 87 per cent of the bears left their dens within two weeks once the average daily temperature rose above 0°C (32°F). But just when it seems that there might be a general correlation between rising temperature and den emergence, the black bears in south-central Alaska throw the pattern off (Schwartz, Miller and Franzmann 1987). They seem to ignore the thermometer, sometimes remaining in their dens for weeks after daytime temperatures rise above freezing.

Finally, another environmental cue that bears may use to time den emergence is the photoperiod. The photoperiod, or number of hours of daylight, is an important biological synchronizer of animal behaviour throughout arctic and temperate regions. The photoperiod coordinates migration in birds, seasonal colour changes in weasels, hares and arctic foxes, antler

Female brown bears with newborn cubs generally remain in their winter dens a month or two longer than other bears. Sometimes they may not emerge until late May.

growth in deer, and hibernation in ground squirrels. Daylight does penetrate to the depths of most bear dens, even those covered with a thick blanket of snow. Perhaps the increasing photoperiod functions like an environmental clock and notifies bears that spring is approaching. This stimulus might then initiate metabolic changes that sensitize the bear to other cues coming from its body and from its environment.

Warm spring temperatures alone cannot lure a bear into becoming active, but midwinter thaws may melt enough snow to flood a bear's den and force the animal to leave. Den flooding is a problem for brown bears and black bears in many areas. After being evicted, a bear may move to another den nearby or build a nest of branches, leaves and grass on the ground and spend the remainder of the winter out in the open. In North Carolina, an adult male black bear abandoned his den site after several days of heavy rains. The bear returned four days later when the water level receded (Hamilton and Marchinton 1980).

During a winter thaw in Minnesota, Rogers (1987) saw an adult female black bear come out to gather additional bedding material when meltwater drained into her den. He wrote that "she brought spruce boughs, shrubs, and pieces of birch bark into the den, elevating herself and her newborn cubs above the water."

The long-term research of Dr. Gary Alt (1984b) in Pennsylvania has revealed yearly casualties caused by the flooding of dens. Nearly all of the cubs that drowned in flooded dens were less than a month old, and Alt believed that the cubs were physically too immature to escape from the water. He also thought that

BEAR MYTH

Before a bear enters its den in the autumn, the last thing it does is plug its intestinal tract. It does this by stuffing a wad of moss or similar material into its anus or by ingesting certain materials that become wedged into place. In spring, the bear is unable to resume eating again until after it has expelled the plug and removed the obstruction. I have been told this story a number of times, and I always marvel at the conviction with which the storytellers recount their tale.

some mother bears may have contributed to the death of their cubs by their apparent lack of concern for the condition of their den. In two dens, Alt was surprised to find females with just their heads, necks and tops of their shoulders protruding above the water.

When I crawled into a flooded excavation den in Pennsylvania, the den floor was a soup of ice water and mud, 15 centimetres (6 inches) deep. I spent only five minutes cramped inside, but in that time my feet became soaked and numb. For me, the flooded den was only an inconvenience; for a bear, it might have been a matter of survival.

Most researchers now conclude that the timing of den emergence in bears is not controlled by one or two factors. Rather, all of the factors discussed, both the physiological ones, such as a bear's fat reserves, sex, age and reproductive status, and the environmental ones, which include snow cover, temperature, photoperiod and the availability of food, act in consort.

Of course, the behaviour patterns outlined here are generalizations, and not all bear behaviour fits into these generalizations. If you watch enough bears for a long enough time, you see them behave in ways you have never seen before. In the beginning, I discounted such behaviour as aberrant and ignored it because it was a rare occurrence. I reasoned that any behaviour that did not happen often or that had not been reported in the scientific literature surely could not be important. I have since learned that bears have a rich behavioural repertoire. They are intelligent, adaptable creatures that readily modify their behaviour in response to the many vagaries in their environment. Thus, den emergence behaviour, and all other behaviour in bears, often varies between individuals, from season to season and from region to region. This behavioural plasticity is at the heart of the bears' success in surviving.

GETTING UNDER WAY

Most bears loiter for a week or two in the vicinity of their den before they finally leave the area. Mothers with newborn cubs may spend up to a month in the vicinity of their den.

During this time, bears build one or more day beds near their den, and sometimes there are well-worn trails leading from the mouth of the den to the beds. Most of the day beds I have found have been simple pits scooped out of the snow, or piles of debris (grass and conifer needles) raked from the forest floor into a mound. In Norway, brown bears flatten anthills, which may be 2 metres (6½ feet) tall, and use these as day beds (Sorensen 1989). The anthills are likely chosen because they are dry and easy to dig.

One biologist watched a grizzly sow and her three newborn cubs in late April in the rugged mountains of Alberta after they had emerged from their den. Each day, the family members spent two to four hours outside; they spent the nights inside their den. During their time outside the bears never wandered more than 50 metres (164 feet) from the den (Vroom, Herrero and Ogilvie 1980).

In Minnesota, Lynn Rogers (1987) watched five families of black bears as they emerged from their dens. All of the bears stayed near their dens for a time. Some days they would return to their dens periodically during the day, and almost always they spent the entire night inside the den. Rogers wrote that "all 5 mothers were lethargic, spending the majority of their time resting in or near their dens. Each raked additional bedding into their dens or constructed beds outside them." He noted that yearling bears that spent the winter denned with their mother were also lethargic, whereas cubs-of-the-year were quite active. He attributed the difference in activity to the fact that yearling black bears hibernate, the same as adults, but newborn cubs do not.

When a bear first leaves its den, physiologically it may continue to hibernate for two or three weeks afterwards (Rogers 1987). Bears probably have a compulsory period of acclimatization during which the animals shift from the energy-conserving metabolism of winter to the energy-burning metabolism of sum-

mer. During the transition days, the bears are sluggish, and they eat and drink very little.

The first bowel movement that all bears have in the spring is likely to consist of hard, dry scats. Often it consists of a single scat 19 to 28 centimetres (7½ to 11 inches) long. One Alaskan researcher found a scat 75 centimetres (29½ inches) long, and 5 to 7 centimetres (2 to 2¾ inches) in diameter near the den of a male brown bear. Although these scats are commonly called fecal plugs, there is no evidence that the scat actually plugs the intestinal tract. There is no logical reason why the intestinal tract should need to be plugged in the first place. Most likely the bowel contents simply consolidate because the bear does not eat or drink for months, and the motility of the intestinal tract stops because of the bear's inactivity during the denning period. When the bear starts to move about again in spring, the bowel also starts to move and expels its contents. The same thing happens to humans when they are bedridden and become constipated.

In all bears, the fecal plug usually consists of hair, grass, leaves and twigs—materials that the bear may have accidentally swallowed when it built its den in the autumn or when it licked itself or groomed its cubs.

Once bears leave the area of their dens, they scatter in search of food, and it is difficult to predict where they might be found. Female American black bears with newborn cubs are an exception; the mother bear heads straight for the largest tree nearby and builds a nest at its base. In Pennsylvania and Minnesota, the mother usually chooses a large hemlock or white pine. In the mountains of Alberta, she may choose a Douglas fir. Dr. Lynn Rogers thinks the mother bears select trees for their large size and their bark characteristics.

In northern Ontario, George Kolenosky (1987) found that when humans approached a mother and her cubs, the cubs immediately climbed to the top of the tree; the mother often positioned herself below them, 4 to 10 metres (13 to 33 feet) off the ground, and huffed and growled.

When danger threatens a family of bears, the mother bear sometimes simply runs away. In Massachusetts, a pack of hounds chased a mother bear 10 kilometres (6 miles) away from her cubs. The sow returned to retrieve her cubs six hours later.

A tree is also a safe refuge for cubs when the mother bear leaves them to look for food. At times like these, she may stray several kilometres from her offspring and she may be gone for three or four hours at a time. Normally, cubs are safe when they are left alone in a tree, but one time in Yellowstone National Park a male black bear spotted a cub hiding in a tree, climbed the tree, and killed and ate the cub (Rogers 1978).

In April and May, food is scarce, and in most years black bears and brown bears continue to lose weight for many more weeks. The situation is quite different for the polar bear. At this time of the year, the polar bear is on the sea ice, where there is an abundance of seals to hunt.

ORIGIN OF THE SEA BEAR

Male polar bears commonly weigh over 500 kilograms (1100 pounds), and some of the largest ones exceed 700 kilograms (1500 pounds). These weights surpass those of the great feline predators of the world, the Siberian tiger (*Panthera tigris altaica*) and the African lion (*Panthera leo*) by two and three times, respectively, making the polar bear the largest and most powerful land predator on Earth.

The story of the polar bear's evolution is a short one and begins when the animal was brown. The polar bear evolved from the brown bear. A closer look at the unusual behaviour of some brown bears may help to understand how a terrestrial omnivore could evolve into a semi-aquatic carnivore.

In the Smoking Hills of Canada's Western Arctic, I have seen brown bears walking along the coast at the edge of the sea ice within a few hundred metres of basking ringed seals (*Phoca hispida*). In the same area,

Young black bear cubs use trees as resting sites when their mother leaves them to go off and forage.

biologist Peter Clarkson (1989) has located brown bears a number of times on the sea ice, several kilometres from shore. Unfortunately, Clarkson could not determine if the brown bears were hunting seals or scavenging the kills of polar bears. Another bear researcher, Dr. Ian Stirling (1988) has talked with Inuvialuit (Eskimo) hunters who have seen brown bears on the shorefast ice, hunting for ringed seal pups in their snow lairs, and Stirling himself saw a male brown bear on the ice, 60 kilometres (35 miles) from the nearest land. Although the bears may have passively drifted on the ice for part of their journey, the animals clearly did not view sea ice as a barrier to movement.

Some brown bears may occasionally eat the same thing that polar bears eat. Coastal brown bears frequently scavenge on the carcasses of seals washed onto

beaches, and in the Okhotsk Sea, Russian researcher Popov (1976) considers brown bears to be significant predators on spotted seals (*Phoca largha*) that haul out on land in the summer. Since some brown bears do hunt seals along the seacoast, it was always tempting to speculate that they may also hunt them on the sea ice.

The final proof of this came on 4 May 1991 on the sea ice in Viscount Melville Sound, 500 kilometres (311 miles) north of the brown bear's usual range in Canada. That day, biologist Dr. Mitchell Taylor was flying over the sea ice tracking polar bears. Taylor told me: "When I first saw the grizzly I thought my eyes were playing tricks on me." His initial reaction was understandable, since a brown bear had never been sighted that far north before. Taylor quickly tranquillized the bear and examined it. It was a healthy adult

The brown bear is a capable swimmer, an attribute inherited by the polar bear when it branched off from its brown bear ancestors.

male weighing a burly 318 kilograms (700 pounds). When Taylor backtracked the bear, he found where it had been hunting ringed seals, and it seemed to have made at least two kills. Taylor found no polar bear tracks in the snow around the seal kills, so the brown bear had not scavenged from its close relative. This was the first solid proof that brown bears could hunt and kill seals on the sea ice.

Polar bears are strong swimmers, and this same characteristic is shared by their ancestor, the brown bear. Biologist Ed Bailey (1984) reported seeing brown bears on forty separate occasions swimming between islands used by nesting seabirds along the southern coast of the Alaskan Peninsula. He wrote to me that bears, especially females with cubs, regularly swim to raid seabird colonies as much as 16 kilometres (10 miles) offshore. In another example of swimming capability, an adult male brown bear swam at least 11 kilometres (7 miles) through strong tidal currents when it moved from Montague Island in Alaska's Prince William Sound to the mainland (Berns, Atwell and Boone 1980).

Clearly, brown bears swim well, hunt seals and periodically move about on the sea ice, characteristics that polar bears inherited and improved upon. It is likely that the brown bear possessed these aquatic and predatory abilities for hundreds of thousands of years before the polar bear appeared. But what happened to the brown bear to finally trigger the evolution of its close polar relative?

The oldest polar bear fossils, surprisingly, come from a site in London, England, and are estimated to be approximately 100,000 years old (Kurtén 1964). The evolution of the polar bear was pieced together primarily by the late Finnish paleontologist Dr. Bjorn Kurtén. Kurtén (1976) joked that he became destined to work with bears on the day he was born, when his parents named him Bjorn, which is Swedish for "bear." Kurtén postulated that during the Ice Age, 200,000 to 250,000 years ago, a population of brown

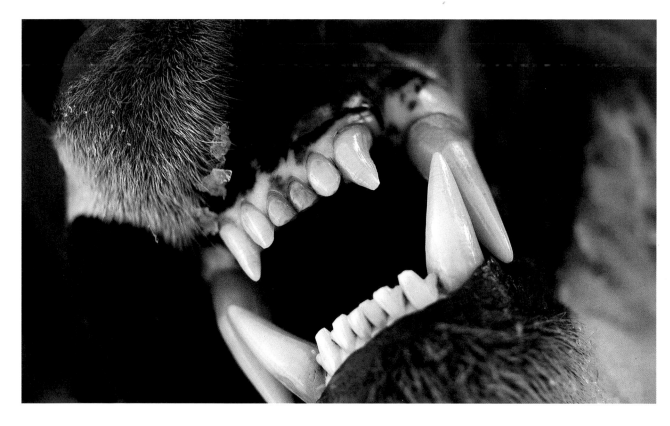

The deadly canine teeth of a polar bear are longer, sharper and spaced farther apart than those of its ancestor, the brown bear.

bears, possibly in Siberia, became cut off from other brown bears by the advance of a glacial ice sheet. These isolated brown bears, finding themselves in an arctic environment filled with seals, and with no other land predators preying on the seals, evolved to fill the vacant niche. In the thousands of years that followed, the brown bear underwent a number of adaptations that honed it to its new environment.

Polar bears have longer necks than brown bears, making it easier for them to keep their heads above water when they are swimming. Their large, paddle-like front paws are a further help in the water. The white fur of the polar bear enables it to blend better with the ice ridges and snowy hummocks of its environs, and its ears are small to lessen heat loss.

The teeth of the polar bear show the greatest change from the ancestral brown bear. This is not surprising, since the brown bear is a grass-and-root-eating omnivore, and the polar bear is a seal-eating carnivore. The brown bear has large rear molars to crush and pulp vegetation. In the polar bear, these rear molars are smaller, since it rarely eats plants. The polar bear's premolars and its front molars—in particular, the so-called carnassial teeth—are pointed and sharp edged to shear like scissors through flesh, whereas in the brown bear the carnassials are flattened. In addition, the polar bear's canines, which are used for seizing prey, are longer and sharper and spaced wider apart than those of the brown bear.

The polar bear is the youngest marine mammal on Earth. It evolved from the brown bear so recently that in captivity the two species can still interbreed and pro-

duce fertile cubs that may be yellowish-white or bluish-brown (Gray 1972).

In the wild, brown bears and polar bears probably never mate with each other because they rarely cross each other's path. In those rare instances when they do encounter each other during the breeding season, the subtle behavioural cues that the animals use to communicate with each other in courtship probably differ enough to prevent the potential mates from becoming synchronized. In time, the two species will evolve greater genetic differences and will eventually lose the ability to interbreed.

HUNTERS ON THE ICE

In May, the sun never sets on Canada's Lancaster Sound, 850 kilometres (528 miles) north of the Arctic Circle. It was 11:00 P.M. and −15°C (5°F). From my vantage point on the top of Cape Liddon, hundreds of metres above the sea ice, I could see the polar bear and the trail of blood where it had dragged the seal for 30 metres (98 feet) across the ice.

The bear looked like a subadult. It had caught an adult ringed seal when the seal surfaced at its breathing hole in the ice. After killing it, the bear played with the dead seal, swatting it with a paw and bouncing on it with its two front feet. Eventually, when the bear began to eat, it ate only the skin and the blubber. A raven (*Corvus corax*) landed nearby, hopped about for a few moments, and then flew off. Four glaucous gulls (*Larus hyperboreus*) were more patient than the raven, and they waited on the ice for the bear to finish its meal.

The bear ate for half an hour, then left the carcass to the gulls and returned to the breathing hole where it had caught the seal. As I have seen polar bears do a number of times, the bear stalked the hole in the ice as if it were prey. When the bear reached the empty breathing hole, it stared for a moment into the water and then moved off to a nearby ice hummock, presumably searching for other seals. When the young bear squatted to urinate, I knew that it was a female.

Satisfied that there were no other seals around, she returned to her kill and dragged the carcass for a couple of metres. After several bites she lifted her nose, as if testing the air, and abandoned the carcass for the final time. For the next hour, the polar bear slowly walked beside a pressure ridge that ran for kilometres across the ice. I lost sight of her as she disappeared into the glare of the midnight sun.

Polar bears locate seals with their acute sense of smell. Throughout the winter, every ringed seal maintains three or four breathing holes by scratching through the ice with the sharp nails of its front flippers. In places where snowdrifts accumulate over a breathing hole, such as in the lee of an ice hummock or pressure ridge, the seal digs out a cave in the snow above its breathing hole so that it can haul out on the ice hidden from view. Most ringed seals whelp in April, and the pups are born in the relative security of these snow lairs (Smith and Stirling 1975), which offer the mother and pup protection from the elements but not necessarily protection from bears.

Dr. Ian Stirling, the eminent polar bear researcher, believes that the months of April through about July, when young, newly weaned seals are abundant and when all seals haul out onto the ice to molt and are vulnerable to predation, are the most important months of the year for a polar bear. This is the time when the bear can replenish its fat reserves. Stirling believes that an experienced bear not only can detect the presence of a snow lair with its sensitive nose but can also determine whether a seal is there or not and whether the lair is being used by a pup or an adult. Although snow lairs can be more than 3 metres (10 feet) long, Stirling has frequently observed that bears break into a lair immediately over the breathing hole (Stirling and Latour 1978). He believes that such accuracy, based entirely on smell, is probably essential to hunting success.

Ringed seals breed in April and May, after the whelping period, and snow lairs used by rutting adult males have a strong, lingering odour, which the Inuvialuit call *tiggak* (Smith and Stirling 1975). *Tiggak*

Harp seals (Phoca groenlandica) are hunted by polar bears on the seals' traditional whelping grounds east of Greenland. On rare occasions, they are also hunted on their whelping grounds east of Labrador.

seals are not eaten by the Inuvialuit in many areas because of the unpleasant odour and taste of the blubber and meat. Smith (1980) found that of all the lairs that had been entered by bears, only 3 per cent had been occupied by rutting male seals, even though male lairs were much more common than this figure suggests. He concluded that polar bears, like the Inuvialuit, do not like to eat *tiggak* seals, and the bears avoid digging into male haul-out lairs.

Polar bears use two methods to hunt seals: stalking and still-hunting (Stirling 1974). The most common method is the still-hunt, in which the bear lies on its stomach next to a lair or a breathing hole and waits. Stirling believed that this posture produced the smallest silhouette when viewed by a seal from below and also was the most comfortable one (Stirling and McEwan 1975). Comfort is probably a consideration,

since a bear must remain motionless for a considerable time when it still-hunts. A still-hunt lasts an average of fifty-five minutes, and Stirling timed some that lasted more than two hours. Any movement that a bear makes, even shuffling its feet, might alert a seal and cause it to use another breathing hole or lair.

Although polar bears stalk prey much less frequently than they still-hunt, the stalk is the most exciting hunt to observe. In Lancaster Sound I watched an adult female with two yearlings stalk a snow lair that contained an adult ringed seal. I wrote in my field notes:

The mother bear turned towards her two yearlings who trailed behind her by about 10 metres (33 feet). The young bears immediately froze in their tracks. I was too far away to know if she vocalized to them or whether her gaze was enough to communicate her wishes. She started to stalk, moving one paw at a time, carefully planting each before she advanced another. After a couple of steps she leaped forward, a distance equal to twice her body length, and plunged through the roof of the lair. The front half of her body disappeared into the snow. She withdrew in an instant, dragging the seal away from the hole. The cubs rushed to her side.

Usually a polar bear is able to crash through a snow lair in a single pounce, but whether or not it can accomplish this feat depends on the weight of the bear and the depth of the snow covering the lair. The snow on the roof of some seal lairs may be hard packed and a metre (3 feet) thick, so it may take the bear several attempts to break through. The bear usually rises on its hind legs and forcefully pounds down on the lair with both front feet together. I watched one small bear pound seven times before the roof of the lair finally collapsed. Another time I saw a subadult bear climb an ice hummock and leap from the top to break through the roof of a lair.

When a bear catches a seal, it immediately drags the animal away from the water to prevent it from escaping down the hole. Once the bear has dragged the seal onto the ice, it bites the seal several times on the head and neck. A seal's skull is very thin, and the animal dies within seconds of its capture.

Surprisingly, until twenty years ago, no one had ever watched the hunting behaviour of free-ranging polar bears. In the summer of 1973, Ian Stirling and his wife, Stella, spent several weeks on the southwest corner of Devon Island, in the Canadian High Arctic, where they logged over six hundred hours of observations. From those observations and later ones, Stirling documented how polar bears hunt and eat seals, which parts of the seal they prefer, and the frequency with which they steal kills from each other (Stirling 1974; Stirling and Guravich 1988).

In April and May, a polar bear usually eats only the skin and blubber of its kill and leaves all of the muscle, bones and viscera. If the seal kill is a newborn pup with very little fat, the bear may not eat any of the pup at all.

Most of the calories in a seal carcass are in the blubber. The entire carcass of a yearling ringed seal contains approximately 60,000 kilocalories, of which 41,000 kilocalories, or 68.8 per cent, are contained in the blubber (Stirling and McEwan 1975).

Researcher Robin Best (1984) calculated that an active adult polar bear requires 12,000 to 16,000 kilocalories per day to maintain its weight. This would be equivalent to a meal of 2 kilograms (4 pounds) of seal blubber or 5 kilograms (11 pounds) of muscle. Since a polar bear has a small stomach capacity, normally 10 to 20 per cent of its body weight, it makes sense for a bear to eat only blubber (Best 1977). By choosing to consume only the high-calorie component of a carcass, a polar bear gains more weight than if it were to eat the less calorically rich parts, such as the bones, muscle and viscera.

There may be a second reason why polar bears often eat only the blubber. When a bear digests blubber, the waste products are water and carbon dioxide. The water is used by the body, and the carbon dioxide is expired through the animal's lungs. When a bear digests muscle and viscera, however, the principal waste product is urea, which is excreted in the urine along with water. The water that is lost in the urine must then be replaced, and to replace the water a bear may be forced to eat snow. The energy that is then required to convert snow, which is at a subzero temperature, to water, which is at the bear's body temperature of 37°C (98°F), is tremendous and greatly reduces the net energy gain derived from the meal (Nelson 1987).

There is one final point to consider. Both subadult bears that are still growing and nursing mother bears with rapidly growing cubs need additional protein in their diets. For these members of the bear population, it may be advantageous to eat the muscle and viscera of a carcass as well as the blubber.

The assumption in all of this, of course, is that the bear can catch enough seals to enable it to be choosy, but that is not always so.

SCAVENGING

When Ian Stirling first began to observe polar bears hunting, he thought that subadults bears, being inexperienced hunters, would likely be the ones to scavenge carcasses left by other bears. From his observations, he learned that all polar bears scavenge, and surprisingly, some subadults are very proficient hunters. One subadult female I watched with researchers in Lancaster Sound was such a successful hunter that we named her the killing machine. She killed four seals in a forty-two-hour span. We lost sight of her for fourteen of those hours, so she may have killed other seals as well. At her last kill, this young bear, apparently satiated, played with the dead seal for nineteen minutes before she began to eat. Six times she dragged the carcass back to the breathing hole and dropped it into the water. Each time, she hauled the wet animal out of the hole, plopped it on the ice, and stood over it. She finally abandoned the carcass after eating very little of it.

Such partially eaten carcasses may be stolen or scavenged by any bear that comes along. One carcass that I watched for several days was visited by at least six different bears. In the end, all that remained was some bloodstained snow, a portion of a rear flipper and a segment of the backbone.

Adult male polar bears are probably the most frequent scavengers because their large size enables them to drive off most other bears and steal the carcass. I watched a large adult male steal a seal carcass from a female and her two cubs twelve minutes after the female had caught the seal. The family got very little to eat. Another time Ian Stirling (1974) observed a mother bear defend her kill from an adult male twice her size. Stirling wrote:

Rather than be displaced, the female lowered her head and charged the male who also lowered his head to meet her. When they separated, the female was bleeding freely from a wound in her right shoulder and the male from a wound on his right side over the rib

cage. The female then made a second charge of about 5 metres [16½ feet] toward the male, but he did not move. The male then returned the charge while the female stood firm. Then, after standing and looking at each other for about 30 seconds, the male, the female, and her cub all began to feed on the carcass together. After 21 minutes of feeding, the female and cub walked away to wash in a pool. Nine minutes later they attempted to return to the carcass but were chased off by the male.

One of the incidental observations that Ian Stirling made in 1973 during his first summer of field work was that polar bears wash after feeding on a seal (Stirling 1974). He wrote in the *Canadian Journal of Zoology* that

after an initial feeding period of 20 to 30 minutes, a bear typically went and stood with its forepaws at the edge of, or actually in, a pool of water. The bear then licked off the upper and lower parts of the paws and its face, alternating between rinsing and licking. The washing procedure was repeated every 5 to 10 minutes thereafter. At the termination of feeding, up to 15 minutes might be spent in a final washing. From its frequent occurrence in all observations, it is apparent that washing is an integral part of feeding behavior in the polar bear.

Polar bears, unlike brown bears, rarely cache their kills for later consumption, although caching of a seal kill under a metre (3 feet) of snow has been reported twice, in the Bering Sea, by an Alaskan researcher (Eley 1978). A polar bear will most often eat at a kill until it is satisfied and then leave. Adult male polar bears have been known to spend more than a day at a bearded seal (*Erignathus barbatus*) carcass, and they presumably feed on it repeatedly. Bearded seals are three or four times larger than ringed seals and may weigh over 350 kilograms (770 pounds). Since there is more to eat, the bears naturally spend longer at the carcass.

When a polar bear leaves a carcass, other arctic animals capitalize on the food bonanza. Ravens, glaucous gulls and arctic foxes (*Alopex lagopus*) are the usual scavengers, but I was surprised by some of the others. In the High Arctic, the hardy ivory gull (*Pagophila eburnea*) will pick at carcasses and also feed on polar bear dung. Ivory gulls may even follow polar bears. Russian researcher Uspenskii (1977) wrote that "in early spring on Franz Josef Land, each bear had its own group of ivory gulls, made up of four to six birds. The gulls evidently did not want to risk being separated from 'their' bear, and when it left the area they also disappeared."

Biologist Cheryl Spencer told me about another unlikely scavenger, the rough-legged hawk (*Buteo lagopus*), which she watched feed on a seal kill on the ice of the Beaufort Sea. The famous arctic explorer Sir John Richardson found the tracks of wolverines (*Gulo gulo*) following those of polar bears on the ice in Canada's Gulf of Boothia. These large, powerful members of the weasel family are common scavengers throughout the North, and it is not surprising to find them venturing onto the sea ice in their continual search for carrion. Finally, along the northern coast of Labrador, both red foxes (*Vulpes vulpes*) and wolves (*Canis lupus*) have been seen travelling on the sea ice and scavenging ringed seals that were killed by polar bears (Andriashek, Kiliaan and Taylor 1985).

The fact that many unlikely carnivores have been sighted on the sea ice suggests that most carnivores—in fact, most mammals—continually test new habitats. If they encounter competition or predators, they may leave the habitat and not return. If they find food—in this case, seal carrion—the rewards may offset the dangers and reinforce such behaviour. Thus, rare behaviour in one carnivore population may be quite common in another.

STARVING WITH A FULL STOMACH

When brown bears and black bears emerge from their winter dens in April and May, many of them have not eaten for months. In the northern latitudes, the bears' fast may have lasted six to eight months. During the denning period, most bears lose 15 to 30 per cent of their body weight, and a lactating female bear with newborn cubs may lose as much as 40 per cent. Although these weight losses are substantial, few bears die while they are in their winter dens. Instead, the greatest nutritional stress on a bear comes one or two months after they leave their dens in spring. At this time, the bear's metabolism is no longer operating in the energy-saving mode of hibernation. The animal is active, so it is burning calories, and food is relatively scarce. For these reasons, most bears continue to lose weight well into June and sometimes even into early July.

As might be expected, the bears most vulnerable during April and May are yearlings and subadults with marginal fat reserves. These animals often exhaust their fat deposits during the denning period, and by the time they leave their winter dens they have no energy reserves; some may starve to death. Lynn Rogers (1987) documented the starvation of one such litter of yearling black bears in Minnesota.

In mid-March the yearlings weighed 3.9, 5.0 and 6.8 kilograms (8½, 11, and 15 pounds). The family left its winter den in mid-April, and the smallest yearling died two weeks later. The famished mother bear skinned and ate the yearling. A week later, Rogers found the mother bear and the largest yearling in an aspen tree eating catkins. The second yearling was lying on the ground nearby, too weak to climb the tree or to run away. It died the following week. The largest yearling managed to survive for more than two months after leaving its winter den, but it too finally succumbed to starvation and died in late June.

The diet of most brown bears and black bears is 80 to 90 per cent vegetable. Thus, it may seem surprising that bears are unable to find enough food in April, or at least in May, to stave off starvation. After all, the forests are full of new leaves, grasses and wildflowers,

An American black bear feeds on dandelions (Taraxacum officinale), one of the earliest flowers to bloom in the spring.

food that many animals, such as deer and elk, are gulping down and using to build strength. The problem for bears is not so much a scarcity of food as their inability to digest the food that is available.

The bulk of the nutrients in a plant's leaves and stem are locked inside its cells, each of which is surrounded and protected by a wall of cellulose. Plant-eating mammals have evolved a number of strategies to extract the nutrients from the cells of plants. Ruminants, such as cattle, sheep, antelope and deer, have a large, multi-chambered foregut where their food is bathed in a broth of digestive enzymes and microbes. The microbes, namely, bacteria and protozoans, break down the cell walls of plants, releasing the enclosed nutrients, which are then easily digested by the animal. Ruminants also rechew their food and mechanically break it down as much as possible before they pass it along to the microbes. Horses, rhinoceroses and tapirs have an enlarged chamber at the end of their gut, called the cecum, where microbes perform the same function they do in the foregut of the ruminants. Rabbits reingest their feces, exposing their food to digestive enzymes twice and extracting more nutrients.

Most herbivores have a long digestive tract. The gut of a sheep is twenty-five times longer than its body. A typical carnivore has a digestive tract that is only four to eight times longer than its body. Clearly, the digestion of meat requires much less intestinal length than the digestion of vegetation.

Bears do not have a multi-chambered foregut and do not rechew their food; they do not have an enlarged cecum; and they do not reingest their feces. Like most carnivores, they have a relatively short intestinal tract. All in all, bears are poorly equipped to feed on vegetation, even though it often constitutes the bulk of their diet. Their poor ability to digest vegetation explains why they may starve in April and May with a full stomach, whereas deer and elk are gaining weight.

Bears overcome the handicap of their digestive tracts by being selective in what they eat. Often they choose the parts of a plant that contain the least amount of indigestible cellulose, such as the flowers, seeds, fruits, bulbs and roots. Bears eat the leaves and stems of a plant after the plant first emerges, when it contains less cellulose, is easier to digest and contains more nutrients. Eating great quantities of a plant is another way that bears compensate for their inefficient digestive systems. Alaskan biologist David Hatler (1972) reported a black bear whose stomach contained nearly 5 litres (5 quarts) of horsetail shoots, a common spring food of bears.

DROPPINGS AND DIGESTIBLES

The diet of bears has attracted more scientific interest than any other aspect of their biology. My reference files just for brown bears include nearly 100 scientific papers that concentrate on diet alone and an additional 354 papers that include some diet information. The reason so much is known about what bears eat is simple: scats, also known as feces, droppings and dung. Scats are abundant, easy to find and cheap to analyze. All you need is a strong stomach, an inquiring mind and a deft hand to tease the turd apart.

A researcher can learn a lot from a bear scat. Viewed under a microscope, the spicules of a feather found in a scat can identify the type of bird that was eaten. The pattern of scales on a hair can distinguish between a mouse and a moose. Claws, teeth, bones and beaks are a cinch to identify, as are the seeds of a fruit, the bristles of an earthworm, the antennae of an ant or wasp and the carapace of a beetle. Scats not only tell you what food a bear has eaten but may also tell you when the bear ate the food. The remains of fly larvae or scavenger beetles in a dropping are a clue that a bear fed on an animal that may have been dead for some time.

There is one pitfall in using scats to determine a bear's diet. A scat represents the parts of a meal that were *not* digested. Thus, any food that is completely digested will not be detected. For example, a re-

A brown bear forages near the tideline on newly emergent sedges. At this time of year, sedges may contain 25 per cent protein.

BEAR MYTH

It is frequently repeated that a grizzly scat has a larger diameter than that of a black bear scat. This is false. The diameter of a bear dropping is most affected by what the bear has eaten, not by the type of bear. I can say from personal experience, however, that you can distinguish between an old scat and a fresh scat by the presence of steam rising from the latter.

PREVIOUS PAGE: *Even four-month-old grizzly cubs will eat fresh green sedges, but milk is the cubs' principal food until late summer.*

searcher may never know that a bear ate a mouthful of mushrooms or a large lump of meat because both of these foods leave no trace in the animal's scats. Nevertheless, scat analysis is an established technique that has taught us much about the diet of bears.

Young spring vegetation begins to appear as soon as the snow disappears. In mountain regions, the snow begins to melt in April and May at low elevations and on avalanche slopes, and these areas attract bears, which feed on the newly emergent grasses and sedges. In coastal regions, bears are attracted to tidal marshes for the same reasons. Along the tideline bears can also feed on seaweeds, mussels and crabs, and a lucky bruin may even find the beached carcass of a whale or a seal. Skunk cabbage (*Symplocarpus foetidus*) is one of the earliest plants eaten by bears in the eastern United States. Despite the plant's fetid smell, it is a botanical wonder. The skunk cabbage generates its own heat and keeps its flower temperature at a remarkably constant 21°C (70°F), which is sometimes 30°C (63°F) warmer than the air. The heated flower can melt its way through ice and snow. Bears never eat anything but the flowers and young leaves of the skunk cabbage. The older leaves and the stem and root of the plant are filled with sharp, microscopic crystals of calcium oxalate, which would inflame the mouth of any bear foolish enough to chew on them.

In spring, both Asiatic and American black bears often climb up 10 to 15 metres (33 to 49 feet) into the crowns of poplar trees to eat the catkins and newly sprouting leaves. As the bears climb, their claws scratch deep furrows into the bark. You can see the evidence of this spring feeding activity many years later, for the scratches remain as black linear scars.

Whereas black bears are built to climb, brown bears are built to dig. The hump on a brown bear's shoulders is a mass of muscle that powers its front limbs. Add to this a formidable set of claws, and you have an impressive digging machine. In Alaska, I watched a female grizzly till up an alpine slope as she dug for

peavine (*Hedysarum alpinum*) roots. The grizzly would plant her front claws into the soil, rock backwards with her entire weight, lift up a section of sod and flip it upside down. She then sifted away the soil with her claws and nibbled off the roots she had exposed.

At this time of the year, brown bears in North America also dig up the roots of other plants, primarily those of glacier lilies (*Erythronium grandiflora*), wild onions (*Allium cernuum*), spring beauties (*Claytonia lanceolata*), and Indian rice (*Fritillaria camschatcensis*). Before the growing season, these plants store all of their nutrients in their roots, and this is when the bears dig them up.

Spring food is often patchily distributed, and bears investigate every potential food source they encounter. Early one May in the Canadian Arctic, I flew over a subadult grizzly that was tearing apart a muskrat pushup in the middle of a small lake. A pushup is a mound of aquatic vegetation pushed through a hole in the ice by a muskrat (*Ondatra zibethica*). Muskrats sit inside these mounds and eat. From the bear's tracks in the snow, I could see that it had investigated three different pushups. Bears eat the vegetation in these mounds, and sometimes they get lucky and find other things to eat as well. Harding (1976) looked at the contents of a dozen or so different pushups. Besides the usual aquatic plants, he found hundreds of snails and three frozen muskrats.

Although bears eat mostly plants in the spring, they will also eat animals. Along the shores of Lake Baikal in Russia, brown bears feed on fish eggs and newly emerging caddis flies. Across Canada and the northern United States, black bears feed on spawning white suckers (*Catostomus commersoni*) that crowd by the thousands into shallow streams every spring.

After reading hundreds of scientific reports on the diet of bears, I still get excited when I learn about a new food, especially when it has an interesting story associated with it. My most recent piece of dietary trivia was observed in grizzly bears in the mountains of western Montana in 1932 (Chapman 1955). The author of the

Yellow skunk cabbage (Lysichitum americanum), a flower of western North America, is eaten by brown bears and blacks, as is the other species of skunk cabbage, which grows in the East.

FOLLOWING PAGE: *An adult American black bear sniffs a tree stump, searching for insect larvae and eggs.*

report watched a dozen grizzly bears in a high, rocky slope above the treeline. The bears were overturning rocks and feeding on ladybird beetles (*Coccinella spp.*) Apparently, these familiar orange and black beetles that many people know as ladybugs overwinter in large aggregations under rocks. The author, an insect collector, stated that in an area where there is a large aggregation of beetles, as many as 38 litres (10 gallons) of beetles could be collected in a day.

Bears most frequently feed on insects that occur in concentrated numbers—the social insects, such as wasps, bees and ants. In the spring in Scandanavia, brown bears tear apart anthills, and in North America black bears do the same. With a swipe of their paw, the bears open the ants' home. When the insects well to the surface to defend their nest, the bears lick them up.

A study in Montana reported ant remains in a third of the spring scats of black bears in that area. Although ants are 50 per cent protein, they are pretty meagre fare for an animal that weighs hundreds of kilograms. What a bear wants to find in spring is something big, something nutritious, something that won't fight back and something that won't run or swim away.

CACHING AND CARRION

Winter in the northern wilderness is a tough season for most ungulates, and the cumulative effects of persistent cold, deepening snow and the gradual decline in the quality of food kills some of them. By April, of the survivors, many are weak. Their weakened condition led one researcher to call them walking carrion. Every

An American black bear moves a dead white-tailed deer (Odocoileus virginianus) into thicker cover, where it will feed on the animal for several days. Earlier, the deer was struck by a car and then died in a woods nearby before it was found and scavenged by the bear.

BEAR MYTH

Bears relish putrid meat. This myth has been around a long time. Possibly the idea that bears prefer decaying flesh fits our notion of what a large, powerful carnivore should eat. Regardless, there is no scientific evidence that bears prefer meat when it is rotten. Bears show up at rotten carcasses more often simply because these are the easiest to smell and locate.

PREVIOUS PAGE: *A subadult American black bear wades into a stream in northern Saskatchewan, searching for spawning white suckers.*

spring, these winter-weakened animals, and those that died earlier, are a food bonanza for bears.

The amount of carrion available to bears in the spring can be tremendous, especially following severe winters. Ecologist Doug Houston (1978) counted the number of winter-killed elk, mule deer, bison and bighorn sheep in the northern third of Yellowstone National Park in two consecutive winters. During his study, most of the deaths occurred in elk; in the worst of the two winters, he found 512 elk carcasses. Estimating the mortality for the entire park, Houston came up with 1200 elk deaths, which would yield 104 000 kilograms (229,277 pounds) of carrion. If all of the carcasses had been eaten by black bears and grizzlies, which in Yellowstone number in the hundreds, the bears would have had an easy spring. You will see, however, that not all the carcasses were eaten by bears.

To begin with, some of the elk died when the bears were denning, and the carcasses were consumed long before the bears showed up. Once the bears were out of their dens, they had to compete with the entire cast of Yellowstone scavengers: coyotes (*Canis latrans*), ravens, bald eagles (*Haliaeetus leucocephalus*), golden eagles (*Aquila chrysaetos*) and black-billed magpies (*Pica pica*). Birds may not seem like much competition, but a flock of ravens can finish off a carcass in a couple of days. In other areas, bears must also compete for carrion with wolves, lynx (*Felis lynx*), red foxes, arctic foxes and wolverines. In fact, many, if not most, carcasses are picked clean long before a bear ever discovers them.

Among the scavengers, the bear is king, and bears will steal carcasses from other predators, such as wolves and cougars (*Felis concolor*). Cougars may hiss and snarl at a thieving bear and offer token resistance, but they invariably run off and surrender their kill. A pack of wolves may stay near a stolen carcass for a time, but it is unlikely they ever recover their kill. Typically, once a bear claims a carcass, nothing can drive it away except a larger bear.

Bears do not differentiate between an elk carcass and the carcass of a cow or a sheep. Meat is meat. Since hundreds, if not thousands, of head of free-ranging domestic livestock die every winter from natural causes, some of these carcasses are naturally found by bears. Often when this happens, the bears are accused of killing these animals. The result is that the bears' reputation is maligned, the ranchers scream compensation, and bears are trapped, poisoned and unjustly shot.

Brown bears, unlike the other northern bears, cache food to hide it from other scavengers. In northern Alaska, Gebhard (1982) observed a female grizzly at the carcass of a dead caribou. When the bear first found the carcass, she spent almost an hour covering it with tussock grass that she raked from the surrounding tundra. After the grizzly ate, she rested for 4½ hours and then worked for another hour covering the carcass with more grass. A second 4-hour rest period was followed by 39 minutes of more raking and burying. Before the grizzly finished this third bout of carcass covering, however, she was chased away by a large male grizzly.

After a brown bear covers a carcass, the cache may become quite large and conspicuous. In Alaska's Denali National Park, Murie (1981) found a cache that was 4 metres (13 feet) wide and 5 metres (16 feet) long. He estimated that the bear had raked about a cubic metre (25 bushels) of sod over the carcass of the dead caribou.

Covering a carcass may minimize telltale odours and also slow down decomposition. In a Norwegian study, half the brown bear caches were covered with sphagnum moss (*Sphagnum spp.*). Sphagnum moss contains phenolic chemicals that kill fungi and bacteria, and the plant has long been known for its antiseptic and preservative properties. Although it could not be shown in the study that bears prefer sphagnum as a covering material, the plant may nonetheless work as a preservative whenever it is used to cover a carcass (Elgmork 1982).

These three subadult brown bears walking across tidal flats might find a marine mammal washed up on shore.

The coyote (Canis latrans) *is one of the most successful carnivores in North America. In the 1850s, it was restricted to the Great Plains. Today the coyote ranges from Alaska to Costa Rica and from the Atlantic to the Pacific.*

Besides covering a carcass with vegetation, brown bears also actively guard and defend it, something that black bears rarely do. A brown bear may spend a week or more feeding on a large carcass. While it guards the carcass, the bear will rest in a day bed nearby or sometimes sleep right on top of the carcass. If another bear approaches, it is aggressively chased away. A brown bear sometimes responds to a human trespasser the same way as it does to one of its own kind; it attacks. A number of maulings have resulted when hikers knowingly or unknowingly came near a carcass that a bear was guarding.

Carrion may go undetected by a bear, but it is rarely missed by ravens. In northeastern Alaska, ravens found every large mammal carcass that researchers observed, and three-quarters of the time the birds were the first scavenger to discover the carcass (Magoun 1979). It seems to me that a smart bear should watch the movements of ravens, just as spotted hyenas and lions in Africa watch the movements of vultures to locate carrion. Although I cannot prove it, I strongly suspect that bears do watch ravens and that they also listen to them and are drawn to a carcass when noisy flocks assemble to feed. In Alberta I once found a moose carcass by following the feeding yells of a flock of ravens. Why would a bear not do the same?

> The scientist does not study nature because it is useful to do so. He studies it because he takes pleasure in it, and he takes pleasure in it because it is beautiful. If nature were not beautiful, it would not be worth knowing and life would not be worth living.
>
> —Jules Henri Poincaré
>
> French mathematician

In 1948, the year I was born, few zoologists studied animal behaviour. Most of them believed that behaviour was genetically predetermined and driven by instincts and thus was an unproductive field of study. Any reports on animal behaviour were largely anecdotal. ¶ In the 1950s, attitudes and biases began to change. Zoologists began to accept the idea that animals can learn and that they also may adapt their behaviour to their environment. It was the dawn of a new field of science—ethology, the biological study of animal behaviour. ¶ As a student of animal behaviour, I could live in no better time. In the past forty years, ethologists have uncovered a wonderful diversity of animal behaviour, a repertoire richer with complexities than anyone imagined. ¶ The premier driving force in all animals is to procreate, to pass on their genes to as many offspring as possible. Not surprisingly, then, some of the most interesting discoveries in animal behaviour involve reproductive biology. The reproductive biology of bears raises several interesting questions. Why are male bears twice as large as females? Why are they promiscuous? Why do they chase and kill young cubs? Why do some female bears begin to breed when they are 2½ years old, whereas others wait until they are 7 or 8? And finally, why would a female bear abandon her cub and let it die? The first half of this chapter looks at these intriguing questions.

▷

A male brown bear may follow a female in heat for a week or more before the pair finally mates. The pair mated shortly after the photograph was taken, and they were coupled for twenty-three minutes.

THE MATING GAME

The breeding season for all northern bears lasts several months. Most brown bears and black bears breed between late May and early July, with the greatest activity occurring in June. Polar bears breed in April and May, a month or two earlier than the other bears (Craighead, Craighead and Sumner 1976; Alt 1989; Ramsay and Stirling 1988).

Bears, for the most part, are solitary animals, so the first problem they face in the breeding season is to find each other. Male bears begin by scouting their home range weeks, if not months, before the peak of the breeding season. Typically, the home range of most male bears overlaps the home range of a number of females. In Minnesota, biologist Lynn Rogers (1987) found that some male black bears shared their home range with as many as fifteen females.

Not all female bears mate in any given breeding season, since some of them are nursing cubs. To detect potential mates, therefore, male bears probably check the resident females in their area repeatedly and continually monitor their reproductive status. In Washington, male black bears sometimes visited as many as five females in a sixteen-hour period. The male might leave after only fifteen minutes, presumably to search for other females (Barber and Lindzey 1986).

You might wonder whether bears ever fail to breed simply because they never encounter a mate. Bears are wide-ranging animals, and their large movements could sometimes result in missed breeding opportunities. This problem might be lessened if female bears also searched for mates as males do, and sure enough, some female bears seem to do just that.

In his study of black bears, Rogers (1987) found that estrous females—females in heat—covered their home territory in less time during the breeding season than at other times. One estrous female completed circuits of her territory in less than a day. When she was not in heat, she normally took about three days to do a circuit.

Greater movements such as these increase the likelihood that a female will intercept a potential mate (Barber and Lindzey 1986; Alt et al. 1977).

Courtship in bears, as in most solitary carnivores, follows a predictable sequence. It begins when the male suitor starts to trail his prospective mate. At first he follows from a distance. He smells her day beds after she has left them, and he sniffs the ground where she urinates. Urine contains the metabolites of sex hormones, and a male bear can probably analyze how receptive a female is.

In the beginning, the female runs away. She fears the male bear because he is much larger than she is and potentially dangerous. In time, however, she allows him to come closer and closer. Sometimes, however, her inherent fear of him causes her to charge him aggressively or even to swat him with a paw. Rarely, though, does the male retaliate. He bides his time.

When contact is finally made, the bears nuzzle and chew on each other's head and neck, and they may even wrestle a little. If the male is an experienced bear, he moves the courtship along as quickly as possible, and soon he is draped over her neck, then her back and finally her rump. The female periodically slows things down by sitting or lying down, but for the most part she willingly participates.

In most bears, the female is in heat for about three weeks or so during the breeding season. During this time, her vulva is greatly swollen. This sign is so conspicuous that I have seen it with binoculars from a distance. Vulvar swelling is probably easiest to detect in polar bears, which have black skin; the swollen genitals appear as a large dark patch against the animal's white fur.

Although a female bear is in heat for a number of weeks, she will only allow a male to mount her during the middle of her estrous period, the three to five days when she is most receptive. When this time comes, the male and female are inseparable. They eat together, sleep together and travel together. They may even re-

▷

Numerous scars are visible on the nose, head and shoulder of this enormous male brown bear, which probably weighed over 450 kilograms (992 pounds). The scars are testimony to the many battles he had fought during a succession of breeding seasons.

verse roles, and the female may follow the male. When the pair finally couples, the event usually lasts twenty to thirty minutes. In the days that follow, the bears mate repeatedly.

I have described a nice, uncomplicated courtship sequence, but life for a bear is rarely so easy. Estrous females are frequently attended by more than one male. In a study in southwestern Washington, when more than one male black bear vied for an estrous female, the dominant male stayed closest to the female, commonly less than 25 metres (82 feet) away from her, whereas the rival male stayed several hundred metres away. In that study, researcher Kim Barber saw male bears chase each other away from females, but she never saw them fight, and the animals had no wounds or scars (Barber and Lindzey 1986). All in all, a relatively peaceful arrangement. Elsewhere, rival male bears are not always so peaceful. Lynn Rogers (1987) wrote in *Wildlife Monographs* that

encounters between mismatched males were settled by the larger ones simply chasing away the smaller, but when contestants were fairly even in size, clawing, biting battles with continuous contact up to 4 minutes were seen in some instances. Two fighting areas were examined, and both were characterized by clumps of fur and trampled, and broken vegetation. . . . Because of fighting, old males had numerous scars on their heads, necks, and shoulders.

Reports of wounds, scars and broken canine teeth are widespread in male brown bears and polar bears as well as in male black bears. During the breeding season, I have seen male brown bears with injured front legs, broken lower jaws and gaping facial lacerations. One year I had a chance to closely examine an adult male polar bear during the breeding season. I wrote in my journal afterwards: "The bear had a number of old scars on his nose and forehead, half of his right ear was missing, and the fourth claw on his left front paw was broken off at its base. There were two fresh puncture wounds on his left shoulder that were draining pus."

The fact that male bears are so much larger than females is another indication that males compete with each other for the privilege to mate. When male and female animals differ in size, they are referred to as sexually dimorphic. Sexual dimorphism exists in many of the carnivores, but it is most evident in the big cats (lions, tigers, jaguars, leopards), weasels and bears. In all of these animals, the male is substantially larger than the female. All species of bears exhibit at least some degree of sexual dimorphism. The dimorphism is very slight in the smallest bear, the sun bear of Southeast Asia. In this species, males are about 20 per cent heavier than females. The greatest difference between the sexes is found in the northern bears that grow the largest, the brown bear and the polar bear. In these bears, males may be more than twice as heavy as females. Between the two extremes are male black bears, which are on average 50 to 70 per cent heavier than females of the species (Stirling and Derocher 1990).

Sexual dimorphism evolved in bears as part of their breeding biology. A big bear packs a big punch, so the bigger the bear, the more males he can dominate, the more females he can breed and the more offspring he can father. Humans are also sexually dimorphic, and I have often wondered if this trait evolved in us for the same reasons that it did in some carnivores.

The serious fights that occur between some rival males explain why they sometimes try to isolate an estrous female from other males until she is no longer sexually receptive. Polar bear researchers Malcolm Ramsay and Ian Stirling (1986) wrote that male polar bears appeared to herd females "into small bays or onto hillsides, away from productive areas of sea ice where most other bears were hunting seals. Although such sequestering was not possible in all habitats or areas, it frequently appeared that males attempted to isolate individual estrous females away from areas where they might encounter other males."

David Hamer and Steve Herrero (1990) have reported similar herding tactics in grizzlies in Alberta.

Also, in Denali National Park in Alaska, I watched a male grizzly bear restrict the movements of his female mate to a small isolated valley for ten days. The bears were courting, although I did not see them mate. Not only are male bears frequently promiscuous, but females may also have more than one sexual partner during a breeding season. Rogers (1987) observed one female black bear in Minnesota that had as many as four mates in one season. The record for female promiscuity, however, belongs to a Yellowstone grizzly that mated ten times with four males in two hours. At the time, the grizzly was feeding at a dump with many other bears. The artificial circumstances may have contributed to her unusual behaviour.

VAGINAL CODES AND PENIS BONES

A number of obvious statements can be made about the vulnerability of mating animals. When animals are coupled together, they are less likely to detect danger, they are less able to escape from predators, and they are poorly positioned to defend themselves. For these reasons, it is advantageous for animals, especially prey species, to mate for as brief a time as possible. Ungulates typically copulate for less than a minute. In muskoxen (*Ovibus moschatus*), for example, the affair is all over in just fifteen seconds.

If ungulates can achieve conception with such a brief copulation, why have long copulations evolved in bears? I wrote earlier that copulation in bears typically lasts twenty to thirty minutes, but it has been reported to last as long as an hour. Long copulation times are common among the carnivores, and every schoolboy in my childhood referred to mink—which sometimes copulate for more than an hour—as the standard for sexual appetite. Of course, none of us understood what we were saying, but it sounded good.

Large carnivores such as bears have little to fear

from predators, so they can afford to copulate as long as they want and still not expose themselves to much risk. The risk, however, is quite different for the tiny least weasel (*Mustela nivalis*), which may mate for ninety minutes or more. This tiny carnivore has many predators that can prey upon it. Therefore, since not all carnivores are immune to predation when they are mating, there must be a good reason why the group as a whole has such lengthy copulation times. The answer, it seems, rests with the females of these species, all of whom need repeated and prolonged genital stimulation to induce ovulation.

Mammals are either spontaneous or induced ovulators. In spontaneous ovulators, such as humans, the female ovulates during her estrous period regardless of whether there is a male around to mate with her. With this strategy, the timing of mating is critical, since a female's ova typically die within twenty-four to forty-eight hours. Thus, if a female were solitary and wide ranging, her ova might die before she encountered a male.

In induced ovulation, a strategy adopted by a wide variety of mammals, including bears, the female ovulates only after she has found a mate and been appropriately stimulated by him. What constitutes appropriate stimulation in an induced ovulator? It is speculated that the trigger for ovulation is simply the mechanical stimulation of the female's vagina and cervix during mating. I should caution that induced ovulation has not been definitely proven to occur in bears, although there is strong circumstantial evidence for it.

There is one more intriguing aspect of copulation in bears. A male bear has a bone called a baculum in his penis. In a large bear, the baculum is about twice as thick as a ballpoint pen and slightly longer. Bacula are present in all mammals that are induced ovulators. It is believed that one of the functions of the baculum is to provide additional mechanical stimulation for the female.

Let me leave you with one final piece of research to

ponder. In some induced ovulators, scientists have found that the key to female ovulation is a specific vaginal code, which may be unique to each animal species. The code includes the frequency of copulation, the interval between copulations, and the design of the baculum. The female ovulates only when all of these factors combine to produce the proper copulatory formula (Diamond 1970). This might mean, then, that if a male were not vigorous enough in his copulatory efforts, he would be unable to properly stimulate the female. Such a code would be advantageous to the female because it would ensure that only a superior male would sire her offspring. The system may not be this elaborate, and a vaginal code may not exist in all induced ovulators. Whatever the final discoveries, the details will undoubtedly exceed our imaginations.

THE BIOLOGY OF MURDER

Until recently, infanticide was viewed by most biologists as an aberrant behaviour. It had been observed frequently in captive rodents, and it was believed to be a reaction to overcrowding. Beyond that, the topic was given little thought. A 1981 biology dictionary I own doesn't even list the word.

In the past twenty years, biologists have spent thousands of hours in the field observing animal species in their natural habitats. From their findings, it is clear that infanticide is not just an artifact of captivity but an established behaviour pattern in many mammals and birds (Hrdy 1979; Hausfater and Hrdy 1984). Infanticide has been described in eagles, wolves, African wild dogs, dwarf mongooses, spotted hyenas, gorillas, chimpanzees, baboons, ground squirrels, tigers, lions, cougars and bears, to name just a few species.

Infanticide has been reported in all of the northern bears in North America (Rogers 1987; Dean, Darling and Lierhaus 1986; Taylor, Larsen and Schweinsburg 1985). In an Arizona black bear study, for example, 50 per cent of the spring cub mortalities were caused by

adult male bears (LeCount 1987). In brown bears, similar infanticidal behaviour is particularly well documented. In Yellowstone, the Craighead brothers saw male grizzlies kill cubs on four separate occasions. A particularly detailed account of infanticide comes from Kodiak Island in Alaska. In May one year, Troyer and Hensel (1962) watched a large male brown bear as he followed a sow and her spring cub. The sow tried to escape from her pursuer by climbing a steep snow slide. The steep slope and soft snow fatigued the cub, and eventually it stopped after climbing for thirty minutes. The big male caught up to the cub, grabbed it by the head and shook it until it was dead while the cub's mother watched helplessly from several hundred metres away. Afterwards, the male continued to pursue the female, and the pair disappeared over a ridge.

Less commonly, female bears are the killers. In one incident witnessed by Murie (1981) in Alaska, a female grizzly with twin cubs of her own killed two cubs belonging to another female when the two families accidentally wandered close to each other.

Three reasons have been proposed to explain infanticide in bears: to reduce the competition for food and space, to provide food and to create a breeding opportunity for a male bear. Of the three explanations, many biologists believe the last one is the most common, although each explanation may operate at one time or another.

It is speculated that killing a cub creates a breeding opportunity in the following way. When a female's only cub is killed, she stops nursing, and often she will come into heat shortly afterwards; the male can then breed with her. Female bears can be induced into heat this way many weeks after the usual breeding season. Black bears in Pennslyvania, for example, have bred successfully as late as 12 September. Biologist Gary Alt (1989) believes that late-breeding females such as these have possibly lost their litters earlier in the summer and then come into heat. It is tempting to suggest that all late-breeding females lose their litters to killer male bears

who are trying to create a mating opportunity for themselves, but infanticide is only one of many causes of cub mortality.

The opponents of the kill-a-cub-so-you-can-breed scenario suggest that this explanation is weak because a male bent on passion, particularly a polar bear or a brown bear, would first have to battle a very dangerous and protective mother bear and risk possible injury from her while attempting to kill her cubs. Even assuming that a male succeeds in dispatching the cubs, possibly by stealth or surprise, he would still have to follow the female for some time until she became sexually receptive. During this time she might elude him or, worse yet, be stolen from him by a higher-ranking male (Ramsay and Stirling 1986).

The logic against this scenario is convincing. But even if male bears do not kill cubs as a reproductive strategy, there is still the documented fact that male bears *do* kill cubs, whatever their reasons.

Mother bears seem acutely aware of the danger that male bears present to their offspring, and female polar bears, brown bears and black bears try to avoid male bears as much as possible. For this reason, female polar bears with small cubs of the year hunt in shorefast ice away from the floe edge and shifting pack ice, where most of the male bears concentrate to hunt. Researchers have observed that during the breeding season in May and June brown bear females with cubs choose elevated steep slopes on which to rest during the day and at night. These isolated sites are well away from the normal travel paths used by bears and provide the family with a good vantage point from which to detect other bears, especially adult males that travel widely at this time of the year (Murie 1981; Darling 1987).

Two decades ago few people believed that infanticide existed in bears. Today we know that it is a relatively frequent occurrence and that female bears protect their offspring from males by specific avoidance behaviour. It is to be hoped that in the next twenty years we will learn why infanticide evolved.

COMING OF AGE IN BEARLAND

Although there is considerable variability in the age at which female bears begin to breed, on average, female black bears reach sexual maturity and breed for the first time when they are $3\frac{1}{2}$ years old. Female brown bears and polar bears breed for the first time when they are $4\frac{1}{2}$ years old. Male bears of all three species reach sexual maturity at roughly the same age as their female counterparts and are then physically able to sire offspring.

Even though a young male bear is fertile and able to breed at three or four years of age, it rarely gets an opportunity to do so in the wild. As we have seen, in most bear populations there is intense male competition for estrous females, and the biggest bears do most of the breeding. In Alaskan brown bears, males do not reach their maximum size until they are eight to ten years of age. Thus, even after a male brown bear reaches sexual maturity, it usually has to grow for a number of years before it becomes a breeding contender. Any young male that loiters around an estrous female is quickly chased away by the larger, more mature males (Glenn 1980).

Most male bears, therefore, probably do not begin to breed until they are nearly full grown, sometime after seven years of age. Once a male bear does begin to breed, however, he may make up for lost time and mate with many females in a breeding season. There are exceptions to this pattern, of course, and an adult male bear might breed when it is younger if there is a surplus of females in the population or a shortage of older adult males to guard the females when they come into heat.

Female bears, as far as we know, do not compete with each other during the breeding season as males do, so as soon as a female bear reaches sexual maturity, she begins to breed. The age at which a female bear begins to breed varies depending on where the bear lives and the quality of her habitat. The most important indicator of habitat quality is food. In good habitats food

FOLLOWING PAGE: *Yearling brown bears, such as these triplets, have been known to survive on their own, but most will spend another year with their mother before the family finally breaks up.*

◁

A mother brown bear and her yearling cub stand up to watch a male bear that has just strolled onto the sedge meadow where the two bears were feeding.

is abundant, and in poor habitats food is scarce.

Food influences most aspects of reproduction in the life of a female bear. It is easy to understand why. Just consider the energy demands of bearing and rearing a litter of cubs. This process, from conception to weaning, takes a minimum of two years in black bears and a minimum of three years in polar bears and brown bears. Adult female bears are consequently the most energy-taxed individuals in a bear population, and their reproductive performance is closely linked to the amount of food they get to eat. Not only does the diet of a female bear determine the age at which she will reach sexual maturity and breed for the first time, but it also affects the average size of her litters and the interval between successive litters. If you compare these three parameters—the average minimum breeding age, the litter size and the interval between litters—in different areas of a species' range, you can appreciate how sensitive and responsive female bears are to the quality of their habitat.

Table 3.1 compares populations of brown bears and American black bears. Polar bear populations do not differ enough, so only one location is listed. The Asiatic black bear has been omitted because not enough is known about its reproductive life, but it is likely that it is quite similar to the American black bear.

Both brown bear studies were conducted in northern North America. The U.S. study examined bears in a treeless coastal region of the Alaskan Peninsula where seasonal temperature extremes are moderated by the nearness of the ocean. Here, in the summer months, the bears have a high-quality diet of salmon and lush coastal vegetation. The Canadian brown bear study was done in the dry, mountainous interior of the southern Yukon, where there are long, cold winters and January temperatures may plummet to −50°C (−68°F). In this part of the Yukon, the bears eke out an existence on a meagre diet of peavine roots and soapberries (*Shep-erdia canadensis*). These two populations of brown bears are less than a 1000 kilometres (620 miles) apart, yet

◁

Individual bears have very distinctive faces that are recognizable even to human observers. This female brown bear with a single yearling was one of the most handsome bears I have ever photographed.

Table 3.1   Minimum age of first successful breeding, litter size, interval between litters and habitat quality in selected populations of brown bears, American black bears and polar bears.

	Minimum Age of First Breeding	Litter Size	Average Litter Interval (Years)	Habitat Quality	Reference
BROWN BEARS					
Coastal Alaska	4½	2.5	3	Good	(Glenn et al. 1976)
Yukon	6½–8½	1.7	3+	Poor	(Pearson 1975)
AMERICAN BLACK BEARS					
Pennsylvania	2½ (82%)	3.0	2	Good	(Alt 1989)
Montana	6½–8½	1.7	3+	Poor	(Jonkel and Cowan 1971)
POLAR BEARS					
Canadian Arctic	4½	1.8	3	—	(Stirling, Calvert and Andriashek 1980)

the females have quite different statistics. As you can see, the females from the food-impoverished Yukon breed much later in life and have smaller litters than the salmon-stuffed bears in coastal Alaska.

The effects of nutrition are even more striking in some black bear populations. The hardwood forests of Pennsylvania yield bountiful crops of beechnuts, acorns, wild cherries and grapes. In the spruce-fir forests of western Montana, a bear must make do with grasses, wildflowers, ants and huckleberries. Not surprisingly, Montana females breed later than Pennsylvania females and have smaller litters. By the time some females in Montana breed for the first time, a female in Pennsylvania may be breeding for her fourth time, and she may already have raised nine cubs. If we assume a lifespan of twenty years for female bears in both regions, then the lifetime cub production of a Pennsylvania female is twenty-eight cubs and that of a

Montana female nine cubs, greater than a threefold difference (Alt 1989). Nutrition also explains the differences in litter size seen from one year to the next in the same area. In Montana, black bear litters were smaller in the year after a poor huckleberry crop, and a similar trend was seen in Massachusetts in the year following a poor crop of beechnuts or wild cherries (Jonkel and Cowan 1971; Elowe 1987).

The next time someone asks you how many bear cubs there are in a litter, how often a bear has a new litter or at what age bears begin to breed, you will know to start the answer with "It all depends on where the bear lives and what it eats."

THE FAMILY BREAKS UP

Usually young black bears leave their mother in their second summer, when they are 1½ years old. Young brown bears and young polar bears stay in the family for a year longer, separating from their mother when they are 2½ years old. Although this is the usual timing of family breakup, families in all of the species may stay together for an additional year. In this case, young black bears would remain in the family until they are 2½ years old, and young brown bears and polar bears would stay with their mother until they are 3½.

In Alaska, at the northern edge of the black bear's range, it may be usual, in fact, for cubs to stay with their mother for an extra year. Biologist John Hechtel, working north of Fairbanks, thinks that the black bears in his area may stay together longer because of the harshness of their environment. The added year of family life might be necessary so that cubs can grow to a sufficient size to survive once they are independent. Hechtel has just begun his study and cautions that no firm conclusions can be made, but the preliminary data are suggestive.

The bond between a mother bear and her cubs is greatest in the first spring and summer of the cubs' lives. During this time, the mother bear is quite attentive to her offspring. She checks their whereabouts constantly, frets when they are missing and responds promptly when they whine. A mother bear may even let a tired cub ride on her back. The family moves as a unit, its daily movements stalled by periodic bouts of nursing when the mother rests on her rump and leans back, often closing her eyes, while her offspring suckle contentedly.

By their first autumn, the mother bear has lengthened the leash on her family, and the trend continues thereafter. By the time the family is about to split up, the cubs have grown into quite independent little bruins. Although the youngsters continue to nurse, the bouts are less frequent and they often skip a session, especially when they become preoccupied with their own feeding activities. At this age, the young bears have the confidence to move away from their mother, and they may feed at some distance from her. Stirling (1974)

noted that whereas yearling polar bear cubs never strayed more than a half kilometre (⅓ mile) from their mother's side, 2½-year-olds often hunted up to 2 kilometres (1¼ miles) away.

A bear family separates in a number of ways. Over the summer, the family members may simply slowly drift apart. Or after spending the summer together, they may separate in August or September. Sometimes the mother bear may force her cubs to leave, woofing aggressively and charging at them until they finally leave her alone.

At times the family separation can be quite abrupt, as Adolph Murie (1981) observed in Alaska. Murie spent twenty-five summers, between 1922 and 1970, observing grizzlies in Denali National Park. He wrote about one abrupt family breakup that occurred like this. On 18 May, he saw a female grizzly and her two offspring nurse and later share a caribou calf carcass. Two days later, on 20 May, the pair of 2½-year-olds were seen feeding alone on some peavine roots, about 5 kilometres (3 miles) from where they were last seen with their mother. Later that day, the youngsters were chased for a short distance by a large adult male bear, which Murie assumed bred with the youngsters' mother. The grizzly family was never seen together after 18 May. The mother bear and her two offspring spent the summer in the same alpine valley, often feeding within a few kilometres of each other, but they never reunited.

Although the time of breakup varies, grizzly bear families, like the family Murie watched, most commonly break up during the breeding season. Up to this point in a young bear's life, its mother would have kept it away from large adult male bears because of the threat these animals pose. During the breeding season, however, the mother is less likely to flee from a male. A young bear's fear of one of these powerful males would keep it temporarily away from its mother, and out-and-out aggression from the male may finalize the separation. Dr. Lynn Rogers (1987) in Minnesota monitored

FOLLOWING PAGE: *The bond between a mother bear and her cubs is strongest in the first spring and summer of the cubs' lives, when they rely on her most for protection.*

A subadult brown bear, in his first summer alone, shakes off after fishing for salmon.

the breakup of fifty-one black bear families during the breeding season, and only one of the families reunited afterwards.

In Idaho, black bear families also broke up in June, but there were occasional reunions between the mother and one or both of her yearlings later in the summer (Reynolds and Beecham 1980). Family reunions sometimes occur in brown bears as well, but most bear biologists believe that mother bears are generally antagonistic towards their offspring once the family splits up, and this attitude discourages most young bears from returning. Of the bear families that do reunite during the summer after the breeding season, most break up for good in the autumn, and the mother and her offspring den separately. However, black bears in both Pennsylvania and Ontario, at least on a couple of occasions, did not do what scientists predicted they would do. One April, when biologist George Kolenosky looked into a bear den in northern Ontario, he found an adult female bear, two three-month-old cubs, and a two-year-old male. He concluded that the young male had probably stayed with his mother during the previous summer and simply extended the association into the denning period (Kolenosky and Strathearn 1987).

Once family breakup occurs, what happens to the newly independent juveniles? In black bears, the yearlings separate from each other at the same time as they separate from their mother, and they move to different portions of their mother's home range. In brown bears, 2½-year-olds may also wander off alone, but many times they stay together for the rest of the summer, presumably for companionship and security. Sometimes these sibling relationships last as long as two years, until the bears are 4½ years old. During this time, the juvenile bears probably den separately and then reunite each spring.

At sites where brown bears gather, such as salmon streams and berry patches, a pair of juveniles may improve their rank in the bear hierarchy by working as a team. The partnership enhances the juveniles' ability

A full-grown cougar (Felis concolor), weighing over 50 kilograms (110 pounds), is more than a match for a young black bear cub. Cougars prey on cubs in several areas of western North America.

to intimidate other bears, and they may benefit by having greater access to contested fishing spots or feeding areas.

ORPHANS AND CASTAWAYS

Although adult mortality is low, usually less than 15 per cent per year, every year some mother bears die and orphan their cubs. Brown bears, orphaned as young as 7 months, have survived. Albert Erickson (1959) has reported that orphaned black bear cubs, aged 5½ months, survived alone in the wild, but in most cases the survival of such young animals may be a matter of luck. Their survival would hinge upon the quality of the habitat in which they find themselves, whether it is a good year or a bad year for berries and

nuts and whether there are predators in the area.

In Arizona, cubs of this age are killed by cougars and bobcats (*Felis rufus*) (LeCount 1987). In British Columbia, a golden eagle swooped down and snatched up one of three cubs and carried the victim to its nest about half a kilometre away (Nelson 1957). And in Wyoming, a trio of coyotes harried a family of bears and escaped with one of the cubs. In all of these cases, the cubs were preyed upon while they were still with their mother. What chance would an orphan cub have against predators with no maternal protection?

Happily, the fate of all young orphans does not end in tragedy. On 21 July 1975, three grizzly cubs were orphaned when their mother died in a back country valley of Jasper National Park in Alberta. The orphans were not seen again that year, but the three showed up

▷

Orphaned brown bear cubs may stay together for several years after their mother dies. This behaviour probably increases the bears' chances of survival.

in the same area the following May. The bears appeared healthy, although they were somewhat small for yearlings. The trio was observed in the area throughout July of 1976 during which time they wrestled and played together, slid down snow drifts, grazed on grasses, dug for ground squirrels, roots, ants and bumblebee nests, and even managed to steal a freshly killed marmot from a coyote.

In August, one of the yearlings disappeared, but the two survivors stayed together. They denned together that winter and emerged on schedule the following spring. The young grizzlies, now a little more than two years old, were captured and examined by researchers in May. The brother and sister were fitted with radio collars and then followed over the summer. When the two bears were recaptured in October, both had almost doubled their weight since May. The orphans remained inseparable for two more years. They denned together and summered together. In 1979, at four years of age, their radio collars were removed (Russell et al. 1979). Fittingly, the grizzlies were then released from human scrutiny, and they melted into the wilderness.

Sometimes mother bears abandon their cubs. In Utah one autumn, researchers found a total of twenty-three black bear cubs unaccompanied by their mothers. Because bear food was scarce that autumn, Fair (1978) speculated that the cubs may have competed with their mothers for what little food was available, and it became necessary for the adult females to abandon their offspring.

In Arizona, LeCount (1987) suspected that black bears in his area sometimes abandoned the remaining cub when the first cub in a litter of two died or was killed by predators. Abandoned bear cubs have also been reported in brown bears in Montana.

Why would a mother bear cast away her cub, sentencing it to death by starvation? From a human perspective, which invariably is lofty and self-righteous, many would decry such abandonments as the actions of a savage, insensitive beast. Humans, then, must also

be beastly, for dozens of human societies, past and present, have abandoned offspring. A 1991 news report estimated that in the slums of Rio de Janeiro there were more than a million orphan children living on the streets and eating garbage. Most of the children were there because they had been abandoned by their parents.

For a moment, let's resist the temptation to interpret animal behaviour, as well as our own behaviour, in sentimental and emotional terms. Instead, if we scrutinize all behaviour in the rational light of evolutionary theory, we may be more forgiving of bears, and of ourselves. According to current evolutionary theory, as every animal evolves, it acquires a set of behaviours that maximizes the number of offspring that an individual can produce (Dawkins 1989). If abandoning her young enables a female to produce a greater number of offspring in her lifetime, then such a behaviour makes sense from an evolutionary standpoint.

Abandonment as a reproductive tactic has been examined in brown bears by David Tait (1980), and he presents a convincing argument. Tait reasoned that the number of cubs a female grizzly can contribute to a population in her lifetime depends upon how long she can expect to live in her area, the average size of her litters and the average interval between successive litters. Using a mathematical model, he concluded that in good habitats, where grizzlies typically produce large litters and have short intervals between their litters, a female would increase her lifetime production of cubs by abandoning a single cub. If she kept the cub, she would not produce any other cubs during the 2½ years the cub was with her. By abandoning the cub, she could breed the following year and likely raise a larger litter.

The strategy of abandonment would not be advantageous in a population of bears living in poor-quality habitat, where bears normally have small litters and long intervals between those litters. In this circumstance, if a female abandons a single cub, she has no

Since polar bears are more predatory than the other northern bears, an abandoned or orphaned polar bear cub would have a harder time feeding itself than other young bears and would likely die.

guarantee that she will breed the next spring or that she will conceive a large litter. Thus, abandoning a cub might reduce, rather than increase, her lifetime production of cubs.

In conclusion, most mothers that abandon their young probably unconsciously assess the liabilities and advantages of continuing to care for an offspring. When a mother decides to abandon and sacrifice that offspring, she surrenders to the directives of her genes and behaves in a fashion that is in her best long-term interest.

SUNBATHING SEALS

In the realm of the polar bear, summer begins in June. In the most northern regions, the sun may not have set for two months, its meagre warmth slowly working on the ice and snow until it finally begins to melt.

June is the month to watch seals. On the sea ice, the ringed seals no longer shelter inside their snow caves. The roofs of many caves collapse on their own, and others are destroyed by the seals themselves, who butt through them with their heads or scratch and bite them full of holes. Now when the seals surface through their breathing holes, they haul out into the glare of the arctic sun and not into the muted shadows of a snow lair. The young seals of the year, who are several months old and layered in fat from suckling for weeks on the rich milk of their mothers, make their first appearance. In addition, all of the older animals haul out into the sunshine to complete their annual molt. On warm and windless days, as many as 70 per cent of the

ringed seals in an area may be seen sprawled on the ice
(Finley 1979).

During the molt, many seals haul out for twenty-four
hours at a time, and some may even stretch out for fifty
hours straight. When seals haul out during the molt,
they feed very little, they lose weight, and they expose
themselves to the risk of predation by polar bears. They
subject themselves to these pressures because they *must*
warm up to molt. When seals swim in ice-choked sea
water, the water penetrates their pelts and cools their
skin to within a few degrees of freezing. For a seal to
molt and grow a new coat of hair, its skin must be
warmer than 21°C (70°F), and this only happens when
the animal is hauled out (Feltz and Fay 1966). Basking
ringed seals orient themselves broadside to the sun to
receive the maximum solar radiation. This works so
well that on a warm, calm day the seals may heat up too
much and be forced to return to the water to prevent
overheating.

Seals are vulnerable to polar bears when they bask.
But in every predator-prey relationship, the armament
and tactics of the predator are balanced by the detec-
tion and evasion strategies of the prey. Hauled-out
seals counter the threat of polar bears in a number of
ways. A seal always approaches its breathing hole with
great caution. If there is the least noise or movement
around a breathing hole, it will use a different one.
When the seal feels it is safe, it pokes its head up
through the hole and examines the surrounding ice for
some time before it finally hauls out. Seal researcher
Tom Smith observed that it was common for a seal to
haul out, plunge back into the water and haul out again
a number of times before it finally settled on the ice
(Smith and Hammill 1981).

Seals may haul out in groups of a hundred or more
along large cracks in the ice, but when seals use breathing holes to haul out, each animal uses a separate hole.
If a seal pops up in a breathing hole already claimed by
another seal, the owner defends the hole by lunging at
the intruder with its mouth open, slapping it with a

▷

The Duke River valley in southern Yukon is characteristic of the tundra habitat of many of the brown bears in northern Canada.

front flipper or biting it. Seals have good reason to defend a breathing hole. When more than one animal basks beside the same hole, they increase their risk of being caught by a polar bear because they can't all dive through the hole at the same time. On Baffin Island in the Canadian Arctic, Smith (1980) watched a polar bear stalk two adult seals stretched out beside the same breathing hole. When the bear made its final charge, the seals tried to escape together. One seal got away, but the bear snagged the second one by its hind flippers.

A basking seal uses a two-part surveillance system to detect stalking polar bears. First, it rests on the ice with its tail facing into the wind, which will carry the odour of any bears lurking behind it. At the same time, the seal can use its eyes to detect any bears that might approach from the front. Second, a basking seal is always vigilant. Bear researcher Ian Stirling (1974) noted that hauled-out seals continuously alternate between lying flat and raising their heads to look around for bears. When he timed them, the seals spent an average of seven seconds looking around and twenty-six seconds lying flat. The times, however, varied greatly, and Stirling wrote that "a polar bear could never learn to alternate between periods of stalking and stillness on the basis of such averages."

Out in the open, a seal can use both its eyes and its nose to detect a bear. This may explain why polar bears are not as successful hunting seals in this situation as they are hunting them in the spring, when they are inside their snow caves. In the spring, polar bears hunt for four to six hours each day. In the summer, when the seals are hauled out in the open, the bears hunt for nine to thirteen hours every day, twice as long as they did in the spring. Not only do they hunt longer in the summer, but they are less succesful. When a polar bear stalks a seal in its lair, it is four times more likely to catch its prey than when it stalks a seal hauled out in the open (Stirling and Latour 1978; Stirling and Archibald 1977).

In the contest of bear versus seal, a bear uses two manoeuvres to outwit its prey. It stealthily stalks the seals over the ice, or it surprises them by swimming underwater and surfacing at their breathing holes. On top of the ice, when a hunting bear first spots or scents a seal, it crouches down. Staying crouched, it then slowly sneaks forward, using any available hummocks or ice ridges to shield its approach. Late in the season, the ice surface may be covered with pools and interconnecting channels of meltwater. When this happens, a stalking bear slips into the water and uses the channels to carefully paddle closer. When it is within 20 to 30 metres (65 to 98 feet) of its quarry, the bear makes a final rush (Stirling 1974).

The more cunning manoeuvre is when the polar bear surprises a seal by popping up at its breathing hole. I try to imagine what must go through a seal's mind when his only avenue of escape is suddenly plugged with a white furry bruin interested in dinner. When polar bears hunt in this way, they actually swim under the ice, and they can stay submerged for over a minute. They work their way closer to the seal by swimming from breathing hole to breathing hole. At each hole, they breathe, look around to get their bearings, and then dive again. Ian Stirling (1974) wrote that "the bears have such control that they can surface, breath, raise their heads slightly to look, and submerge without making a ripple in the water."

Dr. Tom Smith (1980) watched a polar bear stalk a large bearded seal in this fashion. When the bear started to stalk the seal, it was twice the length of a football field away. Surfacing at a number of seal holes along the way, the bear took thirty-two minutes to reach the unsuspecting seal. When the polar bear popped up, the seal plunged into the same hole with the bear. A great deal of splashing ensued, and the bear surfaced about a minute later *without* the seal. The next day the seal was basking in the same spot, but it had a couple of fresh wounds on its neck and shoulder.

HUNTER AND THE HUNTED

For the most part, the June diet of black bears and brown bears is the same as it is in April and May and includes such foods as fresh green vegetation, willow and aspen catkins, roots, ants, bees and wasps, and carrion.

In mountain areas, as the growing season progresses, bears climb to higher elevations, following the retreat of the snow line to eat the new plants that sprout up. In June, they move to shaded north-facing slopes, where the snow disappears last and where they find more fresh vegetation. By making such movements, bears can continue to find the young, succulent plants that they prefer.

When you look at the diets of bears across the breadth of their range, a number of novel foods turn up, further testimony to the omnivorous and opportunistic feeding habits of these adaptable carnivores.

Nearly everyone in eastern North America knows about the snapping turtle (*Chelydra serpentina*), a large, pugnacious fresh-water turtle that gets its name from its strong jaws and lightninglike bite that can sever your finger. Apparently, one snapping turtle in New York state wasn't fast enough or pugnacious enough to escape a black bear. The female turtle was caught by the bear as she was laying her eggs, and all that remained two hours later was a single egg and an empty turtle shell (Behrend and Sage 1974).

In Okefenokee Swamp in southeastern Georgia, June is the nesting season of the alligator (*Alligator mississippiensis*). At this time, female alligators construct large mounds of vegetation in which they lay about thirty large eggs. Afterwards, they lie nearby and defend their nest, hissing and lunging at any intruders. Still, the eggs in over 50 per cent of the alligator nests in Okefenokee are lost to predators. When Howard Hunt, the curator of reptiles at the Atlanta Zoo, set up surveillance cameras at a number of alligator nests, he discovered something quite surprising. The most common predator was the black bear. The bears sit on top of the nests and methodically eat every egg in a clutch. Sometimes they flip the end off an egg with a claw and then lap up the contents, or they take the whole egg in their mouth and then spit out the shell.

Hunt couldn't understand why the alligators never seem to defend their nests against these bruin bandits. At destroyed nests, he never found any signs of a struggle—no blood, no ravaged alligators and no injured bears. Hunt decided to get a bear's eye view of how an alligator responds to a bear at its nest. He located an active nest and approached it to see if the female would defend her eggs, and she did. Typically, a defensive female alligator raises her body high on her legs and walks menacingly towards the intruder, hissing with her mouth open to expose her toothy weaponry. Later in the day, Hunt returned to the same alligator nest, but this time he was dressed in a bear suit and he approached the nest on all fours. The alligator fled. Hunt can't explain why this happened, but some of his colleagues joke that the alligator knew enough not to tangle with anyone who would dress up in a bear suit and walk through the swamp.

Another bear story involving an egg of a different kind was recounted to me by Dr. Tom Barry, an ornithologist who worked for over thirty years in the Canadian Arctic. As part of his work, Barry monitored waterfowl nesting colonies. Over the years, one or two brown bears would periodically raid the goose colonies in the deltas of the Anderson and Mackenzie Rivers in the Northwest Territories, but their raids were nothing compared with the egg-stealing assault mounted in 1986. That June, five brown bears converged on the Anderson River delta and the goose colony was ravaged. Twenty-five hundred brant (*Branta leucopsis*) nests, 3000 to 4000 snow geese (*Chen caerulescens*) nests and 100 glaucous gull nests were destroyed. Barry estimates that the bears probably gulped down 24,000 eggs, shells and all. He told me with delight: "The eggs gave the bears terrible diarrhea."

A final novel-food story comes from Adolph Murie (1944) in Yellowstone National Park in the 1930s. One day Murie watched eleven black bears flip over dried bison chips to lick up the grasshoppers and crickets hidden underneath. Murie wrote that "the hillsides were flecked with bison chips of all ages and I was astonished to see that hundreds of these had been tipped over by the bears." Murie carefully noted that crickets and grasshoppers were only found under those bison chips that had aged a certain amount and that the bears ignored the fresh chips because they stuck to the ground too much to hide any insects underneath, not to mention what a challenge it is for a bear to flip a wet chip.

As a child, I knew from watching nature programs on television that bears ate grass and flowers and insects, but it came as a complete surprise to discover that bears, like porcupines, rabbits and squirrels, also eat bark. Somehow the vision of a mighty grizzly bear nibbling on a tree trunk just didn't fit. Nonetheless, I discovered that not only do grizzlies eat bark but so do most other brown bears, as do American and Asiatic black bears (Poelker and Hartwell 1973; Watanabe 1977; Blanchard 1983; Slobodyan 1976).

In late spring and early summer, the bears strip the bark from the base of tree trunks. First they bite the bark loose with their teeth, and then they strip it upwards for a metre or more, exposing the underlying cambium layer, or sapwood. Often the bark strips stay attached at the top, so they hang about the trunk like a grass skirt. At this time of the year, the sapwood is soft and spongy and easily scraped off by a bear's front teeth. The sapwood is 90 per cent water, but it has a higher sugar content than any other bear food around at this season, so bruins with a sweet tooth attack the trees with zeal (Radman 1969).

When the trunk of a tree is completely girdled by a bear's scrapings, the tree dies. More commonly, however, a bear only eats the sapwood from part of the trunk. Although the tree doesn't die, the exposed sap-

wood allows insects and fungi to penetrate the heartwood, weakening the tree and stunting its growth.

Dozens of species of trees are attacked by bears, but most frequently they are softwoods such as spruces, firs, pines, redwoods and cedars. Generally, bear damage to trees is a scattered problem, but in Japan, Washington and Oregon it is such a serious problem that the black bears in these areas are heavily hunted to reduce the damage that these animals cause to the timber industry. This area of conflict promises to increase in the future as we depend more and more on tree farms to sustain the timber industry. Tree farms present bears with great swathes of densely packed trees, all the same age and all the same species. When a stand is young, bears find a great number of trees close together that have the thin bark ideal for stripping, so they can do considerable damage in a short time.

When bears eat trees, the foresters are unhappy. When they eat fish, the fishermen are unhappy. And when they eat goose eggs, the biologists are unhappy. Unfortunately for bears, their June diet includes other items that displease some people. Newborn deer, elk, caribou and moose are hunted by bears in June and are an important supplement to the bears' diet at this time of the year. These cervids are born in late May and June. At birth, they weigh from 3 to 15 kilograms (6 to 33 pounds). White-tailed (*Odocoileus virginianus*) and mule deer fawns (*Odocoileus hemionus*) are the lightest, caribou (*Rangifer tarandus*) intermediate, and elk (*Cervus canadensis*) and moose calves (*Alces alces*) the heaviest.

Caribou young are strong enough to walk and follow their mothers within an hour of birth, but all the other young cervids spend their first week or so as "hiders." The young animals stay hidden by themselves, except when their mother nurses them a few times a day. If there are twins, they hide separately.

Young hiders are spotted or coloured to blend with their surroundings, and they have little scent. To further conceal their presence from predators, their mothers remove any evidence of their birth by devouring the placenta and eating any vegetation or earth soaked with birth fluids. As well, each time the young nurse, their mother stimulates them to void by licking their groin, and then she consumes their urine and feces. All of the carnivores that prey on young cervids, including bears, have a keen sense of smell, and these maternal measures reduce odours.

Until recently, most biologists believed that it was uncommon for bears to prey on young cervids, since hair rarely showed up in the June scats of bears. What no one realized was that bears rarely eat the hide of their young kills, so normally very little hair is consumed. In addition, since meat is completely digested in its passage through a bear's intestinal tract, it also leaves no incriminating evidence.

Starting in the mid-1970s, biologists began to attach radio collars to newborn cervids to monitor their survival and to determine the reasons why some of them died. What they found came as a complete surprise. In a Utah study (Wilton 1983), black bears killed 9.3 per cent of the young mule deer, and in an Idaho study (Schlegel 1976) they killed 47 per cent of the elk calves. In Alaska, young moose calves fared no better. Brown bears killed 43 per cent of them in one area (Ballard, Spraker and Taylor 1981), and black bears killed 34 per cent in another (Franzmann, Schwartz and Peterson 1980). Other studies have reported that bears preyed on white-tailed deer fawns in eastern North America (Mathews and Porter 1988), caribou calves in northern Alaska (Reynolds and Garner 1987), sika deer (*Cervus nippon*) fawns in Japan and roe deer fawns in Russia. Clearly, predation on young cervids occurs wherever brown bears and black bears are found.

The statistics on how many young cervids are caught by bears are interesting, but what is more interesting is how the bears catch them. Some researchers believe that bears purposefully travel to calving grounds with the sole intention of preying on young cervids. Although I don't doubt that bears are intelligent enough to plan in this way, there may be another explanation why young cervids are hunted as often as they are. In June, bears and pregnant female deer and elk may simply select the same type of habitat, where there is an abundance of fresh green growth for them to eat. If bears and cervids are in the same spot at the same time, it is natural that bears should take advantage of any vulnerable young animals they find.

Because brown bears use open country such as tundra and grasslands, they are easier to observe than black bears, which live in forests. Consequently, most observations of hunting behaviour by bears on young cervids involve brown bears. Since 1986, Dr. Steven French and his wife, Marilynn, have spent every May and June in the rolling meadows of Yellowstone National Park filming and observing grizzly bears hunting elk calves. Their detailed observations have contributed greatly to our understanding of hunting behaviour in bears, and many of the following details were gleaned from their work (French and French 1990).

The most common way that a grizzly hunts elk calves is to simply search a likely area for bedded animals. A bear might spend several hours slowly moving across a sagebrush flat, stopping often to look around, move its ears and sniff the air with its nose held high. When it gets close to a bedded calf, the bear's searching pace may quicken, and it may zigzag back and forth. Elk calves are so well camouflaged and difficult to scent that a searching bear may pass within 2 metres (6½ feet) of a bedded calf without detecting it. Grizzlies also successfully hunt for bedded calves at night, as the Frenches learned when they used a night-vision device.

The other hunting method used by grizzly bears is "the chase," a behaviour one associates more with fleet-footed wolves and large predatory cats than with bears, which often seem to just amble along. Once an elk calf is a few weeks old, it follows its mother during the day and grazes alongside her. Even though young cervids quickly outgrow their hiding phase, they remain vulnerable to bears until they are six to eight weeks old. At this age they generally have the strength and endurance to outrun a bear, which will rarely continue a chase for more than 100 metres (328 feet).

Before a chase begins, a grizzly will stalk along the forest edge to get close to the animals it is interested in. Once it is within 100 metres (328 feet) or less of its quarry, it launches a surprise charge at close range. In the melee, the bear singles out a calf and tries to run it down. When a bear runs at full speed, it cannot make sudden turns, so an elk calf can sometimes out-manoeuvre its pursuer if it makes a sharp turn.

Deer and caribou cows usually offer no assistance to their calves if they are being chased by a bear. At best, they snort, stomp their front feet and circle around the bear. Cow elk are more protective of their offspring, and in Yellowstone they assist their calves in a number of ways. Sometimes a cow runs ahead of her calf. The Frenches thought this not only spurred the calf on to greater speeds but also enabled the cow to select the best flight path. This strategy was very successful, and the calf escaped in twelve out of thirteen chases that they witnessed. Another manoeuvre that cow elk use is to run alongside the bear and the calf and then suddenly swerve between the two of them. I watched one film segment in which three elk cows ran directly in front of the bear, only a few metres from its nose. The bear seemed to momentarily lose its concentration or lose sight of the calf. In any case, the bear slowed down, and the calf escaped.

Even after a bear catches a calf and starts to cart it off into the woods, a mother elk may still not give up. Sometimes a cow will rush at the bear repeatedly and even kick it with her front feet. The Frenches saw female elk kick bears on five separate occasions; twice the bear released the calf, and it escaped unharmed.

The only mother cervid that puts up more of a fight in defence of her young than an elk is the cow moose. In Denali National Park in Alaska, photographer Dave Fritts watched one grizzly try to catch a young moose calf. The bear had killed the calf's twin a few days earlier. When the grizzly returned to finish off the remaining calf, the mother charged the bear, lashing out with her front feet. The bear limped away and left the mother and her calf in peace.

Another moose-bear encounter occurred in Wyoming, but this time it involved a black bear. When the bear first grabbed the moose calf, the calf began to bleat, and the mother moose, with her hackles raised and ears lowered, immediately charged the bear. The moose jumped on the bear's back with her heavy, sharp hoofs and cut a deep gash across the bear's shoulder. The bear immediately freed the calf, and it escaped.

In recent years, the public's opinion of predators has softened. Today most people accept and understand that a predatory bear is just as important to the natural world as the young moose and elk calves it preys upon.

Those things are better

which are perfected by

nature than those which

are finished by art.

—Cicero,

Roman statesman

Covering the northern pole of the Earth is a vast dome of ice that never melts. Because it is permanent, it has sometimes been mistaken for land. Unlike land, however, this massive island of ice floats atop the Arctic Ocean and rotates slowly in a clockwise direction, completing a revolution every three to four years. In winter, the ice fuses with all of the polar lands that circle the Arctic Ocean: Canada, Alaska, the former Soviet Union, Greenland and Norway's Svalbard Archipelago. In summer, however, the edge of the ice is often kilometres from the nearest land. Off the north coast of Alaska, for example, the ice edge may be 100 to 300 kilometres (62 to 186 miles) offshore. ¶ In summer, polar bears try to remain on the pack ice as long as they can so that they can continue to hunt seals, but in some areas of the North the ice melts completely and the bears are forced to spend part of the summer on land (Larsen 1986; Uspenskii 1977; Amstrup 1988). This period of compulsory shore leave is naturally longest for those bears that range the farthest south, namely, the polar bears that live in Hudson Bay, the great body of Arctic water that penetrates the mainland of northern Canada. (Stirling et al. 1977). The bay is covered with ice well into the summer, cooling the surrounding land and resulting in a climate that is much colder than is usual for such latitudes. Thus, some polar bears live at the same latitude as London, England, or as my home in Calgary, Alberta. These polar bears have developed various techniques for adapting to the ice-free conditions and relatively warm temperatures of summer life in southwestern Hudson Bay.

BEARS ON THE BEACH

The polar bears of Hudson Bay begin to come ashore in July, though the last of the ice does not disappear from the bay until the middle of August. As the bears come off the ice, they settle into different areas of the coast, depending on their age and their sex.

The big adult males position themselves along the shoreline on headlands or on small offshore islands, settling on top of old beach ridges that are close to the water. These are the preferred sites because they can be reached with the least amount of walking and they intercept any breeze blowing off the water (Derocher and Stirling 1990). Both male and female subadult bears hang around the coast with the adult males, but since they are subordinate to the adults, they end up in all the spots that the adult males don't occupy.

Adult females, both those with offspring and those that are solitary and presumably pregnant, move 20 to 40 kilometres (12½ to 25 miles) inland. They do this for very good reasons. In this part of Hudson Bay, most of the adult females spend the summer in the same place where they den in the winter to have their cubs. Derocher and Stirling (1990) believe that when mother bears return to the area in the summer with their cubs, the cubs—in particular, the young female cubs— become familiar with the denning area. Later, when the female cubs are pregnant for the first time, they know where to go to den. Another reason for females to move their families inland is to avoid encounters with adult males, most of whom stay on the coast. Derocher, who has seen adult males chase females with cubs during the summer, believes that females may settle inland to reduce the risk of infanticide.

Another of the interesting discoveries that Derocher made was that from one summer to the next all the bears return to the same general area where they spent the previous summer. In fact, when Derocher monitored individual bears for six summers in a row, every year he found the bears within 30 kilometres

(18½ miles) of where they had first been located. Since the bears have hundreds of kilometres of coastline to choose from when they come ashore, the bears seem to know where they want to go and how to get there.

Polar bears are usually thought of as loners. However, Derocher and Stirling (1990a, 1990b) found that once the bears came ashore, though subadults and female adults remained alone, the adult males were often found in small groups. The average group had four males in it, but one exceptional gathering totalled fourteen males. The composition of these male groups constantly changed throughout the ice-free period. Bears would leave one group and join another. When a helicopter would approach a group of males, they might huddle together until they were touching each other, and if they fled, they often ran as a group, shoulder to shoulder. A rare photograph taken by researcher George Kolenosky shows a cluster of nine adult males, sitting on their rumps side by side and facing forward, as though they were part of a circus act.

Derocher speculated that adult males gather together to become familiar with each other. Because the bears return to the same spots each summer, and because they are not competing for food or mates at that time of the year, it is a perfect opportunity to get to know their neighbours, particularly their strengths and weaknesses. In the final analysis, these friendly get-togethers may actually be a method for adult males to assess and establish rank.

Once the bears have settled into their respective locations, they make themselves comfortable. Polar bears in Hudson Bay, and everywhere else in the Arctic, dig shallow pits that resemble the familiar day beds dug by brown bears and black bears. In areas north of Hudson Bay, snowdrifts may survive through the summer in sheltered ravines and north-facing slopes. When this happens, bears may simply park on top of a snowdrift or dig right in and bury themselves inside a snow den. On northern Baffin Island, snow can always be found in the summer, and in a deep ravine, Schweins-

burg (1979) found twenty-two snow dens strung along the top of a single snowbank.

In southwestern Hudson Bay, bears dig earth dens. Most of the earth dens are dug inland from the coast. Typical dens are only 1¼ to 2 metres (3¼ to 6½ feet) deep, but on high banks along lakeshores, some dens are more like burrows. The longest burrows may extend 6 metres (19½ feet) into the earth and terminate at permafrost, which helps keep the dens cool. Researcher Dr. Chuck Jonkel (Jonkel et al. 1972) found one long burrow that was used by a 562-kilogram (1239-pound) adult male.

The deep burrows may not only keep a bear cool but also reduce the mosquitos. I have been in this area of Hudson Bay a few times in July, and the mosquitos are horrific. In July, you cannot talk without inhaling mosquitos. If you try to enjoy a cup of coffee, it quickly fills with floaters, and only the the desperate risk the necessary exposure needed to relieve themselves. Bears are bitten by mosquitos through the thin fur on their faces and bellies, and especially on the bare skin around their eyes, noses and nipples. It is easy to understand the attractiveness of a cool den at the end of a long, dark burrow.

Staying Cool

The average summer temperatures in southern Hudson Bay are in the mid-teens (60s Fahrenheit), but on calm, sunny days the temperatures may rise to over 26°C (79°F). For the polar bears of this region, the warm temperatures come at a time when it is most difficult for them to dissipate body heat. The bears have just ended their most important seal-hunting period, and most have added several hundred kilograms of insulating fat to their bodies. The fat deposits of some bears can be truly unbelievable. One seventeen-year-old female weighed 99 kilograms (218 pounds) when she was caught in November. When she was recaptured the following July, she weighed 410 kilograms (904 pounds), a 311-kilogram (686-pound) weight gain in eight months (Ramsay and Stirling 1988).

Tropical animals that store fat isolate the fat in specific areas of their body where it does not interfere with their ability to dissipate body heat. A few examples are the hump on camels and Zebu cattle, and the fatty tails of Gila monsters (*Heloderma suspectum*) and fat-tailed sheep. Arctic animals, in contrast, deposit fat over their entire bodies, where it serves not only as an energy reservoir but also as an insulating layer against the cold. The fat layer on a polar bear is usually at least 1.5 centimetres (½ inch) thick, and over some parts of its body it may be as much as 11 centimetres (4½ inches) thick (Oritsland 1970). To keep from overheating, polar bears use several strategies. First, polar bears molt in the summer. All mammals molt their pelts periodically because their hair bleaches and wears out. In northern mammals such as bears, the molt occurs in the summer, when the animals are most stressed by the heat. During the molt, polar bears shed their thick winter coat and replace it with a thinner, cooler one.

Second, polar bears cool off by lying on their backs and waving their legs in the air. The fat layer is thickest on a bear's back and rump and thinnest on its legs, so it can lose heat most easily through its limbs. A polar bear can further cool off by panting like a dog (Best 1982).

Third, bears stay cool in the same way as your family car—with a radiator. In your car, water circulates through the radiator, where it is cooled by the flow of air passing through it. A polar bear has two radiators, one over each shoulder blade. A bear's radiator consists of a thin sheet of muscle that lies directly under the skin on top of its fat layer. When a bear needs to cool off, blood is shunted out to these sheets of muscle, which dissipate the heat through the skin (Oritsland 1970).

By now it is probably clear that summer life for a polar bear during the ice-free period is mostly lounging along the coast, trying to stay cool. Indeed, Knudsen (1978) concluded that as much as 90 per cent of a bear's time is spent resting. More recent studies suggest that the bears not only are resting but, from a metabolic standpoint, may actually be hibernating. Since the bears still move around, researchers have coined the expression "walking hibernation." This aspect of polar bear research has only begun. Although summering polar bears are lethargic and show some of the same biochemical changes in their blood that are found in denning brown bears and black bears, it has yet to be determined whether polar bears have the other metabolic adjustments typical of bear hibernation, namely, a reduction in their metabolic rate, heart rate and body temperature (Nelson 1987; Derocher et al. 1990). Polar bears in southern Hudson Bay may be landlocked for three to four months. If they actually hibernate while they are ashore, their energy requirements would be greatly reduced and they would use less of their fat reserves.

The Summer Menu

While polar bears are on land, they survive off of their fat reserves, but that does not mean they never eat. Some bears eat carrion or small amounts of seaweed they find washed up by the tide. Others may forage a little on the tundra and eat grasses or crowberries (*Empetrum nigrum*) or catch the occasional lemming or vole. Some bears, however, are more resourceful.

One August John Hicks and I travelled to Wager Bay, a known polar bear summer retreat in the northwest corner of Hudson Bay. The topography of the southern shore of Wager Bay is quite dramatic. In places, steep cliffs rise almost directly from the water to heights of 500 metres (1640 feet), and here and there the cliffs are split by deep ravines and waterfalls. It is common knowledge among the Inuit of the region that polar bears sometimes climb these cliffs to steal the eggs of nesting seagulls. John Hicks watched a female bear climb the cliffs with her two cubs. Once the family members had cleaned out all the nests on one ledge, they moved up to the next one.

In James Bay, the large inlet at the southern tip of Hudson Bay, molting sea ducks such as oldsquaws (*Clangula hyemalis*) form large flocks on the water in late summer. The ducks stay on the water all the time because their ability to fly is impaired while they are molting. On several occasions, researcher Richard Russell (1975) watched polar bears swim among the ducks, and he believed that some of the bears had learned to capture the ducks on the open water. He wrote: "Polar bears are excellent swimmers, and can dive and swim for considerable distances underwater. A bear could dive and rise under a bird resting on the surface, particularly in stormy weather when the shallow seas are roiled, or in the presence of heavy breakers."

The polar bear and the white whale, or beluga (*Delphinapterus leucas*), occupy the same Arctic range. A number of belugas have been found with linear scars on their bodies, and these injuries have been attributed to polar bears (Heyland and Hay 1976). Marine mammal biologist Thomas Smith is one of the few people to have watched polar bears and belugas interact in summer, and his observations add an another twist to the multifaceted life of the polar bear (Smith and Sjare 1990).

In late July in the Canadian High Arctic, Smith watched belugas approach swimming polar bears on two separate occasions. Each time a group of belugas was involved, and their behaviour may have been an attempt to intimidate and threaten the bear. In the first instance, a group of a dozen belugas swam underneath the bear, passing within 1 to 2 metres (3¼ to 6½ feet) of it. As they swam underneath, they exhaled, sending up a shower of bubbles that burst around the bear. The second time, approximately one hundred belugas approached a swimming bear and formed a semicircle around it. The bear stopped swimming and began to turn around in the water. The belugas stayed about 10 to 15 metres (33 to 49 feet) away from the bear, but occasionally one would approach as close as 1 to 2 metres (3¼ to 6½ feet). The bear finally swam to shore. Smith thought the coordinated behaviour of the belugas caused the bear to retreat.

It has been reported that walruses (*Odobenus ros-*

marus) mounted a similar group threat display against polar bears. Stirling (1984) described a coordinated display given by forty-five walruses to a polar bear on the edge of the ice. Stirling thought that the walruses used underwater vocalizations to alert each other to the presence of the bear and that their vocalizations may have then played a role in coordinating the group display. Belugas are also vocal—they are sometimes called sea canaries—and like walruses, they may use their vocalizations to coordinate defensive action against bears.

Belugas have good reason to be concerned about polar bears. Polar bears hunt them. Twice Smith watched a large bear successfully hunt belugas from an ice floe. Each time, the bear waited on a small pan of ice for belugas to swim nearby. When a beluga calf swam by, the bear jumped into the water on top of the calf and dragged it up onto the ice. Beluga calves are around 1.2 metres (4 feet) long and weigh about 45 kilograms (99 pounds) at birth. The bear killed the young belugas quickly by biting them on the head and neck.

The award for resourcefulness in hunting certainly goes to a bear in Wager Bay that successfully hunted a seal by pretending to be an ice floe. The polar bear caught the seal in late August. When the pair was first sighted, the seal was floating in the water about 60 metres (180 feet) away from the bear. Whenever the seal was on the surface, the bear would swim slowly towards it, but each time the seal dove the bear stopped swimming and floated motionless on the water. The sequence was repeated at least five times, and each time the bear moved a little closer to the seal. The stalk ended when the seal surfaced beside the bear and the bear killed it immediately. The observers speculated that the seal mistook the motionless floating bear for an ice floe (Furnell and Oolooyuk 1980).

The ice-free period removes polar bears for weeks and sometimes months from the pack ice, the environment for which they are best adapted. Nonetheless, on land the polar bear continues to display the same adaptability and flexibility that enabled it to first exploit the pack ice thousands of years ago.

SALMON AND BEARS

The Life of the Salmon

The salmon is the fish that most people associate with bears. In the North Pacific, there are five kinds of salmon that breed in both Asia and North America. They are, in order of increasing size, pink or humpback salmon (*Oncorhynchus gorbuscha*), sockeye or red salmon (*O. nerka*), chum or dog salmon (*O. keta*), coho or silver salmon (*O. kisutch*) and king or chinook salmon (*O. tschawytscha*). The salmon differ greatly in size, from the lightweight, 2.5-kilogram (5½-pound) pink salmon to the heavyweight king salmon, which can weigh over 50 kilograms (110 pounds). The length of their life cycle also varies. The small pink salmon has a two-year cycle, whereas the large king salmon lives eight years or more.

In general, the lives of all salmon follow the same pattern. The fish spawn in late summer or autumn in gravel beds in freshwater streams or lakes, sometimes 1600 kilometres (1000 miles) from the sea. The eggs overwinter under the ice and then hatch in the spring. Most of the newly hatched salmon, called fry, migrate downstream to lakes, where they stay for up to three years. Once they grow to a certain size (7 to 10 centimetres, or 2¾ to 4 inches), they migrate to the sea, where they do most of their growing to reach adult size. A salmon may live in the sea for up to four years, during which time it ranges widely.

Once a salmon is large enough to spawn, it returns to the same river system in which it was born. The fish locate their birthplace by smell. Every river has its own unique signature odour, imparted by the combination of bedrock, soil and vegetation over which the water flows. When salmon are fry, they seem to imprint on that odour in an irreversible way.

Some sockeye salmon may swim more than 1600 kilometres (994 miles) after they leave the sea to reach their fresh-water spawning grounds.

Once a salmon leaves the ocean, every fibre in the fish is focused on one activity: reproduction. From the moment it enters freshwater, it barters its survival for a one-time opportunity to procreate. None will survive the ordeal; in fact, once a salmon enters fresh water, it stops eating and its digestive tract slowly deteriorates. Instead of eating, the fish draws upon its body reserves, and once its reserves are depleted, it digests its own tissues.

One year I swam with schools of spawning sockeye salmon to get a closer look at these remarkable creatures. Afterwards, I wrote in my journal:

The spawning stream was a chamber of horrors filled with dead and dying salmon. The crimson bodies of the fish were covered with pearly white scars. Some of the fish had loose flaps of skin that

pulsated slowly in the current. Others had clouded eyes. All faced death, a death that none could escape. As I floated in the 12°C [55°F] water in my rubber wetsuit, the salmon swam within centimetres of my mask. They brushed against my arms and legs. None seemed alarmed by my presence. The spectre of death had dulled their reactions.

The salmon faced into the current. Their hooked snouts opened and closed slowly, but even that seemed to be a labour. A few salmon among the hundreds were new arrivals on the spawning grounds, and these fish bullied the others, rushing and biting them. Males bit other males, and females bit females. The bullies needed a place to nest and spawn, and time was running out.

A female salmon lays four thousand to eight thousand eggs. Of those thousands, only about ten salmon reach maturity and begin the return journey to their

After a brown bear catches a salmon, it will often leave the river to eat the fish in privacy, away from other bears that might steal its catch.

natal spawning grounds. In their homeward journey, salmon must skirt fishing nets, thrash through rapids, scale waterfalls, endure pollutants from paper mills, mines and agriculture, avoid capture by eagles and ospreys, and escape from bears. Because of these many hazards, only two or three salmon out of the original ten that begin the homeward journey ever survive to spawn.

Scenes from a Salmon Stream

The spawning runs of many salmon begin in late July and August, and from then on the salmon are hunted by bears. Salmon fishing by bears is a widespread occurrence. Black bears from Washington to Alaska fish for salmon along a multitude of coastal rivers (Frame 1974). Even polar bears have been known to fish for salmon, albeit Atlantic salmon. In 1778, George Cartwright wrote in his journal that he counted thirty-two polar bears fishing for salmon along the Eagle River in Labrador. There are no recent records, however, of fishing polar bears.

Of all the bears, the brown bear has the greatest reputation as a salmon fisherman. Brown bears fish for salmon around the entire perimeter of the North Pacific, from Russia's Kamchatka Peninsula in the west around to southern British Columbia in the east.

Salmon are caught by bears on their spawning grounds and during their upstream journey. A popular place for bears to fish is below a waterfall or along a stretch of shallow rapids. In these areas, the upstream progress of the fish is slowed, and great numbers of exhausted salmon crowd together in quiet eddies and pools to rest. Here salmon are especially vulnerable to bears.

I have watched brown bears fish for salmon in a number of locations, but the best bear-salmon show in the world is at McNeil River Falls on the Alaskan Peninsula. Here, in late July and early August, an observer can watch dozens of bears chasing, pinning and grabbing salmon only a few dozen metres away. Many of

A snorkelling brown bear searches for tired salmon that it can snag.

the bears of McNeil, after fourteen years of careful management, have become completely habituated to humans. Every day of the summer season, the bears go about doing the things that bears do in plain view of a dozen gawking people.

A brown bear may use as many as two dozen different fishing techniques, but a few of these techniques are more successful than others (Luque and Allen 1976). In shallow water, the run-and-scatter technique is popular. A bear charges into a spawning stream, and as the water flies in all directions, it locks on to a fleeing fish and doggedly chases it around and around and back and forth in the shallows. Eventually, if the bear is lucky, the salmon is herded into water where the fish can no longer manoeuvre, and it is quickly caught. I have watched bears chase salmon for hours in this way,

and at times it seems that the chase is more important than the capture. Many times I have watched a bear splash towards shore with a plump salmon in its mouth and then abruptly release its catch to chase another salmon that suddenly swims across its path.

Another fishing method is the snorkel-and-lunge technique. A bear swims or walks through the water with most of its head submerged, and when it spots a salmon it lunges forward and tries to grab the fish. Typically, a snorkeling bear only submerges its face, so as it swings its head back and forth through the water searching for salmon, its ears resemble twin periscopes riding along the surface. If that is not endearing enough, a bear often blows bubbles while its face is submerged.

A female brown bear with yearling cubs will often choose a fishing spot apart from other adults. When she and her cubs fish downstream from other bears, they can scavenge the injured fish that escape from other bears.

An adult brown bear catches a sockeye salmon in mid-air, snagging the fish by the tail. A fishing brown bear may catch ten or more salmon in an hour.

The most common way for a bear to fish is to simply stand in the current and wait for a hapless salmon to swim within reach. For several weeks one year, I photographed sockeye salmon and brown bears along a small stream in Alaska, and most of the bears fished in this way. I wrote about one female in my journal:

For hours, the bear scanned the foaming water at the base of a small waterfall. After each successful catch, she always returned to the same spot in the river, backing into position like a runner into her marks. Frequently, when the time between catches became long, she would paddle the churning water several times with a paw, almost, it seemed, to break the tedium of her vigil. At other times she would balance on three legs with her left front paw cocked in the air ready to strike. As soon as the bear spotted a fin breaking the surface she sprang forward with remarkable speed and grabbed the fish with her jaws, or pinned it to the bottom of the stream with her paws.

Every salmon was brought to shore and eaten in a predictable sequence, as though the bear were adhering to the etiquette of an ursine Amy Vanderbilt. First, the head and gills of the fish were chewed with noisy relish. Then the skin, garnished with fins, was stripped and eaten. And finally, the bulk of the salmon was consumed in several quick gulps. Invariably the bear teased out the entrails from her meal and left these for the gulls.

When salmon are migrating upstream, they often seem to assault a waterfall as a group. One moment the water will be quiet, and the next there are salmon erupting everywhere. During such a flurry of action, salmon often miscalculate their leaps. Sometimes the fish leap in the wrong direction and end up in the bushes along the shore. More amusing is when a leaping salmon collides in midair with a bear, spearing the bear in the rump or crashing into the side of its head. Once I even saw a leaping salmon arc completely over a bear's back. You would think that such salmon were doomed to capture, but often the bear's reactions are too slow to catch the fish before it falls back into the water and escapes.

Bears, like all patient fishermen, eventually catch their limit. On that small stream in Alaska that I monitored for almost a month, I saw one adult female brown bear catch 8 sockeye salmon in just forty minutes. Along the McNeil River, it is common for bears to catch 50 salmon in a single day. According to biologist Larry Aumiller, the record catch was made by an adult male bear named Groucho who caught 88 salmon in one day. Groucho also holds the record for the greatest number of salmon caught in one season, 1018—and those are just the fish that Aumiller saw the bear catch during the day. Bears can fish after dark, and Groucho may have caught other salmon at night. The salmon that bears catch at McNeil Falls are chum salmon, which commonly weigh 2.5 to 4.5 kilograms (5½ to 10 pounds). If Groucho had eaten all of the salmon he caught on the day of his record catch, he would have consumed a minimum of 200 kilograms (441 pounds) of salmon—a physical impossibility.

When a bear first arrives at a salmon stream, it is usually quite hungry and eats all of the salmon it catches. Once it has eaten several fish, however, a bear's hunger slackens, and then it eats only the parts of the salmon that are high in fat content, namely, the eggs, skin and brain. Since a gram of fat yields twice as many calories as a gram of protein, it makes sense calorically for a bear to ignore the protein-rich flesh of the salmon (which, incidentally, is the part that humans relish) and eat only the fat-rich parts. In this way, a bear can consume a greater number of calories and build up its fat reserves more quickly. You may recall that polar bears also show a similar preference for the fat-rich parts of seals.

Half-eaten salmon carcasses are never wasted. Subadult bears that are excluded from the prime fishing spots along a salmon stream can do very well just by scavenging the carcasses abandoned by other bears. Of course the young bears have to be quick to compete with the retinue of avian scavengers that invariably flock around the streams. I have seen ravens steal a salmon right from under a bear's nose, and a feeding bear is often surrounded by a dozen or more squabbling glaucous-winged gulls (*Larus glaucescens*), which pour onto an abandoned carcass the instant the bear turns away.

EAGLES AND BEARS

Of all the avian scavengers that associate with bears, the largest and most powerful are the eagles. Ornithologist Leslie Brown (1976) wrote that "an eagle in masterful flight combines grandeur and grace in a manner no bird can eclipse." Although no eagles live on the pack ice with polar bears, eagles are found in most other areas where there are black bears and brown bears. Four species of eagles regularly associate with bears.

Three species are fish eagles. They live along seashores and around large rivers and lakes. Because of their similar diets and requirements for nest sites, these eagles would be in competition were it not for the fact that their ranges overlap very little. The bald eagle (*Haliaeetus leucocephalus*) is found only in North America. The white-tailed sea eagle (*H. albicilla*) inhabits Greenland, Scandinavia and the western former Soviet Union. And Steller's sea eagle (*H. pelagicus*), the largest of the three with a wing span of 3 metres (9¾ feet), is found only in a small area of eastern Russia on the Kamchatka Peninsula and along the coastal regions of the Sea of Okhotsk (Palmer 1988a).

The fourth eagle species is the golden eagle (*Aquila chrysaetos*), a large, powerful raptor that ranges across the breadth of northern Asia and throughout most of North America, especially in the West and the North. The golden eagle prefers open country, so it occurs most commonly in mountainous regions, tundra and deserts (Palmer 1988b).

All of the eagles are rapacious hunters preying on everything from game birds and other birds of prey,

◁

When salmon are abundant, a brown bear may eat only the fat-rich parts of the fish, namely, the skin, brain and eggs. This bear had caught eight sockeye salmon and only eaten the choice parts.

The bald eagle is one of the fish eagles that regularly associate with bears.

such as peregrine falcons (*Falco peregrinus*) and great horned owls (*Bubo virginianus*), to rabbits, sea otter pups (*Enhydra lutris*) and even pronghorn (*Antilocapra americana*) that are many times larger than the eagles themselves. Even though eagles are capable hunters, all of them scavenge and feed on carrion, and this is when they commonly come into contact with bears.

Golden eagles, like bears, frequently feed on ungulates that have died from disease, injury or malnutrition, and eagles and bears may compete for the same carcass. In Alaska, I watched a golden eagle circle several times over a foraging grizzly. I wondered at the time whether the eagle did this to see if the bear had found something, such as carrion, that the eagle might also scavenge. Biologist Adolph Murie (1981) thought that golden eagles do such bear surveillance as a matter

of course. He wrote that "any bear on the landscape is worthy of at least a brief inspection by an eagle or other animal interested in carrion, for the bear may be at a carcass. I have watched eagles perch on a slope near a bear at a carcass, patiently waiting and hoping for a chance to eat. And I have often watched an eagle circling over a bear, alighting nearby or diving low over him."

Also in Alaska's Denali National Park, Murie watched a golden eagle follow a grizzly along a ridge for 1½ hours as the bear dug for ground squirrels in half a dozen different locations. Each time the bear moved, the eagle followed and perched on the ground nearby. Another time, a grizzly digging for ground squirrels attracted three eagles at the same time. Two rested on the ground nearby, while a third alternately hovered and

The golden eagle acquired its name from the straw-coloured plumes at the back of its head and neck.

soared low overhead. In none of these instances did the eagles obtain anything to eat. Nonetheless, since golden eagles still follow bears, their efforts must be rewarded often enough to reinforce this behaviour. Indeed, a photographer in Denali saw an eagle swoop down and capture a ground squirrel as it escaped unseen from a grizzly that was busy digging up the rodent's burrow.

Most commonly, fish eagles and bears come together at salmon streams, and any stream that attracts bears invariably also attracts eagles. Like the golden eagle, the fish eagles are not above scavenging. In fact, the bald eagle may even prefer to feed on carrion and steal from other birds than to hunt and kill for itself (Stalmaster 1987).

Typically, along most salmon streams in North America, bald eagles course up and down a stream or slowly circle overhead. As soon as a bear abandons a partially eaten salmon, an eagle swoops down and snatches up the remains in its talons and flies away with its prize. Often a cluster of gulls descends on the salmon first, before the eagle can reach it. Then the eagle simply scatters the gulls with a power dive and pirates the booty. But the drama may not end there. Eagles often steal from each other, and if the pirate is noticed by a larger eagle, a chase may ensue. In these eagle chases, adults usually chase subadults, or adult females chase adult males. Adult females are able to dominate males because female eagles are as much as 20 per cent larger than males.

It is easy to understand why eagles watch bears, but how might a bear profit by keeping an eye on eagles? First of all, bears are opportunistic predators, and they are not averse to adding an eaglet to their diet if the opportunity presents itself. In the northwestern former Soviet Union, a researcher reported that a female brown bear killed a white-tailed sea eagle nestling. Although the report did not mention any details, it is likely that the bear plundered a nest that had been built on the ground. In a similar situation in the McNeil

River Sanctuary, a brown bear pillaged the ground nest of a bald eagle and ate the single chick.

My favourite bear-eagle story comes from the Columbia River valley in southern British Columbia. McKelvey and Smith (1979) were conducting an aerial survey of bald eagle nests in the area when they sighted a pair of adult eagles excitedly circling a stand of cottonwood trees. In the top of one of the trees was a large nest. As the men flew over, they saw no eggs or nestlings, but they did see a black bear sitting in the nest.

Often when bald eagles are not actively searching for food, they will soar in groups of a dozen or more in giant funnels high above a salmon stream. When eagles soar as a group against an open sky, they are conspicuous to other eagles. It is believed that eagles, which have a visual acuity six to eight times greater than that of humans, may spot such groups as far away as 65 kilometres (40 miles) and key in on these to locate sources of food. Although I cannot prove it, bears may also watch eagles to learn of possible food sources. One experience I had in coastal Alaska convinces me that this is sometimes so. At low tide, a bald eagle flew down and snagged a large salmon with its talons. The fish was too heavy for the bird to carry away, so it flopped to shore, dragging the salmon with it. Almost immediately, another eagle that had been soaring around spotted what had happened, and it dropped from the sky like a stone. At that moment, about 300 metres (984 feet) away, a brown bear was walking along the tide flats in the general direction of the eagles. As soon as the bear spotted the plummeting eagle, it galloped towards the birds and stole the salmon from them.

When I first began to study animal behaviour, it never dawned on me that animals might use other animals just for the information they could provide. I overlooked this possibility because I never attributed thought to animals. I arrogantly believed that only humans think. I was wrong. I now believe that many animals other than humans also think. They assess, analyze and choose, and as you will see, of all the animals,

bears are among the brainiest.

SOCIAL RANK

A bear spends a large part of its life alone, but sometimes it may join other bears, especially at sites where food is concentrated, such as in berry fields, along salmon streams and at large carcasses. On a mountain slope in Montana, eleven black bears fed together in the same patch of huckleberries (*Vaccinium membranaceum*) (Jonkel and Cowan 1971). On Kodiak Island in Alaska, researchers (Atwell et al. 1980) counted thirty-two brown bears grazing in alpine sedge meadows within an area of only 10 square kilometres (4 square miles). Bears sometimes associate in even denser aggregations, and the groupings along salmon streams are a good example of this. At McNeil Falls, an observer can see as many as sixty brown bears fishing together in a area the size of a football field.

Even the normally reclusive polar bear forms feeding aggregations. In 1980, the carcass of a right whale (*Balaena mysticus*) was found floating in the drifting pack ice among the islands of Norway's Svalbard Archipelago. A fully grown right whale can weigh 80 000 kilograms (88 tons) and provide a sizable parcel of food. Biologists believed that the carcass may have drifted in the ice for months and attracted bears from kilometres around. A total of fifty-six polar bears had gathered in the area, and eight adult bears were feeding shoulder to shoulder at the carcass (Larsen 1986).

Such feeding aggregations may occur only a few times in a bear's life or, at most, for a few weeks each year. Still, bears need some method to maintain social order in these crowded situations, and they do this by adhering to a hierarchy or pecking order. In brown bears, and probably most other bears as well, a bear's rank depends upon its age, sex and reproductive status. At the top of the hierarchy are adult male bears. Females with yearling and two-year-old cubs rank sec-

Typically, an adult female brown bear with a yearling cub is superior in rank to all other bears except an adult male.

ond, and solitary adult females rank third, followed by subadult bears. Cubs rank the lowest (Egbert and Stokes 1974).

Females with cubs-of-the-year do not readily fit into a particular slot in the bear hierarchy. Sometimes a mother bear with young cubs may defer to all other bears, and at other times, especially if she is hungry, she may dominate every bear she encounters, including some adult males. This illustrates an important point about bear hierarchies, namely, that they are flexible.

Hierarchies frequently develop wherever animals must compete with each other for a limited resource, whether it is food, space or mates. When a hierarchy exists, an animal's rank determines what it gets. The alternative to this system is for animals to fight and

possibly risk serious injury every time two of them want the same resource. If they fought, they might be injured over a matter that was relatively trivial. Thus, hierarchies serve to decrease injuries and generally are a peaceful way to settle confrontations. When the stakes are high, however, an animal may challenge the established hierarchy and risk injury to get what it wants.

From the time a bear is a cub, it learns to assess its own rank in the hierarchy and to recognize the rank of other bears. Generally, big bears dominate small bears, and older bears dominate younger bears. But as suggested above, bear hierarchies are flexible, and an animal may not always exercise its dominance. Consider a group of brown bears fishing along a salmon stream. At the beginning of the salmon spawning season, most bears are hungry. At this time, a bear aggres-

When a brown bear is around other bears, as occurs at a salmon stream or other concentrated food source, it must constantly watch what the other bears are doing to avoid a dangerous confrontation.

Newborn black bear cubs have the lowest rank of any bears in the population, and their survival is totally dependent on their mother's protection.

sively defends its fishing spot and the area around it from all subordinates. A dominant bear tolerates few challengers. As the season progresses and the bears become satiated with salmon, a dominant animal may gradually allow other bears to fish closer to it, and it may even relinquish its fishing spot to a subordinate. It is clear that rank alone does not determine the outcome of an encounter. The stakes involved and the motivation of the animal are also important. For example, a satiated bear is less motivated to defend its position than a hungry bear.

There is a second circumstance in which bears may not strictly adhere to the established hierarchy. Bears, like humans, can form alliances to improve their rank. Chapter 3 describes how some subadult bears stay together for several years after the family breaks up. At a salmon stream, such a pair of subadults have a higher status than a lone subadult, and the two bears can use their enhanced status to obtain better fishing spots. Another example of an alliance was observed by biologist Tom Bledsoe (1987). Bledsoe watched an estrous female brown bear that was followed by a male suitor use her association with the adult male to temporarily roust higher-ranking females from choice fishing spots.

Most interesting is the alliance that bears sometimes form with people. Biologist Larry Aumiller has worked in the McNeil River Brown Bear Sanctuary for fourteen years, and he knows most of the bears by sight. Aumiller believes that some bears that are tolerant and unafraid of people may use humans to shield themselves from other bears. I recall one time when a female bear named Teddy was chased by another female.

◁◁
Polar bears frequently begin a bout of adult play by jaw wrestling. The bear in the background is a spectactator.

A mother brown bear with two cubs charges another female bear that has ventured too close to the family while they were fishing for salmon.

Teddy, who is quite habituated to humans, ran straight towards Aumiller and me as we sat on a slope beside the river. The other bear, who was more wary of people, stopped the chase when she saw that we were there. It appeared that Teddy had used her tolerance of humans to shield herself from her adversary.

A final factor that can modify a bear's rank is its temperament. Anyone who spends more than a couple of days observing a group of bears at a salmon stream soon discovers that bears are individuals, each with its own personality and temperament. At one end of the scale are bears that are extremely placid and rarely become aroused. I have seen some placid adult females who would allow almost any bear, including subordinates, to steal a fish from them. At the other extreme are bears that are quick-tempered and aggressive.

These bears will not tolerate another bear anywhere near them when they are fishing, and they are quick to charge and attack any bear that dares to provoke them.

The differences in individual temperament in bears may also explain the different reactions that bears display when confronted by a human. Some bears may charge immediately and make contact; others may charge but then veer off or stop suddenly before they reach the person. More tolerant bears may simply walk away when they meet a human, and some timid animals may flee in fright, crashing noisily through the bushes. This variability in the behaviour of bears explains in part why humans find them unpredictable.

Bears are frequently classified as solitary animals, but in fact there is no such thing as a solitary animal. Not only may bears end up side by side when they feed

A polar bear has a short tail and small ears, so, unlike many other carnivores, it cannot rely on these body parts to communicate a great range of information.

in groups, but males and females must come together when they mate, and females and their offspring travel together for years during lactation. In all of these circumstances, bears need some method to relay their intentions and wishes to each other, and they do this with a communication system that uses the animal's eyes, ears and nose.

THE LANGUAGE OF BEARS

Visual Signals

Carnivores, as a group, use a rich array of visual signals to convey information to each other. Typically, visual signals are used to communicate over short distances, generally in face-to-face encounters. Long tails can be held level with the body, tucked between the legs, dragged on the ground or held erect above an animal's back. Each position conveys a different message. The tail can be further enhanced as a signal if it is tipped with white, as in the cheetah (*Acinonyx jubatus*), the African hunting dog (*Lycaon pictus*) and the red fox, or if it ends in a terminal tuft, as in the African lion. Even when an animal's tail is short, as in the bobcat, the presence of a white underside can draw attention to the tail and make it an effective signalling device. Carnivores also use the position of their ears to relay information, and ear spots or tufts have evolved in a number of species to enhance their conspicuousness.

Carnivores use other visual signals as well. Long, dark hair on the shoulders and back of some species can be raised to make an animal appear more imposing. Many carnivores that roll on their backs to signal sub-

The lowered head position and flattened ears signal aggression in this polar bear. The bear charged moments later.

mission have white belly fur, which accentuates this display. And finally, many carnivores, especially the social carnivores, have a rich repertoire of facial expressions, including snarls, licks and grins, to convey a range of intentions (Ewer 1973).

Bears have short tails and small ears, and they lack accentuating tufts and white belly fur. Nonetheless, bears have other markings that are thought to function as visual signals. All Asiatic black bears and many American black bears have a white chest patch, and both species have a tan muzzle, which contrasts with the black fur of their faces (Stirling and Derocher 1990). In addition, American black bears have tan-coloured areas above their eyelids (Henry and Herrero 1974).

A bear can send visual signals in a number of ways:

through its body posture, the position of its head (for example, held high or low, facing forward or looking away), the position of its ears, which can be held erect or flattened, and the position of its mouth, either closed or open, combined with subtle lip gestures (Egbert and Stokes 1974; Stonorov and Stokes 1972; Herrero 1983). Henrey and Herrero (1974) believe that bear visual communication is very similar to basic canid communication.

Vocal Signals

In contrast to visual signals, vocal signals can frequently transmit information over great distances and are also effective where visibility is impaired—for example, in thick vegetation or in darkness. The howls

◁◁
The ears of a young black bear reach adult size before any other part of its body. Large, conspicuous ears probably help the young, inexperienced bear to communicate its intentions more clearly.

A hierarchy exists even among young brown bear littermates. The yearling on the right was dominant over its smaller sibling.

of wolves and coyotes and the roars of tigers and African lions are well-known examples of long-distance vocal communication.

Bears have no long-distance vocal signals, but they do have many vocalizations that they use in close-range communication. Bear cubs of all species whine and cry like children when distressed and "hum" contentedly when they nurse. Mother black bears can huff once and send their cubs scurrying up a tree, then simply grunt a few times to summon them down. When annoyed, all bears snap their jaws together and smack their lips, and in a fight, bears often growl, snort and bellow (Jordan 1976; Pruitt 1976; Wemmer, Von Ebers and Scow 1976).

Veteran bear biologist Stephen Herrero has studied both the brown bears and black bears of North Amer-

ica. He believes that black bears are the more vocal of the two species because they evolved in a forested environment where visibility was restricted. North American brown bears, which evolved in the open tundra where there is good visibility, depend more on visual cues for communication. Polar bears are also less vocal than black bears, probably for the same reasons.

Odour Signals

The third way in which bears and other carnivores communicate with each other is with odours. Humans have a relatively poor sense of smell, so it is sometimes difficult for us to appreciate the amount of information that can be gleaned from a scent. Kenneth Grahame described it best in *Wind in the Willows* when he called scents "fairy calls from the void," for which "we have only a word *smell*, to include the whole range of delicate thrills which murmur in the nose of the animal night and day, summoning, warning, inciting and repelling."

All carnivores use the odours from their urine to communicate (Ewer 1973; Gorman and Trowbridge 1989). Many of the large cats intentionally spray urine on bushes, rocks and termite mounds to advertise their movements. I have found trees in Africa where the bark on the lower trunk was markedly discoloured by cheetahs that had repeatedly sprayed urine on them.

When bears urinate, they do not use a special site but appear to relieve themselves wherever the urge strikes them. However, something I have seen in the wild makes me wonder whether bears might sometimes use urine to communicate. A strong odour often lingers around bear trails during the breeding season. In addition, the vegetation along the middle of these trails is often dead or yellowed. I suspect that bears, possibly both males and females, dribble urine as they walk along these trails during the breeding season. At this time of the year it would be logical for these animals to advertise their presence to potential mates as well as rivals.

The odour from feces is another way that carnivores communicate. In the featureless tundra, arctic foxes carefully deposit scats on boulders and ridges and even on the tines of discarded caribou antlers. Some carnivores use the same defecation sites over and over again so that their feces accumulate in piles and are more noticeable. Spotted hyenas (*Crocuta crocuta*) use this method, and they have the further advantage that their feces are often chalky white from the bones the animals ingest, making the feces even more conspicuous.

Bears display the same lack of interest in where they defecate as where they urinate. Even so, bears frequently sniff each other's feces, and I have sometimes watched them change direction and walk over to a fresh scat for a closer sniff.

Scent glands, usually found on the animal's face and

tail and in its groin and anal area, are also very important for communication in carnivores. These glands are well developed in many carnivores but are poorly developed in bears, with the exception of the giant panda. Nevertheless, body scent is still used by bears to exchange information.

In summary, the odours from these three different sources—urine, feces and body scent—can tell a lot about a bear. They can identify an individual, divulge its sex, disclose whether it is an adult or a youngster and reveal whether it is sexually receptive or not. From the smell of another's breath, a bear may even know whether it is fasting or feasting.

BEAR TREES

One of the most fascinating bear behaviours is tree biting. This behaviour has been observed in black bears and brown bears in both Asia and North America, but it has not been observed in polar bears (Burst and Pelton 1983; Bromlei 1965).

Animal signs have always excited me as much as seeing the animal itself. A fresh track, a day bed, a scrape on the ground, a chewed tree—all of these signs arouse the sleuth in me. I try to imagine the details of what happened, what the sign means and why it is located where it is. I began to do this when I was a boy on my uncle's farm and wandered in the woods nearby. I soon discovered that animal signs were everywhere, and I was never disappointed when I went for a walk, because there was always something to capture my attention. Even now, as a wildlife photographer, I am still intrigued by animal signs. One of my most memorable bear experiences was a time when I never saw a bear. It was in the rain forests of coastal British Columbia, where I tramped along bear trails for a week, sat in day beds, inspected scats and examined bitten and clawed trees. The experience left me with a greater sense of what a bear was than many other times when I had photographed bears for hours.

Bear-bitten trees are at the top of my list of favourite animal signs. Minnesota biologist Dr. Lynn Rogers (1987) described how one male black bear bit three different trees along a one-kilometre (half-mile) stretch of dirt road. According to Rogers, the bear stood on his hind legs and rubbed his upper back, especially his neck and shoulders, against the trees. As he rubbed, the bear frequently twisted his head around to bite the bark. At one of the trees the bear dropped down on all four feet and then rubbed his hindquarters against the trunk. At a fourth location, the bear rubbed against a fallen wooden signpost. He lay on his back and squirmed with his four feet in the air, twisting occasionally to bite the post.

Trees are the most common objects bitten by bears, but they will chew on trail signs and telephone poles, and in one instance they even chewed on the corner post of a farmer's porch.

Bears may chew on trees at any time of the year, but the behaviour is most common during the months of the breeding season. Most often it is the work of adult males, although adult females may also be involved.

In a thorough search of an area in the Smoky Mountains of Tennessee, Burst and Pelton (1983) found 691 trees bitten by black bears. The trees were found along ridge tops, in valley bottoms and along game trails, hiking trails and roads. In Minnesota, virtually all of the bear trees were in openings or at the edge of openings. In northern and western North America I have found many bear trees bitten by brown bears, and the trees were in the same kinds of locales as those chosen by black bears.

It is important not to confuse a bear tree with other trees that bears have clawed or bitten. You will recall that black bears may climb trees for any number of reasons, and when they do they frequently scratch the bark with their claws. Chapter 3 describes how both black bears and brown bears may tear off the bark on trees to feed on the sapwood. Trees marked in these ways are not called bear trees.

BEAR   MYTH

Bears who bite or claw a tree at the highest point they can reach scare away smaller bears from the area. Any rival bear that later comes along and cannot reach as high immediately realizes that it is outranked and leaves. Bear biologist Dr. Gary Alt jokes that if this were so and he were a black bear and could climb as well as black bears do, the first thing that he would do is locate the tallest tree in the area and climb up and chew off the top.

This well-chewed bear tree was used by brown bears near a salmon stream in south-central Alaska.

A bear trail from coastal British Columbia. Large, deep impressions such as these may have started the legend of the Sasquatch.

The marks on a bear tree are easy to recognize. Often the bark, and even some of the sapwood, has been completely removed from a section of the trunk, leaving a large oval depression up to a metre (3¼ feet) in length. Most bite marks occur about 1.5 metres (5 feet) above the ground and face towards an open area or trail. A bear tree may be used year after year, and many of these trees, especially the hardwoods, develop a thick callus around the site of the damage, making it even more conspicuous. As further evidence of their repeated use, many bear trees have stepping places, or depressions worn into the ground, that lead to the tree. When you take a closer look at a bear tree, individual tooth and claw marks are clearly visible, and sap often oozes from the site, especially if the tree is a conifer. Every bear tree I have ever found also had strands of hair stuck in the resin or in the cracks in the bark, and some even had some mud smeared on them.

A bear tree can be any size, from one as narrow as your wrist to one that is so large you cannot encircle it with your arms. Bears appear to select trees for their strategic location rather than their size or kind.

Bear-bitten trees have been called marker trees, challenge trees, scratching trees, rub trees and bear blaze trees. This confusion of names reflects the lack of agreement among early observers about the purpose of this behaviour. One hypothesis was that bear trees assist in grooming and help bears dislodge parasites and remove old fur during the molt. Another was that bear trees define the boundaries of an animal's range. Neither of these ideas is in fashion any longer. It is argued that the grooming hypothesis fails to explain why primarily adult male bears would need to scratch but not females and subadults, and the boundary hypothesis makes no sense since bear trees are found throughout a bear's range and are not concentrated along borders as you would expect if they were boundary markers.

Bear trees clearly serve as signposts. They are visually conspicuous, and since bears rub and bite these trees, their scent may linger and act as an odour signal for other bears in the area. I have never been able to detect any odour around the bite marks, but that doesn't prove anything.

The most comprehensive look at bear trees was done by graduate student, Thomas Burst (1979), from the University of Tennessee. In his thesis he proposed four possible functions for bear trees: (1) To help adult male bears avoid each other and thus minimize conflicts. Bears using an area would mark the trees, and their odour would then yield up-to-date information about how long ago they were there. (2) To advertise an individual's movements so that any bear that followed behind would know to change course if it wanted to find an untouched area in which to feed. (3) To help a bear orient itself in rarely visited areas. This may explain why some female bears mark. (4) To promote estrus in females. The odours left by male bears might promote estrus in a nearby female, synchronizing it with the male's presence.

Although these ideas are attractive, they are still just hypotheses, and all of them remain untested. Nevertheless, one or more of them may operate in concert.

Bears trees, like many aspects of bear biology, remain tantalizing tidbits of unexplained behaviour that contribute to the mystique of bears. But even if I never learn the purpose of a bear tree, it won't lessen the excitement I feel every time I find one.

A LOOK AT DAILY LIFE

In recent years, our understanding of the daily life of bears has greatly increased. In this area, some of the most innovative field research was recently done by Minnosota bear biologist Dr. Lynn Rogers and his assistant, Greg Wilker (1990). Rogers habituated black bears to himself and Wilker so that the two men could tag along with the bears in the forest and observe the animals at close range, monitoring their every move, right down to the number of bites they took of every food they ate.

Other researchers, namely the gorilla researcher Dian Fossey and the chimpanzee researcher Jane Goodall, proved that habituated animals could yield rare insight into the fine details of an animal's life. Still, it took a researcher like Rogers with twenty-five years of field experience to attempt such a study with black bears.

Rogers habituated his study bears by first establishing a feeding station where the animals received handouts of beef fat. Once the bears became accustomed to people at the feeding station, Rogers approached them in the forest, away from the feeding station. At first the bears were uneasy, but after fifty to one hundred hours of contact each bear became totally accustomed to being approached, fed and accompanied in the forest. Once this stage of habituation had been reached, Rogers stopped feeding the bears. Now he could follow a bear from less than 10 metres (30 feet) and be ignored by the animal.

It took another 100 to 150 hours to totally accustom the bears to the foibles of their human observers. During this time the bears learned not to be frightened by a human sneeze or a cough and not to be startled when an observer tripped or fell, even when the bear was accidentally hit by its human companion. Through all of this, the researchers were never once attacked by a bear. In the end, Rogers and Wilker sometimes stayed with a single bear continuously for up to 48 hours. They ate with the bear and rested with it. At night they even slept with it, curling up in a sleeping bag as close as a metre (3¼ feet) from the sleeping bear. Typically, all of the bears slept from 1 to 2 hours after sundown until a half hour before sunrise, remarkably similar to the sleep pattern of humans.

The black bears of Minnesota are mainly diurnal, but the daily activity pattern of bears varies greatly from one region to another. Some bears are diurnal, some are nocturnal, and others crepuscular, or active at dusk and dawn. The activity pattern of many bears, in fact, changes throughout the year. This variability is another example of the flexible nature of bears.

Human activity has a great influence on whether bears are nocturnal or diurnal. Generally, the more that bears are disturbed by humans, the more nocturnal they become. Some of the remnant brown bear populations in Europe illustrate this point. In the Cantabrian Mountains of northern Spain and in the Trentino area of the Italian Alps, where there is a lot of human activity, bears are most active at night and at dusk and dawn, and they are rarely seen by humans (Roth 1983; Clevenger, Purroy and Pelton 1990). Human disturbance includes hunting, logging, mining, farming, ranching, and oil and gas development. Even the simple presence of vehicles travelling on a road can disturb bears and influence their movements and activities.

The season also determines whether a bear is active at night or during the day. In spring, the Asiatic black bear and the brown bear of southeastern Russia are most active during the day. In the summer, both species become more nocturnal (Bromlei 1965).

In Tennessee, the black bears are diurnal in the spring and summer and then become more nocturnal in the autumn. Researchers speculate that the bears' changing diet may explain the shift in their activity pattern. In summer, the bears eat berries. Because berries are small and dispersed on branches, the bears rely on their colour vision to find them, and so they forage primarily during the daylight hours. In autumn, Tennessee bears gorge on acorns, which are larger than berries and may be perceptible in darkness, thus allowing the bears to forage at night. Autumn is also when black bears spend more time eating in preparation for winter denning, and it may be that the added hours of nocturnal foraging simply give the bears more hours in which to eat (Garshelis and Pelton 1980).

Whether they are active at night or during the day, many black bears and brown bears use a system of well-worn trails that crisscross their home range. Troyer and Hensel (1969) described the trails on Kodiak Island, Alaska, in this way:

A striking feature of brown bear country is the characteristic bear trails. These are especially pronounced in marshy ground where the bear trail forms a well-indented path, and from the air these trails appear like so many interlaced highways.

On firm gound, trails may consist of two well defined furrows with a high center or a deeply worn, smooth trail. They may be worn three feet [1 metre] deep by continual use, but generally are only 12 to 16 inches [30 to 40 centimetres] wide. One often finds trails in which individual foot outlines are preserved with each bear having trod in the same footprints as his predecessors until the trail becomes a uniform series of holes.

In coastal British Columbia, I found one such bear trail that was a series of depressions, 30 centimetres (1 foot) across, worn into the soil. The trail led to a pool in the middle of a sedge meadow. A side trail of similar depressions ran off the main trail and led to a bear tree at the edge of the forest. I have always felt that someone else finding such a trail could envision that it was made by a tall bipedal creature, larger than a man, and in a flash of imagination, the legend of the Sasquatch is born.

Bear trails not only make it easier for the bears to move around but may also keep the bears informed about their neighbours' movements. When the bears of an area use a common trail system, they know from the odours that linger along the trails which bears have passed by recently. A bear can use this information to decide whether to continue its course or change direction.

A facet of the bear's daily life that is frequently overlooked is how they cope with the common summer annoyances, heat and insects. On hot days, when the mercury climbs into the 30s Celsius (90s Fahrenheit), bears can overheat. On such a day, a bear will dip its front paws in water and rub it on its head or soak its entire body in a pool to cool off. These bear bathing pools, called wallows, have been reported from many

On hot days, a black bear will cool off by taking a swim.

areas. They are common enough that a small community of fifteen houses in rural Kentucky calls itself Bear Wallow.

Some bears escape the summer heat, as well as insects, by returning to their winter dens. I have crawled into some rock-cavity dens that were 7 metres (23 feet) deep, and these would be a cool refuge in summer. Such dens would be well known to all the bears in an area. You will recall that summering polar bears also use dens to cool off and to escape from mosquitoes.

Since many dens collapse in the summer, not all bears can retreat to one to escape from the insects. In northern Alaska, the brown bears are so harassed by mosquitoes that their behaviour changes noticeably for several weeks in mid-July, when the mosquitoes are at their worst. At this time of the year, bears rarely stand still to feed, and when they graze they move along at a rapid walk with sudden changes in direction. Sows with cubs nurse much less than at other times, and the cubs will sometimes break into a run, vigorously shaking their heads. Like caribou in the same area, the bears choose gravel bars and any remaining snow patches for resting places to obtain some relief from the mosquito harassment (Gebhard 1982).

When the insects and heat become intolerable, black bears, unlike brown bears, can climb trees and sprawl out on a limb where there is a breeze.

BROWN VS. BLACK BEARS

Trees are essential to the black bears' survival, and their reliance on trees has influenced their behaviour,

For a young black bear cub, climbing a tree is its only defence against a predator or other danger.

their distribution and their relationship with other bears. For black bears, trees not only lessen the impact of warm temperatures but are also a refuge whenever the bears feel threatened. The sense of security that black bears feel when they are aloft in a tree extends well beyond the early years of their lives. Adult female bears sleep in trees with their cubs and sometimes nurse them while straddling a limb. Even large male bears, when they have no other recourse, will climb a tree to escape a baying pack of hounds or a similar threat. This ability of black bears to climb trees and their reliance on trees as a haven is an important difference between black bears and brown bears. Brown bears can climb some trees when the limbs are well spaced, but they do not rely on trees to the same extent that black bears do.

Biologist Stephen Herrero (1972) has suggested that trees have been critical to the survival of black bears wherever their range overlapped that of brown bears. Black bears have been in North America for several million years, but brown bears are relatively recent immigrants, having migrated from Asia to Alaska across the Bering Land Bridge some 30,000 years ago (Kurtén and Anderson 1980). Brown bears will kill black bears if they can, and the ability to climb trees may have been the black bears' main protection against these new arrivals.

After brown bears arrived on this continent, black bears were restricted to forests because they needed the sanctuary of trees. Many observers have noted that black bears always seem reluctant to venture far from trees. In contrast, although brown bears use the forest for travel routes, shelter and some feeding, they are more often found in open areas. Consequently, when brown bears spread across North America, they acquired exclusive dominion over the open, treeless areas of the arctic and alpine tundra and the Great Plains.

It is important to appreciate that black bears were excluded from treeless tundra and grassland because of the threat posed by brown bears, *not* because black bears were unable to survive in these environments. Recent evidence suggests that when brown bears disappear from an area of tundra, black bears leave the security of the trees to inhabit the tundra, filling the niche formerly occupied by brown bears.

Brown bears disappeared from Labrador and the Ungava Peninsula in eastern Canada about 150 years ago (Elton 1954). In the past thirty years, black bears have been seen in the Ungava Peninsula in increasing numbers. In 1967, for example, a black bear was seen on the tundra at Povungnituk, about 320 kilometres (200 miles) north of the treeline (Jonkel and Miller 1970). In the last five years, there have been many sightings of black bears in the Torngat Mountains, almost at the tip of Labrador in a region of open tundra, hundreds of kilometres from the trees.

Researcher Alasdair Veitch is studying the black bears in this region of Labrador. Veitch wants to learn whether the black bears that now occupy the area have adopted brown bear behavioural strategies to contend with the open, treeless terrain. Do the black bears dig for rodents, prey on caribou and aggressively defend their offspring, as brown bears would? After two years of research, Veitch suspects that they do, though he has not completely analyzed his data and further years of study are needed.

Let's backtrack for a moment to explain why a bear that lives in open country would be more aggressive in defence of its young than a bear that lives in the forest. An understanding of this will help you to appreciate why black bears are normally less inclined to attack humans than are brown bears. When black bears are threatened, they usually climb a tree and escape from the danger, and they have probably done this from early in their evolutionary history. A mother black bear whose cubs are safely perched up in a tree has a number of options open to her. She can climb the tree herself, she can bluff-charge her enemy and try to scare it away, or she can run away. Of course, she also has the option to attack, but that always carries the risk that she may be injured in the skirmish. Since mother black bears rarely attack, even when researchers are examining their squealing cubs, it seems that aggressive behaviour has never become ingrained in them by natural selection. In the test of time, the black bears that survived were those that were *not* aggressive, and this behavioural trait has been passed on to succeeding generations.

Brown bears in North America, in contrast, evolved in open, treeless habitats, and they must have frequently found themselves in vulnerable, exposed situations. The cubs of a brown bear mother have no trees to climb for safety. To protect her offspring, a brown bear mother has no option but to charge. She may bluff first, but when that fails, she fights. For the brown bear, aggressiveness was an essential behavioural trait for survival.

Writers do an injustice to bears when they label brown bears vicious and black bears timid or cowardly, based on the belief that the one animal is aggressive and the other is not. It is better to understand how natural selection has endowed each bear with the temperament that best enabled it to survive in its environment.

The grizzly is a symbol

of what is right with

the world.

—Charles Jonkel,

**American bear
biologist**

September continues to be a lean month for many polar bears, especially for those in the south. The polar bears that were forced ashore in July and August as the sea ice melted must wait for the chill of winter to lock their world solid so that they, can once again walk and hunt on the water. ¶ The situation is quite different for brown bears and black bears. These are the halcyon days of clement temperatures and bountiful food. For these bears, September is one of the most important feeding times of the year.

THE FALL FEEDING FRENZY

When biologists speak about the autumn diet of black bears and brown bears, they talk about two kinds of food: soft mast and hard mast. Soft mast consists of fruits and berries, foods that are typically soft and juicy. Hard mast includes beechnuts (*Fagus spp.*), hickory nuts (*Carya spp.*), acorns (*Quercus spp.*) and other such nuts. Bears prefer hard mast, since it often contains twice the fat content of berries (Landers et al. 1979), and bears must ingest as many calories as possible in autumn. A recent study suggests that the bear's digestive physiology may also shift in autumn to increase the animal's ability to digest fat, and this further facilitates rapid weight gain (Brody and Pelton 1988).

Acorns and Other Nuts

Hard mast is eaten by many bears throughout the animals' range. Brown bears in the Apennine Mountains of central Italy and in the Pyrenees of southern France eat beechnuts, hazelnuts (*Corylus spp.*) and acorns (Zunino and Herrero 1972;

Soapberries, or buffalo berries (Shepherdia canadensis), are a critical autumn food for grizzlies throughout the Rocky Mountains, especially in the Yukon.

Berducou, Faliu and Barrat 1983). In Japan, Asiatic black bears eat the nuts of oaks, beeches and chestnuts (*Castanea spp.*), and these foods comprise 87 per cent of all the plant matter eaten in the autumn (Nozaki et al. 1983). And throughout the hardwood forests of the eastern United States, hard mast is a staple fall food of black bears (Bennett, English and Watts 1943; Garner and Vaughan 1987; Beeman and Pelton 1980).

Brown bears can feed on hard mast only after the nuts have fallen to the ground. The tree-climbing black bears, which also include the Asiatic black bear, can go after the acorns and beechnuts before they fall off the trees. This gives black bears several advantages. In the eastern United States acorns are a preferred autumn food of many animals, including white-tailed deer, wild turkey (*Meleagris gallopavo*) and European wild hogs (*Sus scrofa*), but these animals can only eat the mast once it is on the ground. In the Southeast, over a third of all fallen acorns become infested with the larvae of nut weevils (*Curculio spp.*), and they are then further damaged by fungal and bacterial decay. Climbing oak trees allows black bears to obtain the acorns before these infestations lessen their nutritional value.

Biologist Larry Beeman (Beeman and Pelton 1980) described how black bears forage in trees: "Adult males and females as well as cubs were observed pulling in limbs with their paws and using their mouths to pick cherries, acorns, beechnuts, and hickory nuts. In addition, limbs as large as 10 cm [4 inches] in diameter were torn or chewed off and dropped to the ground. This 'pruning' by bears allowed them to consume mast that otherwise would have been unavailable."

Bears will sometimes wedge the broken limbs under themselves and create a crude nest. Pennsylvania bear biolgist Dr. Gary Alt found such a nest in a beech tree, 14 metres (46 feet) off the ground. The nest was 2 metres (6½ feet) in diameter and was constructed of twenty-seven limbs, some as large as 7 centimetres (2¾ inches) in diameter. The nest was such a sturdy one that a bear used it to den during the first half of the winter.

Tree nests are made by both Asiatic and American black bears, and they are particularly common in the hardwood forests of eastern Canada and the northeastern United States (Schaller et al. 1989). A stand of oak or beech trees may contain dozens of tree nests. The nest-building exploits of local black bears were such a common occurrence in 1821, that the town of Antigonish, Nova Scotia, derived its name from the Micmac Indian words meaning "where branches are torn off."

In Minnesota, Lynn Rogers (1987) reported that bears in his area often made special fall feeding trips to areas that were known to have acorns. The longest such trip was 201 kilometres (125 miles) and was made by an adult male. The bear was gone from his usual home range for thirteen weeks. Females with cubs also move to stands of oaks in autumn, and they may travel as far as 107 kilometres (66½ miles) on these trips. Rogers believes that cubs remember the food-rich areas they visit with their mothers, and they return to them later in life when they are on their own.

Pine nuts are an important fall food for bears in the Yellowstone area, especially once the berries and green vegetation have dried up. Pine nuts are the seeds of a family of pine trees, called stone pines, which grow not only in the cold, high altitudes of the Rockies and the Sierra Nevada but also in the high mountains of northern Russia and northern Japan (Stroganov 1962). The stone pine species in North America is the whitebark pine (*Pinus albicaulis*), and its large, oil-rich nuts are 78 per cent fat. Not surprisingly, the nuts are prized by many animals, especially bears, both blacks and browns. In northwestern Montana, researchers can easily recognize black bears that have been climbing whitebark pines to secure the cones. Many of these bears have no hair on their entire front legs. As the bears climb and claw the trees, their front limbs become coated with pine gum, and when enough dirt and debris stick to the gum, the whole conglomeration peels off, taking the animal's hair with it (Mattson and Jonkel 1990).

A grove of beech trees (Fagus grandifolia) *is an attractive lure to black bears in the autumn. The bears eliminate competition from white-tailed deer by climbing the trees and feeding on the beechnuts before they fall from the branches.*

In September, stands of whitebark pines are a strong lure to brown bears as well. The non-climbing brown bear must scrounge for cones that fall naturally from the trees. Unfortunately, in both Russia and North America, any cones that happen to do this are immediately carted away by rodents. In Russia, the culprit is the Siberian chipmunk (*Eutamias sibiricus*), and here in North America it is the familiar red squirrel (*Tamiasciurus hudsonicus*). Nevertheless, the bears are not deterred by this, because the rodents save them time. Both Siberian chipmunks and red squirrels cache pine nuts, which bears can then uncover.

The Siberian chipmunk removes the nuts from the cones and stores them in underground caches. A typical cache contains 1 to 2 kilograms (2¼ to 4½ pounds) of nuts, but a large stockpile may contain as many as 6 kilograms (13¼ pounds) of pine nuts, all shelled and ready to be eaten. Russian bears sniff out these caches and raid them.

In Yellowstone National Park, biologist Katherine Kendall (1983) looked at red squirrel caches. Red squirrels cache whitebark pine cones from August through October, and unlike the Siberian chipmunks, the squirrels usually cache the entire cone, not just the nuts. The squirrels hide from one to fifteen cones in a hole and bury them 2.5 to 20 centimetres (1 to 8 inches) deep. At other times, the squirrels may simply store the cones in a pile at the base of a tree. Kendall found some piles that contained three thousand pine cones. Bears break open the cones by stepping on them or biting them, then they spread out the debris with their nose or a paw and lick up the nuts. Bears rarely cleaned out an entire cone cache in a single visit, and they returned repeatedly to large piles.

Bears in Yellowstone also raid cone caches in the spring when they first emerge from their winter dens. Pine nuts help to offset the nutritional stress of this period, especially after a mild winter when there is little carrion available (Kendall 1983).

There is a postscript to the story of grizzly bears and whitebark pines. These trees grow in cold, high altitudes, and it takes a tree a hundred years or more to produce its first significant cone crop. Thus, when mature trees die, they are not replaced quickly. Since the 1970s, many whitebark pines have died from infestations of mountain pine beetles (*Dendroctonus ponderosae*), white pine blister rust (*Cronartium ribicola*) and dwarf mistletoe (*Arceuthobium ssp.*). This disturbing trend recently prompted scientists to convene an international symposium on whitebark pine ecosystems. Researchers at the symposium cautioned that the plight of the whitebark pine may have serious implications for the maintenance and restoration of grizzly bear populations in the lower forty-eight states (Kendall and Arno 1990).

Berries

As I watched the grizzly, its nose was never still but twisted from side to side, distorting the massive face with comic affect. Its snout reached up to the moist autumn air, teasing out my odour from the background odours of pine, damp earth and decaying leaves. The bear stripped the frozen red berries from one more branch, then it turned and disappeared into the tangle.

As much as bears prefer hard mast, the trees that produce these nuts do not grow in every area where bears are found. Throughout the North (Hatler 1972; Raine and Kansas 1990), in most areas of western North America (Mealey 1980; Grenfell and Brody 1983) and in many parts of the former Soviet Union (Sharafutdinov and Korotkov 1976; Slobodyan 1976), black bears and brown bears must consume soft mast to fuel their autumn appetites. Dozens of kinds of berries are eaten by bears, but the common ones include crowberries (*Empetrum nigrum*), bearberries (*Arctostaphylos spp.*), blueberries (*Vaccinium spp.*) and mountain ash (*Sorbus spp.*).

When a bear becomes engrossed in berry picking, it may lie spread-eagled in the patch and swing its head from side to side, stripping the fruit from one branch af-

Bearberry (Arctostaphylos rubra) is the common name for this alpine plant, which, as the name suggests, is eaten by any bear that discovers the juicy red fruit.

ter another. Once it cleans out one swath, it slides forward on its belly and starts on a fresh one.

Anyone who has examined bear scats at this time of the year knows that bears are quite clean feeders, ingesting very few leaves or twigs when they pluck the berries. The berries are devoured with a minimum of chewing, and there may be a good reason why bears *do not* chew the fruit. Plants produce berries to entice mammals to eat them. Later, when the seeds are passed, the plants benefit by having their seeds dispersed. But the plants would not benefit if their seeds were chewed and destroyed during ingestion. To prevent this, the seeds are impregnated with toxins that are distasteful; some of these toxins can even poison an animal.

Not only do some plants benefit from having their seeds scattered by bears, but the seeds do better when they pass through a bear's digestive tract. The germination rate in cow parsnip (*Heracleum lanatum*) seeds is 16 per cent higher in seeds found in grizzly bear droppings than in seeds collected directly from the plant (Applegate et al. 1979). Even more impressive are the germination rates of seeds found in black bear scats. These seeds showed consistently higher germination rates—twice as high for raspberry seeds (*Rubus strigosus*), three times as high for chokecherry seeds and seven times higher for dogwood seeds (*Cornus stolonifera*). Biologists believe that the action of digestive acid and the mechanical abrasion of the seeds during their passage through a bear's digestive tract makes

*The salmonberry (*Rubus spec-tabilis*) grows along the coast of the Pacific Northwest. The native Indians named the plant for the globules of the berry, which look like salmon eggs.*

the seedcoats more permeable to water and gases and, as a consequence, dramatically improves their germination rate (Rogers and Applegate 1983).

Mast Failures

Crops of berries, acorns and pine nuts vary dramatically from autumn to autumn. Some years, oak and beech trees may produce few nuts at all, and commonly they only produce a good crop every three years or more. Weather also affects mast crops. Sudden spring freezes can kill the flowers of berry bushes; without flowers there are no seeds, and without seeds there are no berries. Even when spring conditions are ideal and all of the flowers survive into early seed development, dry, hot summer conditions can dessicate the berries and ruin the crop.

Biologists call these poor berry and nut crops mast failures, and mast failures mean nutritional stress to bears. To compensate for mast failures in one area, bears may wander outside their normal home range in search of more productive areas. In 1968, there was a complete failure of the acorn crop in Great Smoky Mountains National Park in Tennessee. In response, many black bears dispersed out of the park into unprotected areas and ended up as hunting statistics. Twenty-five bears were killed in areas adjacent to the northern perimeter of the park, a fourfold increase over the usual autumn bear harvest (Beeman and Pelton 1980).

Even if you live in the centre of a big city, you can learn about mast failures by reading your morning newspaper. When mast crops fail, bears will be on the move. Park authorities will announce a sudden rash of bear break-ins involving cars, tents and coolers, and local municipalities will report a surprising influx of bears into residential areas. It is not that bears are suddenly anxious to be around humans; it is just that they are hungry and have no other choice.

The claw design and shoulder muscles of a black bear evolved to enable it to climb trees, not to dig out rodents.

Boozer Bears

The September diet of bears naturally includes foods other than hard and soft mast. They will clip off any green vegetation that is still around, ravage any wasps' nests they find and scavenge the carcasses of spawned-out salmon. They will even exploit a food that they may never have encountered before, as an incident from Montana clearly illustrates.

In February 1985, there were two separate train derailments near the town of Essex, in northwestern Montana, that spilled over 400 metric tons (363 tons) of corn beside the tracks. The bears discovered the corn in the spring, and by the following year it had fermented. Residents from Essex reported as many as a dozen drunken bears, both grizzlies and black bears, sitting placidly on their butts around the corn pile. Bear researcher Dr. Chris Servheen said the area "smelled like a brewery."

Railroad crews tried to discourage the bears by covering the corn with dirt, but that hardly slowed them down for a moment. By the next year, there were complaints of dazed bears wandering in front of trains, and the railway workers were desperate. They mixed lime into the corn mash and hoped that the taste would dissuade the bears. No such luck. The bears continued to return to the corn pile for more than five years afterwards. Biologist Bart O'Gara was quoted as saying: "Bears are awfully hard to stop once they're on to something good" (Richie 1988).

Digging for Dinner

Brown bears everywhere dig for a variety of rodents. In many areas, they tear up the nests and tunnels of mice and lemmings (*Lemmus sibiricus*). In Alaska and the Yukon, grizzlies loot the underground food caches of singing voles (*Microtus miurus*). A single cache may hold several litres of peavine roots, sedge and knotweed (*Polygonum spp.*) rhizomes, lupines (*Lupinus spp.*) and horsetails. In former times, the Inuit also raided these caches for the roots and greens, which the native people

◁◁
In early September, a young arctic ground squirrel is driven out of its natal burrow and must disperse to a new area. At this time, the young, inexperienced squirrels— seven to nine in each family—are very vulnerable to predation by grizzlies.

The prominent shoulder hump of the brown bear is the mass of muscle that powers the animal's front limbs when it is digging. The presence of this hump is a good way to identify a brown bear and distinguish it from a black bear, which has a flat back and no hump.

ate as vegetables.

In Yellowstone National Park, grizzlies frequently dig up pocket gophers (*Thomomys talpoides*), large prairie rodents that maintain a labyrinth of underground tunnels. Coyotes (*Canis latrans*) in the park sometimes tag along behind the bears to catch mice and voles that the bears disturb. The bears occasionally chase the coyotes away, but usually they just ignore them.

The North American rodent that is most often hunted by the brown bear is sik sik, the Inuit name for the arctic ground squirrel (*Spermophilus parryii*). The range of the ground squirrel in Alaska and arctic Canada roughly coincides with that of the brown bear, so the two species frequently cross paths. Brown bears will stop to dig up a sik sik any time the opportunity arises, but they are most systematic about it in late

summer and autumn. This is the time when naive young ground squirrels are dispersing from their natal burrows and when all squirrels are layered in fat in preparation for winter hibernation.

As soon as a squirrel spots a grizzly, it gives a shrill alarm cry. The squirrels recognize the threat that a bear poses. Arctic ground squirrels live in colonies, and once one squirrel begins to shriek, others join in the chorus, all of them sitting or standing like picket pins at the mouth of their burrow. When the bear gets too close, the squirrels zip down their holes, and silence is restored.

A ground squirrel colony may be honeycombed with tunnels and peppered with holes. A hunting bear moves from hole to hole, sniffing each one carefully. When a hole smells promising, the bear begins to dig,

During the fall feeding frenzy, an American black bear may gain 1 to 2 kilograms (2 to 4 pounds) of body weight a day.

in much the same way as a dog does. The bear uses a single front paw, or both paws together, to shovel out the dirt and rocks, which are thrown out behind. One sow grizzly in Alaska took an average of ten minutes to dig out a ground squirrel, but at times she dug for over an hour before she finally caught her quarry. Some excavations were so large that the bear was lost from view (Gebhard 1982). One summer in Denali National Park, I hiked several kilometres with all my photo gear down a mountain, across a valley through thick willows and up the other side to investigate what I thought was a grizzly den. It turned out to be one of these large excavations, and I cursed the bear for hours as I puffed back up the mountain to my truck.

While a bear is digging out a ground squirrel it stops repeatedly to sniff the hole, possibly gauging how close it is to its prize, and it constantly looks around to make sure that the squirrel doesn't escape out another hole. Bears sometimes halt their digging and bounce on the soil near the hole as if to jar the earth and frighten the squirrel into abandoning its tunnel. At times the squirrels do try to escape, and the bears chase after them. Ground squirrels are surprisingly quick and agile despite their short legs, and they often lead the bear on a zigzag chase that ends with the squirrel diving down another hole.

Of course, many ground squirrels do not escape, and in some areas, ground squirrels are a major part of the brown bears' diet. A female in the Brooks Range of northern Alaska caught 396 ground squirrels in one year. She caught none in the spring, 36 in early summer, 3 in late summer, 168 in early autumn and 189 in late autumn. The energy value of an average adult ground squirrel is roughly 3800 kilocalories, so the bear's fall diet of sik siks yielded about 22,000 kilocalories a day (Gebhard 1982).

Most bears gain a tremendous amount of weight in the fall, which will sustain them through hibernation, but female bears have extra energy needs, and as you will see, the amount of weight they gain each autumn determines many events in their life.

Packing on the Pounds

The annual weight cycle of most brown bears and black bears follows the same general pattern. The bears lose weight during winter hibernation and in spring, maintain a steady weight during the summer and then gain weight in the fall. The tremendous weight gains of bears in the fall occur not just because more food is available but also because the bears' appetites increase.

Appetite, like many bodily functions, is controlled by biochemical factors in the animal's blood. Something happens in the blood of bears at the end of summer that drives them to feed for as many as twenty hours a day and to increase their food intake from 8000 kilocalories a day to 15,000 to 20,000 kilocalories a day (Nelson et al. 1983). This phenomenon is readily observed in captive black bears, which normally eat 5000 to 8000 kilocalories per day, even when more food is available to them. In the fall, their appetites suddenly increase, and they eat three times as much as they did before. There appears to be some kind of biochemical switch that shifts the bears into this exaggerated eating mode, called hyperphagia.

How much weight do bears actually gain? In Yellowstone one fall, two subadult male grizzlies gained 1.3 kilograms (3 pounds) a day (Blanchard 1987). On the Tuktoyaktuk Peninsula in Canada's Northwest Territories, an adult female brown bear did even better, packing on 1.75 kilograms (4 pounds) every day for a month from mid-August onwards (Nagy et al. 1983). On salmon-rich Kodiak Island in the Gulf of Alaska, a young male brown bear put on 20.5 kilograms (45 pounds) in just twelve days. Another male on Kodiak gained 93 kilograms (205 pounds) in seventy days (Troyer and Hensel 1969).

Black bears also pack on the pounds. In Pennsylvania, a ten-year-old male that weighed 158 kilograms (348 pounds) in midsummer was recaptured and weighed on 19 September. He had gained 58 kilograms (128 pounds) in two months (Alt 1980).

The amount of weight that a bear gains in the fall is regulated by its appetite, which in turn is regulated by the amount of fat that it has stored. Once its fat reserves reach a certain level, a feedback mechanism turns off the bear's appetite, and the animal stops feeding.

In female bears, another factor influences their weight gain. The amount of fat that a female puts on in the fall varies depending on whether she is pregnant or nursing cubs at the time. In Pennsylvania, when a female black bear is pregnant, she gains an average of 40 kilograms (88 pounds) in the autumn. The following fall when she is accompanied by cubs, she gains only 11 kilograms (24 pounds). The next year, after her cubs have left and she is pregnant again, her average autumn weight gain jumps back up to 40 kilograms (88 pounds). This pattern suggests that every autumn the female black bear assesses her energy needs for the coming winter and spring. In the winters when she is bearing cubs and nursing, she needs greater fat reserves—apparently three times greater—than when she is denning with her yearling cubs, and she adjusts her autumn weight gain accordingly (Alt 1980).

A female bear's fat reserves control more than her appetite; they also control the outcome of her pregnancy. To fully understand how and why this happens you need to understand some basic reproductive biology.

In a typical mammal, fertilization of the egg occurs within a few hours of mating. The fertilized egg then begins to divide until it is a hollow ball of cells, the size of a pinhead, called a blastocyst. Within a week or so of mating, the blastocyst implants into the wall of the female's uterus. From that point on, the growing embyro is fed by its mother through the placenta in the wall of her uterus. After a set number of weeks or months of development, the young mammal is born.

The pattern is different in bears. After bears mate, the egg progresses to the blastocyst stage, but then everything stops. For the next five months or so, the pregnancy is put on hold, and the blastocyst simply floats in the cavity of the female's uterus. Then in late November or early December the pregnancy suddenly starts up again, the blastocyst implants and the pregnancy proceeds to completion. This pattern of reproduction is called delayed implantation (Daniel 1974; Kordek and Lindzey 1980).

Examples of delayed implantation are found in many groups of mammals, including marsupials, rodents, bats, armadillos and seals. Among the carnivores, delayed implantation is widespread in the members of the weasel family, and it is believed to occur in all species of bears. In all of these mammals, delayed implantation allows the animal to mate at one time of the year and then continue its pregnancy at a later date, when it is physiologically possible (Mead 1989).

Bears may benefit from delayed implantation for the following reason. If bears were to mate in the fall, breeding activities would seriously disrupt this important feeding period, making it harder for the bears to accumulate the fat reserves they need to sustain them through the winter. Delayed implantation is a practical strategy that allows mating to occur early in the summer when feeding is not so critical. Female bears benefit from delayed implantation for a second reason. In bears, implantation of the blastocyst occurs only if the female has stored enough fat during the fall to sustain the energy demands of a pregnancy. In this way, pregnancy only proceeds when the nutritional condition of the female is ideal (Barber and Lindzey 1986).

The suspected signal for implantation is a simple and reliable one, the daylength, or photoperiod. In late autumn, the daylength gradually decreases. When it reaches a critical threshold, it signals the brain of the bear to release hormones that restart the pregnancy and initiate implantation. Implantation in polar bears occurs between mid-September and mid-October, and in brown bears and black bears it occurs between late November and early December (Mead 1989; Hellgren et al. 1990).

The daylength is the same for all of the bears that live

in an area, so implantation occurs roughly at the same time in all of them, regardless of when they mated, and the birth of their cubs is more or less synchronized. In northeastern Pennsylvania, for example, all of the monitored female black bears gave birth to their cubs between 1 January and 27 January. In addition, it seemed that each individual bear had her own daylight threshold to which she was very sensitive. As a consequence, all of the females gave birth to their cubs within eleven days of the dates of their previous litters. Nearly half of the females were even more precise in the timing of their litters; they had their cubs within three days of previous birth dates (Alt 1989).

The control of implantation by the size of an animal's fat reserves and the synchronization of implantation with the photoperiod are remarkable refinements in the reproductive biology of bears. They illustrate how sensitively attuned these animals are to their environment.

GAMES THAT BEARS PLAY

It was early September in the Arctic. As I looked into the morning sun, I spotted the mother grizzly by the halo of golden fur that rimmed her bulky body. She was digging for roots, followed by two small chocolate-brown cubs.

In the hours that I watched the family of bears, the cubs played many times. Sometimes they would play by themselves. They would lie on their backs and claw at their hind feet or chew on a toe. One cub drapped itself over a small hummock and wrestled with the hummock as if it were some phantom adversary. It chewed and clawed at the hummock, and when it was satisfied that it had subdued its opponent, it bounced off to make a surprise attack on a clump of willow, a piece of wood or some other imaginary foe.

At one point as the bear family moved across the tundra, it was joined by a black-billed magpie (*Pica pica*). The magpie searched for insects in the soil dis-turbed by the digging activities of the mother grizzly. Such a colourful, long-tailed playmate was too much for the cubs to resist, and they repeatedly chased the bird. Each time, the magpie flew a few metres and then landed on the ground. The game finally ended when one of the cubs chased the bird from one spot to the next until the pair was 100 metres (109 yards) from the mother grizzly. When the cub suddenly noticed how far it had strayed from its mother, it raced back to the security of her side, and the magpie flew away.

Often, the young grizzly cubs played with each other. It usually started with one cub making a surprise rear attack on its littermate. As soon as the attack had been launched, the attacker would then run off, hoping the other cub would chase it.

The object of play in all mammals is not to win but to keep the game going. There appear to be rules, however: don't run off too far, don't bite too hard, and don't use your claws when you wrestle and kick.

In bears, most play bouts last only a few minutes, but I once spied a mother brown bear and three yearlings that played together for almost half an hour. Bears may play many times during a day, as often as twenty-five times (Pruitt 1976; Henry and Herrero 1974).

As in humans, play behaviour in bears is probably a good measure of health and well-being. Thus, bears are most likely to play when their basic physiological needs have been satisfied; a well-fed bear is often a playful bear. In a study of brown bears that had gathered along a salmon stream, biologists (Fagen and Fagen 1990) found that as salmon numbers increased and the bears became satiated, the time they spent playing also increased.

Play behaviour varies depending upon the age of the bear. Not surprisingly, cubs are the most playful bears, but mothers frequently play with their offspring, especially if their cub is alone and without a littermate. In the Canadian High Arctic, I examined a large snow-bank along the coast after a female polar bear and her

▷▷

A mother polar bear with a single cub plays with her offspring more often than she would if she had a larger litter.

Even when a yearling brown bear has littermates to play with, it will often play by itself, chasing birds, gnawing on a stick or chewing on its own feet.

solitary cub had left the area and travelled out onto the sea ice. From impressions the bears had left in the snow, it appeared that the female had slid down the slope no less than a dozen times. Sometimes she skied, and sometimes she rested on either her back or her belly and tobogganed down. I couldn't tell whether the cub had joined her on all of these runs, but there were three narrow slide marks that suggested that the cub had sometimes slid down separately. Nearby, at the top of the snowdrift, the mother polar bear had dug a pit in which she and her cub had rested, either before or after they played.

Young bears do not stop playing once the family breaks up. Subadults that stay together after they leave their mother also play together. Subadult bears will also play with other subadults even when they are un-related. Chapter 4 describes how solitary subadult

bears sometimes join together and form an alliance to improve their status in the bear hierarchy. These young bears, naturally, often wrestle and box with each other.

Adult female brown bears also play together at times, and sometimes adult males do too, but I have only seen this happen in brown bears around a salmon stream. These bears may play because they spend considerable time together and they have a surplus of food at their disposal.

Play behaviour in bears also varies among individuals. Some bears are just naturally more playful than others, and often these animals retain their playfulness throughout their life. Thus, a particularly playful cub frequently becomes a playful adult (Fagen and Fagen 1990).

The Purpose of Play

After watching bears play on many different occasions, I find it difficult not to believe that they sometimes play for no other reason than sheer enjoyment, or what we call fun. Of course few "serious" scientists believe that animals play just for fun, and a number of more scientifically acceptable explanations have been proposed to explain why animals play.

Play serves at least four possible biological functions: (1) it promotes healthy bone growth, (2) it is an opportunity to practise survival skills, (3) it reinforces social bonds, and (4) it refines social behavior. Let's take a closer look at each of these functions.

The bones of young bear cubs need the constant pull of muscles on them if the bones are to grow properly and attain their correct shape and density. As a consequence, the play activities of cubs, and all other young animals, are a way to physically challenge their growing skeltons and promote healthy bone growth (Bassett 1965).

Play behaviour is common in many mammals and typically involves activities that the animals will use in their adult life. For example, in deer that depend on flight to escape from predators, play consists of jumping and running with sudden changes in direction and speed. Play in predatory cougars and wolves involves bouts of chasing, stalking, leaping and play biting, behaviours that the adult animals use to subdue prey. In river otters (*Lutra canadensis*), which frequently secure food with their paws, play often consists of manipulating objects and tossing them around, activities that involve manual dexterity.

For bears, play activities are a way for a young animal to practise escape, stalking, capture, killing and fighting techniques. Thus, play activities consist of chewing on each other's face, ears and neck, swatting, chasing and jaw wrestling. In jaw wrestling the bears grab each other's jaw in a restrained fashion and try to wrestle each other down. It always surprises me when I watch bears playing that they are completely silent, unlike some other carnivores, which growl and bark.

The third possible function of play, the reinforcement of social bonds, seems obvious. In play bouts, alliances between animals can be strengthened, and between a mother bear and her offspring, play may enhance the mother bear's attentiveness to her cubs and thus improve the cubs' chances of survival.

Finally, the language of bears is a subtle combination of visual and vocal signals. This bruin vocabulary must be learned by young animals, and play is one way to do this. In play, participants learn the language of dominance and submission, aggression and solicitation.

Adult Polar Bear Play

One of the most exciting bear behaviours a person can witness is play in adult male polar bears. Whereas play between 15-kilogram (33-pound) cubs is always entertaining to watch, a play bout between 450-kilograms (992-pound) adult male polar bears is a spectacle never to be forgotten.

All of the research on adult polar bear play has been conducted in Hudson Bay, where the bears spend months ashore during the late summer and autumn when the bay is free of ice. Gradually throughout the autumn, the bears gather on points of land along the coast and wait for the bay to freeze. Most of the bears in these fall aggregations are adult males and subadults. Aerial surveys of one such point, Cape Churchill, often tallies over 120 bears in that one area, and it is common to see as many as 50 to 80 polar bears along a narrow, 2-kilometre (1¼-mile) sandspit extending out from the cape. Although autumn concentrations of polar bears have been reported in Russia, the density of bears is much less than that along Hudson Bay. The concentrations of polar bears near Churchill, Manitoba, have been widely publicized in books, magazine articles and documentaries on television. The polar bears are now such a popular tourist attraction that they draw almost ten thousand visitors a year to this small coastal town

Play is most common in young bears, but adult brown bears, especially adult females, may play together when their appetites have been satisfied and the bears have leisure time.

When polar bears play, they generally pair up with other bears that are the same size they are, although I have seen small subadult animals wrestle with large adult males twice as big as they were. Typically, a play session involves only two bears, but as many as four may join together. When polar bears play, they wrestle and repeatedly roll over each other. Sometimes they rear up on their hind legs, standing more than 2.5 metres (8 feet) tall, and push and cuff each other in the shoulders and chest until they fall to the ground, when one of them dives forward and tackles his rival. Wrestlers chew and tug on each other's ears and neck, sometimes drawing blood, but the injuries are trivial and the play goes on. When one bear finally tires, he may try to walk away, only to be tackled again, starting a new round of grab, twist and tumble. The big bears rarely make sudden moves, and most play bouts look as though they are performed in slow-motion. The restraint the bears display seems to accentuate their power and self-control, making the spectacle that much more impressive.

The question that no one can answer yet is whether the adult male bears come together in autumn to play, or whether they play because they have come together for some other reason. The bears have 600 kilometres (373 miles) of coastline along which they can lounge and wait for the bay to freeze in the autumn. So there must be a reason why they aggregate.

During late autumn around Hudson Bay, male polar bears are not competing with each other for food or mates, and the bears have a surplus of time on their hands. Their bones have stopped growing, they don't need to practise their hunting skills, and they are completely fluent in bruin body language. Thus, these big bears probably play for completely different reasons from cubs and subadults.

The autumn play sessions may be a way for an adult male polar bear to test opponents and gain experience in assessing size and strength and other cues of superiority. Then, months later in April and May during the mating season, when the males encounter one another on the sea ice and compete for a breeding female, they can better assess each other and avoid dangerous fights in which they might be seriously injured and yet have no hope of winning. In this way, autumn play bouts may teach a male polar bear when to be prudent and retreat and when to challenge a rival. This system of testing and learning is a further testimony to the intricacies and strategies of animal behaviour. In these bears, the lessons learned in simple bouts of play set the stage for the serious, and sometimes deadly, conflicts of the mating season (Latour 1981a and 1981b).

A BEAR'S DOMAIN

No mammal is truly nomadic, and all mammals, including bears, confine their activities to an established area called a home range. The concept of home range in mammals was first defined by William Burt (1943), an American biologist, who defined a home range as the area traversed by an animal in its normal activities of food gathering, mating and caring for young.

Humans have a home range as well, but we don't often view our movements in this way. Consider a hypothetical urban resident in a large city. This person's home range includes key areas that are frequently used, such as his or her home and place of work, the grocery store, restaurants, the dry cleaner and the health club, as well as the routes that link these areas. The person's home range also includes less frequently visited spots such as the shoe repairer, doctor and dentist, and rarely visited spots such as the police station and the funeral home. If you marked all of these areas on a map and then joined the outside points with a line, you would have defined that person's home range.

Bears, like people, have key areas in their home range and other areas that they visit less frequently. Food sites and travel routes that link these food sites to-

The home range of a female brown bear and her family of yearling cubs encompasses a variety of habitats, including tidal flats, willow scrublands and tundra extending up to snow-capped mountains.

gether are important in a bear's home range. Bears also need areas where they can hide, sites where they can den and areas where they can find shelter from inclement weather. They also need other bears if they are to breed, so their home range must overlap the range of potential mates.

A home range is not a specific shape, such as circular, oval or rectangular. It is the shape required to provide the bear with all of the resources it requires to survive. As a consequence, home ranges are dynamic. Their size may vary from area to area, and they may even vary from year to year in the same area.

Researchers (Miller, Barichello and Tait 1982) studied the grizzlies of the Mackenzie Mountains, in Canada's Northwest Territories, for five years and found that the home ranges of some individuals varied tremendously from year to year. An eleven-year-old female bear, nicknamed Killer, had an annual home range that varied from 67.7 square kilometres (26 square miles) to 265 square kilometres (102 square miles). One year, the area Killer used did not overlap any portion of the area she had used the year before. When all of the areas that she used in the five years were combined, the total home range was 456.9 square kilometres (176 square miles).

Variations in home range from year to year often reflect the unreliability of many bear foods. Caribou may change their migration routes, berries and acorn crops can fail, and salmon runs may falter. To cope with the unpredictable nature of their environment, bears require large tracts of land, some parts of which they may visit only once or twice, during hard times.

◁◁
Generally, as a brown bear cub gets older, the size of the family's home range increases.

The polar bear has the largest home range of any of the northern bears.

Males range over much greater areas than females. Reynolds and Hechtel (1979) found that male grizzlies in the Brooks Range of Alaska had an average home range of 1350 square kilometres (521 square miles), almost four times larger than the females' range of 344 square kilometres (133 square miles). In Pennsylvania the home range of adult male black bears was four times that of females (Alt 1980), and in Idaho the home range of black bear males was six times that of the females (Reynolds and Beecham 1980). Males have larger home ranges than females primarily because of their extensive travels during the breeding season. An adult male's range may overlap the home range of two or three females and as many as fifteen.

The size of a female's home range is greatly influenced by the age of her offspring. Females with two-year-old cubs have the largest home ranges. Females with yearlings have smaller ranges, and females with newborn cubs have the smallest home ranges of all. There are frequent exceptions to this pattern, but it is a good general rule.

Females with newborn cubs often choose rugged and isolated areas that are not used by other bears, especially during the breeding season in late spring and early summer, when the cubs are still quite small. Concern for the safety of the cubs and their limited mobility restrict the overall movements of the family and probably explain why these mother bears have the smallest home ranges. As cubs grow and become yearlings and two-year-olds, the mother's home range expands to reflect their increasing food requirements and their increasing ability to travel over greater distances.

The home range size of subadult bears is the most difficult to predict. When young bears first leave the family, they frequently occupy a portion of their mother's home range. Young male bears, however, eventually leave the familiarity and security of their mother's range and disperse to distant areas. Young females, in contrast, may stay and permanently inherit part of their mother's home range. This usually occurs only in areas were the mother's range is rich enough to support her daughters as well as herself; otherwise, the young females, like their brothers, must search out a new area in which to settle. Subadults that are looking for some place to settle often travel widely, and until they establish themselves in an area, their home ranges may be larger than those of many adult bears.

The abundance and distribution of food affects the size of a bear's home range more than any other factor. In general, bears that live in areas with abundant food have small home ranges, and those that live where food is scarce have large home ranges. For example, a male brown bear that lives in the coastal regions of Alaska, where it can fish for salmon, needs only 2 per cent of the area that is needed by a male bear in the Brooks Range, where food is much less abundant (Berns, Atwell and Boone 1980; Reynolds and Hechtel 1979).

Polar bears have the largest home range of any bears. In a study in Alaska (Amstrup 1986), the average home range of just one polar bear was forty-five times greater than the area of Great Smoky Mountains National Park in Tennessee, where there are four hundred black bears. The largest polar bear home range was 269 622 square kilometres (104,101 square miles), an area the size of Iceland.

TERRITORIALITY

A discussion of home range is not complete without a look at territoriality. In the strictest sense, a territory is simply a defended home range. When an animal patrols and guards its home range and excludes others of its own kind, it is said to be territorial. Many carnivores, including the hyenas, the big cats, wolves, foxes, mongooses and others, are territorial.

Territoriality has not been observed in brown bears, polar bears, or most black bears. The most common reason for an animal to be territorial is to protect its food supply. As we have seen, many bear foods are patchy in distribution and unreliable from year to year, and as a consequence a great many bears have large home ranges. If bears were territorial, the energetic cost to patrol and defend such large areas would exceed the nutritional benefits. In polar bears, for example, the distribution of seals changes so greatly from year to year, because of shifting ice conditions, that if the bears were territorial, an individual might have an abundance of seals one year and absolutely none the next.

What about bears that have a small home range with a rich food supply, such as a salmon-spawning stream? For example, why doesn't the largest male brown bear at McNeil Falls in Alaska stake out a territory and claim the falls and all of the salmon for himself? The problem with such a strategy is that other bears would constantly challenge him, and sometimes he would be forced to fight and risk injury to maintain exclusive ownership. Since there are enough salmon for many bears, it is a better strategy for the big male to share the falls than to try to monopolize the area and risk injury from challengers.

In the end, because most bears do not defend their home range, their ranges overlap each other, and a number of animals may occupy the same area. As bears move around in their daily activities, they generally try to avoid each other, but should they confront one another, the outcome of the confrontation is determined by their rank in the hierarchy.

Although most bears are not territorial, territorial behaviour has been reported in adult female black bears in three areas—Minnesota, Montana and Alberta. In Minnesota, Lynn Rogers (1987) found that adult females actively defended their home ranges, and they would vigorously chase intruders out of their territory. Rogers did not witness any fights between neighbouring females, but wounds on a number of them indicated that fights sometimes occur. One year Rogers examined two females that held adjacent territories, and the bears had fresh puncture wounds on their heads and necks. Beforehand, one of the females, an eleven-year-old, had made regular incursions into the other bear's territory. After the fight, the female whose territory had been violated was never seen again in the contested area, and the victor added the new area to her own territory. It is difficult to explain why some female bears are territorial when most other bears are not. It may simply be that in these areas the home ranges are small enough to defend, and the benefits derived by the female from exclusive use of her home range offsets the energy costs of defense and the risks of injury.

The most important point to retain from this discussion is that bears are behaviourally flexible and that they will always adopt the strategy that is most beneficial to them.

THE BRAINY BRUIN

In the 1700s, the Scottish philosopher David Hume wrote that "no truth appears to me more evident, than that beasts are endowed with thought and reason as well as men." Two hundred and fifty years later there are still many people who do not believe animals can think. Perhaps by dividing the world into "them" and "us," it is easier for these people to rationalize humans' self-serving behaviour and manipulation of the environment. Delusions are wonderful tricks of the mind, for they remove guilt and responsibility and give us mental peace, but they also cloud our vision and lure us into making unwise decisions—decisions that not only will affect "them" but will also affect "us," in irreversible ways.

Donald Griffin, in his fascinating book *Animal Thinking* (1984), argues that the more we learn about the in-

genuity of animals in coping with problems in their everyday lives, the more difficult it is to defend the idea that humans have a monopoly on conscious thinking. A few examples of how bears use their minds to cope with their world may help you decide for yourself whether bears are conscious thinkers.

If any animal were to operate strictly on programmed instinctive behaviour, it would need a voluminous set of instructions in its brain to cover all possible contingencies. It is more efficient for an animal to think. Conscious thought is especially helpful to any animal that is long lived and that must cope with a variety of habitats. Bears in the wild can live for twenty-five years or more, and they thrive in a diversity of environments. The versatile American black bear, for example, can reside in cypress swamps, coniferous forests, desert scrub and arctic tundra.

Any time an animal makes a decision, it draws on its previous experience to help it decide what to do. In this way, learning is an important part of conscious thinking, and the years that cubs spend with their mothers are important learning years. A brown bear cub that is abandoned when it is five or six months old dies, not because it can live on nothing other than its mother's milk, but in part because it has not yet learned what else to eat, where to find it and how to catch it or dig it up.

Bear cubs learn by closely observing their mother. Black bear cubs shove their nose into logs and anthills torn apart by their mothers, and grizzly cubs investigate every ground squirrel excavation. One May in Alaska, I watched a female grizzly dig for peavine roots on an alpine slope. A pair of spring cubs followed behind her. Between bouts of play, the cubs examined every clump of sod their mother overturned. They would thoroughly sniff each clump and sometimes nibble at the remnants.

I was never more impressed by the way cubs learn than when I watched a polar bear and her offspring hunt for ringed seals in the Canadian High Arctic. The

PREVIOUS PAGE: *During the 2½ years that a young brown bear stays with its mother, it must learn many important lessons—which foods to eat and which to avoid, where and how to dig a den and much more.*

bears hunted around one snowdrift complex for over an hour. The mother bear dug into a dozen snow caves without catching a seal. Every time she moved to another drift, her cub lagged behind and explored the hole she had just dug. The cub would disappear completely into the snow cave, presumably investigating every nook and cranny, and in the process learning the subtle sights, sounds and smells of a seal lair. During its years of family life, a polar bear cub will investigate hundreds, if not thousands, of seal lairs and learn the locations of the exit holes, the depth of the snow on the ceilings, and the many details it will need to know if it is to catch its wary prey.

Later a bear cub may imitate its mother's behaviour down to the most minute details. At McNeil Falls in Alaska, a female brown bear called Lanky and her cub, Teeny, were a good example of this. Of the several dozen fishing spots at the falls, Lanky always used the same spot. Once in position, she would stand with her two front feet in the water, then raise one leg and lean forward expectantly. Her cub, Teeny, would sit or lie down behind her while she fished. Years later when Teeny grew up and returned to the falls without her mother, she fished in the exact spot that had been used by her mother, and she used the same fishing posture, leaning forward over the water with one paw cocked in the air.

One aspect of conscious thinking that has been investigated in bears is their curiosity. Researchers measure curiosity based on how an animal responds to a novel object placed in its environment. In one study, a pair of captive black bears was given two lengths of steel chain, two pine blocks, two pieces of water hose and two wooden dowels. Afterwards, the bears were watched to see how they investigated the objects and how long they stayed interested (Bacon 1980). Both bears reacted to the test objects in the same manner. Once the object was introduced into their cage, they would approach, sniff the object, manipulate it with

their forepaws and then chew on it.

Since the bears were captive animals, the sterility of their environment may well have increased the time they spent with the novel objects. Nevertheless, it is possible to compare the observations made of the black bears with those made of other captive animals tested in a similar fashion and thereby gain some insight into the different curiosity levels demonstrated by different animal groups. The bears demonstrated a higher curiosity level than all other carnivores tested, including big cats, raccoons, weasels and dogs. In some cases, the bears investigated the test objects for twice as long as some of the other carnivores.

Intense curiosity is a characteristic of mammals, and many early researchers, including Darwin, recognized that curiosity was particularly evident in primates. When captive primates were challenged with the same novel objects as the black bears, the primates displayed substantially *lower* levels of curiosity than did the bears. The higher degree of curiosity displayed by bears does not mean that bears are more intelligent than primates. It does mean, however, that their highly investigative nature may predispose them to discover novel food sources in their environment, and this predisposition may contribute to their adaptability.

I have previously discussed numerous examples of how local populations of bears have learned to exploit a novel food source. Brown bears in coastal Alaska swim to distant islands to raid the nests of seabirds. Mountain grizzlies feed on aggregations of ladybird beetles found under rocks. Black bears feed on alligator eggs. And polar bears catch ducks on the water, and also climb cliffs to loot seagull nests. The inherent curiosity of bears enables them to take maximum advantage of their environment and to capitalize on changes and new developments.

A bear's curiosity sometimes gets it into trouble. The same behaviour that drives a brown bear to discover a razor clam (*Siliqua patula*) hidden in the sand of an

Alaskan beach prompts other brown bears to pry open a cooler, panhandle beside the road or tear the door off of an automobile when there is food locked inside. There is a story about one enterprising black bear in California that specialized in assaulting Volkswagens. The bear would climb on the roof of the car and then jump up and down a couple of times until the air pressure inside the car popped open the doors. Who says that bears can't conceive and execute a plan?

Bear biologists love to regale each other with stories about the intelligence of bears—how the animals avoided their snares, learned to raid a trap and steal the bait without getting caught, and even learned to recognize the researchers themselves. At one time there was a brown bear, named Sister, in Katmai National Park that learned to steal salmon from fishermen after the fish were hooked on a line. The rangers started a campaign of deterrence against Sister, but she quickly learned to avoid any fishermen that were accompanied by a person in uniform. The rangers eventually had to resort to disguising themselves in street clothes.

In a study in Great Smoky Mountains National Park, panhandler black bears were watched to see how they interacted with park visitors who fed them. The bears begged from any visitor who stopped along the road. The researchers never fed the bears, and the bears quickly learned to recognize the researchers and never wasted their time begging from them (Tate and Pelton 1983).

One of my favourite bear stories involves a 225-kilogram (496-pound) male black bear that was followed by biologist Gary Alt (1978) through the swamps of Pennsylvania for two days in March 1975. Alt tracked the bear in the snow to evaluate how the animal would respond to being followed—in particular, which parts of its habitat it would use and how it would avoid the tracker. In the two days, Alt followed the bear for 23 kilometres (14½ miles), and the animal demonstrated how crafty bears can be. Aside from

travelling through thick cover and thus reducing its vulnerability to hunters, the bear used a number of tactics to thwart its tracker. Alt described the pursuit in entertaining detail:

On several occasions when moving north along a stream, his [the bear's] tracks disappeared in the water. I assumed he would either cross the stream or continue north in the water. However, he did neither. He turned and walked south in the stream, then left the water heading in a different direction.

As the afternoon progressed, I realized the bear was reaching into his bag of tricks. The bright afternoon sun was melting the snow from the rocks, and he began to use this to his advantage, jumping from rock to rock. He left little sign this way, making tracking much more difficult.

After a while he reached even deeper into his bag of tricks and came out with something new—backtracking. The first time it happened, I was moving along his trail at a good rate when, suddenly, his tracks simply vanished. There were no rocks, no water, nothing to conceal his tracks. My first thought was that he had climbed a tree. After scanning the treetops until I was dizzy, I half expected Captain Kirk or Spock to appear and tell me that the bear had been beamed aboard the Starship Enterprise.

I examined the tracks again, and this time I noticed there were toe marks at both ends, even though there was no evidence in the snow to indicate the bear had turned around. I followed the tracks for about 50 yards [5 metres] and found where the bear had jumped off the main trail, walking away in a direction perpendicular to his old tracks. He pulled this backtracking stunt on six separate occasions. Each time he placed his feet accurately in his old tracks and changed direction by about 90 degrees when leaving the original trail.

Bears are well equipped to learn and remember. Add to this a highly investigative nature, and you have a well-adapted animal capable of being both opportunistic and flexible. As continued research erodes our predjudices against the thinking abilities of other animals, I won't be surprised if we learn that bears are brainier than we imagined.

OCTOBER / NOVEMBER / DECEMBER

What is man without the beasts? If all the beasts were gone, man would die from great loneliness of spirit, for whatever happens to the beast also happens to the man. All things are connected. Whatever befalls the earth befalls the sons of the earth.

—Chief Seathl, Duwamish Tribe

In the 1970s, researchers (Burghardt, Hietala and Pelton 1972) conducted a survey of visitors who came to Smoky Mountains National Park in Tennessee. All of the respondents overestimated the weight of black bears by at least 50 kilograms (110 pounds), and some of them guessed that the bears weighed over 363 kilograms (800 pounds). A few even went as high as 907 kilograms (2000 pounds). ¶ Bears may not be as big in life as they are in our imagination, but they are still large animals. Black bears weighing over 272 kilograms (600 pounds) have been reported from Pennsylvania, Michigan, Newfoundland, New York, Quebec, Louisiana, North Carolina and California. Brown bears weighing 680 kilograms (1500 pounds) have been recorded in the coastal regions of both Alaska and Russia, and polar bears reach similar weights. On Southampton Island in northwestern Hudson Bay, biologists captured an adult male polar bear that weighed 803 kilograms (1770 pounds)! ¶ All bears except polar bears are at their heaviest weight during late fall. The bears have fed voraciously for weeks in preparation for one of the most important activities in a bear's life—denning.

BEDDING DOWN FOR WINTER

By late autumn, food becomes scarce for many black bears and brown bears. Most berries and nuts have dried up, frozen or fallen to the ground and have been eaten by a legion of furred and feathered creatures. Late salmon runs still offer a few

In late autumn, many brown bears along the coast return to salmon spawning streams to scavenge the remains of dead fish.

bears some final days of fishing, and in other areas there are fish carcasses from earlier runs that can be scavenged. Also at this time of the year, bears may happen upon elk, moose and deer that have been injured in battles during the autumn rut or wounded by hunters, and these weakened warriors are sometimes easy prey. For the most part, however, bears gradually spend less time feeding, and they begin to prepare for denning.

Much has been written about the factors that induce a bear to den in the autumn. Like den emergence in the spring, autumn denning is controlled by environmental and physiological factors acting in consort (Johnson and Pelton 1980).

The two most important environmental factors are the availability of food and the weather. In general, black bears den earlier when mast crops are poor than when they are good, and coastal brown bears that can feed on salmon often den later than bears farther inland, where such food is not available. Weather also influences the behaviour of bears, but it is difficult to determine how great this influence really is. In northern bears, it is rare for an animal to den before autumn temperatures fall below freezing, and yet freezing temperatures alone do not inhibit the movements of bears. Snow is more likely to deter a bear, but that also depends upon how motivated the animal is to move around.

. In Yellowstone, one research team noted that grizzlies frequently moved to their dens during a snowstorm and that their tracks were then obliterated during the storm. It was suggested that denning during a snowstorm would conceal the location of a den and make it a safer refuge. Later studies in Yellowstone and elsewhere failed to corroborate these observations (Judd, Knight and Blanchard 1986).

The primary physiological factor that influences denning is undoubtedly the size of a bear's fat reserves, which when scanty compel the bear to remain active but when ample signal it to den. The timing of den entrance, like the timing of den emergence, is also influ-

enced by the age and sex of the bear.

Most black bears and brown bears enter their dens from early October to early January, depending upon where they live. As a rule, pregnant female bears and bears with cubs enter their dens earliest, followed by subadults, and adult males are the last to enter their dens. The timing of denning for any bear is likely governed by a balance between the costs and the rewards of remaining active.

Finding a Den

For many mountain and coastal bears, moving to their denning area is a simple matter of climbing a short distance from a valley bottom or a tidal wetland up to the adjacent tree line or alpine region. In other regions, bears may travel many kilometres from their fall foraging area to their winter denning area. In Alaska's Brooks Range, six radio-collared brown bears travelled an average of 8 kilometres (5 miles) to their den sites, but several other bears made journeys of over 50 kilometres (31 miles). Some brown bears in Yellowstone also travelled over 50 kilometres (31 miles) to reach their denning area (Reynolds, Curatolo and Quimby 1976; Craighead and Craighead 1972).

It is common for bears to move to the area where they will den a week or more beforehand. In the Rattlesnake Mountains of Montana, some grizzlies arrived in their chosen denning area three to four weeks before they actually denned (Servheen and Klaver 1983; Beecham, Reynolds and Hornocker 1983). During this time, observers have noted that bears often appear lethargic. It is quite likely that many bears slip into the hibernation mode before they retire to their dens, just as many bears continue to hibernate for several weeks after they emerge from their dens in the spring.

It is important not to confuse hibernation and denning. Hibernation is a lowered metabolic state in which an animal's energy costs are reduced. Denning is simply when a free-ranging animal rests in one location for an extended period.

A black bear in Pennsylvania used the hollow base of this large white ash (Fraxinus americana) as a den site.

Some bears travel more than 50 kilometres (31 miles) to their den sites. Why do they make such lengthy journeys? It seems safe to suggest that the animals have a den site in mind and are looking for certain features. Black bear cubs den with their mother for two winters, and young brown bears den with the family for three winters, so the bears undoubtedly remember the characteristics of the den sites chosen by their mothers. It is likely that they try to match these characteristics when they choose their own sites.

As bears travel through their home range during the year, they may note potential denning areas and return to these in the autumn. Large trees with cavities in them often have many claw marks etched into the bark from black bears that have climbed the trees, presumably to investigate the cavity as a potential den site. In Russia, Asiatic black bears are thought to examine many tree cavities to assess their suitability.

The qualities that a bear is looking for in a den site are difficult to determine, but there are a few common features. Bears seem to like seclusion in a den site, and they frequently choose areas where they are least likely to be discovered and disturbed. In mountainous regions they often den in remote, isolated valleys, and in populated regions they commonly hide themselves in dense thickets where people are not likely to find them.

Den sites are usually in locations that are dry and well drained. If it snows in the area, dens are often situated where the snow cover is deep and does not disappear too early in the spring. Although bears are quite resistant to cold, the fact that they often choose den sites that retain an insulating layer of snow suggests that the snow benefits the bears in some way. The most obvious benefit is that it reduces the calories they must burn to maintain their body temperature.

Bear Bunkers

Bears choose a variety of sites for their dens. I have seen dens in brush piles, at the base of uprooted trees and under fallen logs. The bases of hollow trees are also popular as dens for black bears and some brown bears. Since black bears are good climbers, they frequently use cavities produced by wind and lightning high in trees. Such tree cavities are used by bears in North Carolina, Georgia, Tennessee, Louisiana, Arkansas, Ontario and Washington (Wathen, Johnson and Pelton 1986; Pelton, Beeman and Eager 1980; Lindzey and Meslow 1976b), and they are the preferred sites for Asiatic black bears throughout eastern Russia (Bromlei 1965).

To house a bear, a tree must have a diameter greater than a metre (3¼ feet), and in North America trees of that size are most common in the hardwood forests of the eastern half of the continent. In Tennessee, such large trees are usually yellow birches, black gums, red maples or red oaks, and they are often 275 to 300 years old. The cavities in these trees were sometimes 21 metres (69 feet) off the ground. The average entrance hole is just 30 centimetres by 55 centimetres (12 inches by 21½ inches), which is remarkably small when you consider that bears over 140 kilograms (309 pounds) squeeze through them.

Naturally, because of the size of tree cavities, they are most often used by the smaller bears in a population, namely, the subadults and the females. In Tennessee, however, a third of the adult males also curl up high inside a tree.

Besides offering greater security than a den on the ground, a tree cavity also provides a thermal advantage. A cavity is usually dry and shields the bear from the chilling effect of the wind. These benefits translate into a 15 per cent energy saving for the bear, and energy conserved in this way improves the survival of young cubs that are born in these dens (Johnson, Johnson and Pelton 1978; Lentz, Marchinton and Smith 1983). Bears, in Tennessee at least, recognize the benefits of tree cavity dens because they select these sites more often than any ground den, even though ground dens are five times more abundant than tree cavities (Johnson and Pelton 1981).

If you rely on cartoons for your information about bears, you already know that bears love to den in caves. The cartoons are partly correct. Bears definitely den in caves, or rock cavities, but the cavities that bears choose are not the size of cathedrals, and I have never found one that echoes inside.

In Yugoslavia, 80 per cent of the brown bear dens examined by Huber and Roth (1989) were in rock cavities. Similar rock dens were used by brown bears in Yellowstone National Park, in the Brooks Range of northern Alaska and on Admiralty Island in southeastern Alaska (Reynolds, Curatolo and Quimby 1976). On Admiralty Island, the rock cavities varied from deep caves that were 7.5 metres (22½ feet) long to small crevices under large boulders. A number of the caves had more than one entrance, and several of them had been slightly modified by digging. From the wear on the rocks, the researchers suspected that some of the caves had been used many times before, possibly for centuries (Schoen et al. 1987).

Black bears also use rock cavities throughout their range whenever such sites are available. In Pennsylvania I have climbed inside half a dozen rock cavities. Many of them had two or three entrances, and some had multiple chambers that were used by different family members over the winter denning period.

In many areas, these same rock cavities are attractive to porcupines (*Erethizon dorsatum*) as winter dens, and I have always wondered how the bears and the "quill pigs" resolve ownership. Both brown and black bears have been seen with quills in their faces, but it is a surprisingly rare event, considering that bears and porcupines must often confront each other. In Alaska, a porcupine provided the bedding for one brown bear that spent the winter in a rock cavity den. The bear slept on a thick heap of droppings, courtesy of the cave's previous occupant (Reynolds, Curatolo and Quimby 1976).

Most reports that discuss bear denning sites never mention whether bears compete for prime locations.

FOLLOWING PAGE: *A black bear may investigate many potential den sites, including rock cavities, before it decides on the final location.*

A common den site for brown bears and black bears is a simple excavation dug into the ground. This site, in the hardwood forests of eastern North America, was home to a mother black bear and her three newborn cubs.

Certainly tree cavities and many rock dens are preferred sites, and if such sites were limited, you would expect bears to compete for them as they do for many other things. The Craighead brothers in Yellowstone did not believe that grizzlies in their study area defended their den sites, but black bear biologists in Alaska observed competition for rock cavities on three different occasions. On two of those occasions the researchers located two black bears at the same rock cavity, and on a third occasion there were three bears around another rock cavity. The biologists did not witness how the bears resolved the issue, but in all cases only one bear ultimately used each rock cavity for denning. When there is competition such as this for den sites, it may be advantageous for a bear to enter its den early (Schwartz, Miller and Franzmann 1987).

The denning location that surprised me most when I first started to study bears was the surface nest. To make a surface nest, a bear chews off branches from nearby trees and bushes and arranges them in a pile about 1.5 metres (5 feet) across. One surface nest I examined had been used by an adult female black bear and her two newborn cubs and was constructed of hundreds of rhododendron branches that had been neatly chewed into 0.3- to 0.6-metre (1- to 2-foot) lengths. A bear may line the pile with leaves and grass. In many ways, the nests resemble elaborate day beds.

Some surface nests have been built in novel locations. One was built on top of a muskrat house, and another was built in the middle of a beaver (*Castor canadensis*) dam.

Surface nests are built by brown bears and both species of black bears. In the United States, the nests are a typical denning method for black bears that live in Florida, Georgia, the Carolinas and other places in the South. In areas farther north, surface nests are not as common. When they do occur, they are mostly used by adult male bears.

Surface nests have not been reported for any bears in Canada or Alaska. It may be that the climate is too severe in these regions for a bear to remain exposed to the elements for the entire winter.

The most common place for bears to den, throughout their range, is a simple hole in the ground, called an excavation den, that the bears dig for themselves. In the eastern United States, one observer (Matson 1954) thought that black bears occasionally enlarged the burrows of red foxes and woodchucks (*Marmota monax*) to use for their dens, and in the West, researchers (Beecham, Reynolds and Hornocker 1983) believed that bears sometimes enlarged portions of abandoned badger (*Taxidea taxus*) and coyote (*Canis latrans*) dens for the same purpose.

Many excavation dens collapse after a year or two, so a new hole must be dug every fall. Usually the dens consist of a single tunnel leading to a single chamber. The tunnel is frequently 1 to 2 metres (3¼ to 6½ feet) long, but there is one record of a brown bear den in the Alaskan Peninsula that had a tunnel 6.5 metres (21¼ feet) long. Some dens have no tunnel at all, and the chamber opens directly to the outside.

Typically, the chamber is egg-shaped—about 1.5 to 2 metres (5 to 6 feet) across and 1 metre (3¼ feet) high. Bears appear to fashion a den so that it is large enough for them to twist around inside, but no larger. In this way, they minimize the size of the air space that must be warmed.

A grizzly may move 900 kilograms (a ton) of dirt and rock in digging out its den, and the excavated soil forms a characteristic mound at the mouth of the den that can be recognized from a distance. Even though most dens collapse in the spring, an experienced spotter can locate abandoned excavation dens that are fifty years old.

Many excavation dens are dug beneath the roots of trees so that the roots form the ceiling of the den. At other times—in the treeless tundra, for example—the dens may be dug beneath a clump of willows or alders. In these circumstances the roots of the bushes stabilize the soil in the ceiling and keep it from collapsing. The

overhanging bushes also trap snowdrifts and increase the insulation over the den site. According to one researcher (Harding 1976), the average depth of the drifted snow that covered brown bear dens in the Northwest Territories was 76 centimetres (30 inches). Away from the dens, the snow was only 15 centimetres (6 inches) deep.

Thermal considerations may also influence the altitude where bears choose to den. In the Canadian Rocky Mountains, both black bears and brown bears den near the tree line, between 1676 and 1981 metres (between 5500 and 6500 feet). At lower altitudes, the conditions are less favourable. Here, the snow arrives later, it is not as deep, and it is generally more dense, meaning that it traps less air and thus does not insulate as well.

Denning at higher altitudes may have an another advantage. The air temperatures at these altitudes are often warmer because of thermal inversions. In a thermal inversion, an upper layer of warm air traps an underlying layer of cold air, so the colder temperatures occur in the valley bottoms (Vroom, Herrero and Ogilvie 1980; Kansas, Raine and Gibeau 1989).

Bears dig their dens in about five to seven days, even though they may be in the denning area for several weeks. They rest in day beds nearby before they begin digging and while they are digging. Sometimes they will start a den and then abandon the site before the den is completed. These "false dens" are believed to be failed attempts. The soil may turn out to be too crumbly or too moist, further digging may be obstructed by a large rock, or the bear may be young and inexperienced and may have chosen a poor location. Usually when this happens the bear just moves to another site and starts again.

Often black bears and brown bears line their dens with some kind of vegetation—generally whatever material is nearby. They rake in grass, leaves and conifer needles and also bite off small branches. The bears may gather several bushels of bedding and pile it into a nest

A black bear may slip into hibernation weeks before it actually enters its den. It is quite lethargic at this time and spends a great deal of time resting in day beds.

about 0.3 metre (1 foot) deep. Around some black bear dens I have examined, the area looks as though someone has cleared it with a garden rake. One enterprising black bear in Michigan stole hay from a stack in the middle of a farmer's field and carried it 100 metres (100 yards) into a swamp to line its winter nest. Even bears that den in tree cavities often scrape wood shavings from the inside of the tree to line the bottom of the den.

Bears can be very fussy about lining their dens. Biologist Lynn Rogers (1981) watched an adult female black bear rearrange the bedding in her den twice. Each time, the bear would scoop out the den, sending the material flying backward between her hind legs, and then she would organize it again.

Lining a den insulates the bear from direct contact with the ground, and this may lessen the drain on the animal's body heat and thus conserve energy. In some studies, females with newborn cubs used more bedding than other bears, but this is not a consistent finding. More often there is no correlation between the amount of bedding and the presence of young cubs in the den.

I have discussed the typical types of dens, but being opportunists, bears sometimes choose unusual sites. In the Pocono Mountains in northeastern Pennsylvania, bears regularly den in the crawl space under homes. Often the owners never learn that a bear has spent the winter under their bedroom, and the animal leaves unnoticed in the spring. I crawled under one house and discovered that the bear had chewed halfway through a beam that was supporting the floor and had used the wood chips to line her den.

In Yellowstone there are reports of black bears denning in old hot springs and near geyser openings in steam-heated rock cavities. In Alberta, Wyoming and

A frequently used rock cavity den in a housing development in the Pocono Mountains in northeastern Pennsylvania.

Pennsylvania bears have used drainage culverts as dens (Barnes and Bray 1966). The report from Pennsylvania is a heartening story.

In mid-January 1983, biologist Dr. Gary Alt (1983) located a radio-collared female bear denning inside a concrete drainage culvert that ran under Interstate 84, a major four-lane highway. When Alt checked on the bear, he could hear the cries of newborn cubs. He knew from the topography of the surrounding area that the culvert would flood if it rained or whenever the remaining snow melted, and the cubs would probably drown. He decided to leave the family where it was for the time being to allow the cubs more time to mature.

On 2 February, the weather forecast predicted 2.5 centimetres (1 inch) of rain, and Alt knew he could wait no longer. He returned to the culvert to find that the runoff had already begun to trickle through. He tranquillized the mother bear and pulled her and her three cubs out of their den. Alt said that while he was inside the culvert it rumbled as if a volcano were erupting each time a transport passed overhead. He wondered how the bear family had gotten any rest at all.

Later in the afternoon on the day of the rescue the culvert had 30 centimetres (1 foot) of water in it, and the bear's nest had been completely washed away. The mother bear and her three cubs, each of which weighed less than half a kilogram (1 pound), were transported to a another den, where they spent the remainder of the winter in a safer haven.

DANGER IN THE DEN

Even though bears are large, powerful carnivores, other carnivores will prey upon them when they are

A brown bear not only may prey on other brown bears but may also kill a black bear if the opportunity arises.

denned. Sometimes these carnivores are other bears.

Females and subadult bears are normally the first animals to den in the fall and the last to emerge in the spring. While they are in their dens, these bears are vulnerable to predation from larger bears, especially from adult males. In northern Alberta, Tietje, Pelchat and Ruff (1986) reported three instances of such behaviour in black bears.

In the first case, an adult female black bear was killed in October shortly after she entered her den. When biologists approached her den, a large black bear fled from the area. The female's remains, which were partly covered with grass and litter, were found 5 metres (16 feet) from the mouth of her den. The ceiling of her den had been torn apart and had collapsed into the den chamber.

In another instance, an adult male weighing 139 kilograms (306 pounds) killed a juvenile male that weighed only 60 kilograms (132 pounds), after the smaller bear had denned up for the winter. The victim had a broken neck and an extensive hemorrhage over its head. The larger bear had consumed half of the carcass when it was discovered by researchers. It was believed that the cannibal was en route to its own den when it accidentally discovered the smaller bear and killed it.

Even adult male bears are not immune to attack. In Alberta, a 5½-year-old adult male black bear that weighed 111 kilograms (245 pounds) was attacked in his den, but he escaped with superficial wounds to his head, shoulders and right front leg. A larger male that was estimated to weigh 160 kilograms (353 pounds) was thought to be responsible for the attack.

There are a number of reports of adult male brown bears and polar bears killing and consuming females, smaller males and cubs, but none of these attacks occurred while the victims were denned.

Black bears are the smallest of the northern bears, and not surprisingly, they are sometimes preyed upon by the larger bear species. Brown bears have preyed on denning black bears on at least one occasion. In Alberta again, a large female grizzly with two yearlings followed the tracks of a smaller black bear and her two cubs through the snow to the black bear family's winter den. The grizzlies killed and ate the two black bear cubs, but the mother bear escaped (Ross, Hornbeck and Horejsi 1988).

Tigers and Bears

Throughout the world, there is only one other terrestrial carnivore that at times can match the power and size of a bear, and that carnivore is the tiger. The subspecies of tiger (*Panthera tigris altaica*) found in southeastern Siberia and Manchuria is the largest living cat. Males can weigh up to 300 kilograms (661 pounds), which is more than any of the Asiatic black bears and most of the brown bears that share their range with the tiger. Not surprisingly, then, tigers in this area prey on denning bears.

During a study done in the 1950s in eastern Russia, there were more than fifteen cases of tigers attacking bears in their winter dens. Most often the tigers preyed on brown bears because the Asiatic black bears in the area denned in tree cavities and caves where they were more difficult for the tigers to reach (Bromlei 1965).

Another report from Russia described the details of how a tiger killed a brown bear in its den. The bear was denned in an excavation den under a cedar tree. A small entrance hole led to the den chamber. The tiger stalked the den from 50 metres (55 yards) away and began to dig into the den from the side opposite to the entrance hole. When the bear was flushed from its refuge, the tiger grabbed it by the neck with its teeth and killed it instantly by dislocating the vertebrae at the base of the bear's skull. The tiger then killed the two yearlings that were in the den with their mother. In the classic cat fashion, the tiger killed both yearlings with a bite to their throats.

The authors of this account made the point that the relationship between tigers and brown bears is not sim-

There are many records of wolves killing denning black bears in Alberta, Manitoba and Minnesota.

*Pregnant polar bears along south-
ern Hudson Bay frequently travel
inland and dig their dens in the
deep snowdrifts that accumulate
around clusters of trees.*

ply that of predator and prey. Brown bears often consume the remains of tiger kills, and the bears may even
deliberately track the big cats to scavenge from the carcasses they leave behind (Matjushkin, Zhivotchenko
and Smirnov 1980).

Wolves and Bears

The carnivore that shares most of its range with one
bear species or another is the grey wolf (*Canis lupus*).
What the wolf lacks in size, it makes up for in numbers,
and there are numerous accounts of interactions between bears and wolves.

In the Owl River denning area in Manitoba, there
are two reports of wolves preying on a denning polar
bear, although this undoubtedly is a rare occurrence,
considering that most adult female bears weigh 180 to
270 kilograms (between 397 and 595 pounds), four to
five times more than a wolf.

In Finland, a large pack of wolves was seen feeding
on the carcass of a brown bear. The bear's den was
nearby, but it was unclear whether the wolves killed
the bear or whether they were simply scavenging
(Pulliainen 1972).

In incidents involving black bears and wolves in
North America, the picture is much clearer. In Minnesota, a pack of six to nine wolves attacked an adult female bear and her newborn cubs. The female only
weighed 72 kilograms (159 pounds) and her den was a
shallow depression under a pile of logs, a location that
afforded her little protection. The observers, veteran
field researchers Lynn Rogers and David Mech (1981),
described the events in the *Journal of Mammalogy*:

*The wolves apparently attacked from both sides and drove the bear
from the den. The bear fought her way 22 meters [72 feet] to the
nearest big tree, a mature aspen (*Populus tremuloides*), leaving
a path of broken brush and bear fur. At the tree, the fight
continued; trampled brush, part of a wolf canine tooth, tufts of
wolf fur, and much bear fur were concentrated in a 3 meter [10
foot] radius around the tree. The bear possibly was injured as there*

*were drops of blood on the tree, but claw marks indicated that she
climbed to the safety of the crown. She eventually came down and
returned to the den where she died or was killed. Bear fur covered
the snow within 2 or 3 meters [6 to 10 feet] of the den.... the
wolves dragged the carcass beyond the fur-covered area to consume
it.... all that remained of the carcass was fur, fragments of bone,
and the nearly intact skull. Wolf droppings in the vicinity contained
claws of the newborn cubs.*

There is another account of eight wolves killing a
denning black bear in Alberta (Horejsi, Hornbeck and
Raine 1984). In addition, in three incidents wolves dug
up, killed and ate black bears in Riding Mountain National Park in Manitoba.

In one case in Manitoba, two wolves killed an
eleven-year-old bear that was denned in an excavation
between two stumps. The wolves attempted to dig the
bear out of its den, and it was wounded in the struggle.
There were large patches of sprayed blood around the
entrance to the den. When the bear emerged from its
den to continue the fight, it was killed. Later, when the
bear's skull was examined, it was learned that earlier in
the fall it had been shot in the face by a hunter. The bul-
let had struck the bear below its left eye, penetrated the
roof of its mouth and exited through the angle of its jaw.
The injuries may have debilitated the bear so that it
could not properly defend itself against the wolves (Paquet and Carbyn 1986).

Bears are not always the losers when they deal with
wolves; at other times of the year, the score often evens
out. Bears frequently steal the prey that wolves have
killed, and the wolves are then forced to hunt again.
Near Churchill, Manitoba, Steve Miller, a helicopter
pilot, spotted a polar bear feeding on a caribou carcass
while three wolves lay nearby.

In an Alaskan wolf study, the wolves generally de-
ferred to adult brown bears whenever the ownership of
a carcass was contested, but they did not consistently
do so for black bears (Peterson, Woolington and Bailey
1984; Ballard 1982).

Wolves have ample reason to defer to brown bears, as an account from Alaska will illustrate. In late autumn, a pack of nine wolves killed an adult moose. By the following day, the carcass had been confiscated by a brown bear, and there was a dead wolf lying 10 metres (33 feet) from the moose. The wolf had puncture wounds on its throat, and the base of its skull had been crushed (Ballard 1980).

S N O W   D E N S

Brown bears and black bears live in many areas where winter lasts for six months or more and where the annual snowfall is measured in metres. It would seem natural that some bears in these areas would den in snow caves. Nevertheless, aside from two reports of brown bears, one from Kodiak Island in Alaska (Van Daele, Barnes and Smith 1990) and the other from the Northwest Territories (Harding 1976), browns and blacks rarely dig snow dens. Such behaviour is left to the most northern of bears, the polar bear.

The earliest record of a polar bear den comes from a sailor stranded on Novaya Zemlya, an island group off the northern coast of Russia. He wrote in his journal, dated 1597, that

there came a great bear towards us, against whom we began to make defence, but she perceiving that, made away from us, and we went to the place from whence she came to see her den, where we found a great hole made in the ice, about a man's length in depth, the entry thereof being very narrow, and within wide; there we thrust in our pikes to feel if there was anything within it, but perceiving it was empty, one of our men crept into it, but not too far, for it was fearful to behold.

As described in Chapter 1, denning behaviour in polar bears serves a more limited function than in the other species of bears. Polar bears are able to hunt seals during the winter months, so they are not driven to den because of a scarcity of food, as are brown bears and black bears. Denning for polar bears is primarily a reproductive strategy, and a winter den is simply a sheltered environment in which to raise cubs. Consequently, it is primarily pregnant female polar bears that den, and the other bears in the population remain on the ice hunting seals.

In a magazine article several years ago, I described denning in polar bears as a behaviour of pregnant females. I should have written that denning in polar bears is *primarily* a behaviour of pregnant females. After the article was published, I received a letter from Father Franz van de Velde, an oblate priest in Belgium. As soon as I saw his name, I knew I was in trouble. Father van de Velde (1957) travelled with the Inuit in the Canadian Arctic in the 1950s and made detailed notes on the polar bears he encountered. On a number of occasions, he and his Inuit companions flushed adult males and subadult bears out of snow dens in the middle of winter. The good father knew that winter dens were not just used by pregnant polar bears. In the end I learned a valuable lesson as a science writer: Never use absolutes when you are writing about bears.

Since my correspondence with Father van de Velde, I have found scattered references to the fact that polar bears of all ages and both sexes spend time in winter dens. Nonetheless, it is *not* a common phenomenon in polar bears *other than* pregnant females. Probably these other bears den for a short time during periods of bad weather or when hunting is poor to reduce their energy expenditures until conditions improve. Because pregnant females are the most common occupants of dens, the dens are often referred to as maternity dens (Harington 1968; Schweinsburg, Spencer and Williams 1984).

Pregnant polar bears leave the pack ice and come ashore to den in September or October, depending on the ice conditions where they live. In Hudson Bay, the landlocked females simply stay put in the area where they spent the summer and wait for the snowdrifts to pile up.

Polar bears dig their dens in deep snowdrifts. The usual den is an oval chamber, 2 to 3 metres (6½ to 10 feet) in diameter and 1 to 1½ metres (3¼ to 5 feet) in height. A tunnel, several metres long, leads to the outside.

Polar bears, unlike other bears, do not line their dens with vegetation. They differ as well in having multichambered dens. In one Alaskan study, a third of the polar bear dens examined had two or three chambers, and some of them had an adjoining small alcove less than a half metre (1½ feet) in height. The alcoves were believed to have been dug by cubs (Lentfer and Hensel 1980). On Wrangel Island off the northeastern coast of Siberia, a polar bear den with five chambers was found. The multichambered den was inside an immense snowdrift that ran along a rock wall. The whole chain of dens was 13 metres (42½ feet) long and was linked to the outside by a single entrance tunnel (Uspenski and Kistchinski 1972).

The ceilings on some snow dens may be 2 to 3 metres (6½ to 10 feet) thick, so the temperatures inside a den are generally much less severe than outside. A probe was passed through the roof of one maternity den in January, and the inside temperature was monitored for a month. Whereas the temperatures inside the den fluctuated around the freezing point, between −3°C and +2°C (27° to 36°F), the temperatures outside ranged from −30°C to −10°C (−22° to +14°F). At times, the den was 33°C (60°F) warmer than the outside air (Watts 1983).

A layer of snow is best at retaining heat when it is thick and fluffy. As snow compacts, it loses its insulating qualities, and by the time it has compacted into ice, it has virtually no insulating ability. When temperatures inside a polar bear den creep above the freezing point, the snow melts on the inside of the den. Later, when the den cools down again, a layer of ice forms. Over the course of the winter, as the overlying snow compacts into ice, the temperature inside the den may slowly drop.

Most polar bear dens have claw marks etched into the walls and the ceilings. Many researchers believe that the bears periodically scratch away the ice that forms, not so much to affect the insulation of the den but to improve gas exchange. Oxygen does not diffuse through a layer of ice, and the oxygen levels inside an ice-encrusted den might drop. In a black bear den plugged by crusted snow, the oxygen level dropped by 25 per cent (Rogers 1987).

The multiple chambers sometimes seen in polar bear dens may be attempts by the bears to excavate a fresh chamber with better gas diffusion. Often the ceilings of dens have a ventilation hole in them, either melted by the bear's body heat or scratched out by the animal. A ceiling vent, of course, would allow fresh air to readily enter the den and would remedy any oxygen depletion.

Maternity Denning Areas

In most areas of the Arctic, polar bears den within 15 kilometres (9 miles) of the coastline, although in southern Hudson Bay the average female dens 61 kilometres (38 miles) from the coast, and some as far inland as 118 kilometres (73 miles). In Hudson Bay, potential den sites do occur closer to the coast, and it is not known why the females move so far inland. Since all of the bears in this area are landlocked for three to four months, the females may move inland simply to avoid the adult males that remain near the coast (Kolenosky and Prevett 1983).

Polar bears can den just about anywhere in the Arctic where there are deep snowdrifts, but often the females concentrate in specific denning areas. These core denning areas are found in each of the five polar nations where polar bears occur.

In the former Soviet Union, there are core denning areas on each of the five island groups north of the mainland coast. The greatest number of dens is found on Wrangel Island, where an estimated 150 to 200 female bears den annually. In Norway's Svalbard Archipelago, about 150 to 175 polar bears den on a few key

FOLLOWING PAGE: *A female polar bear usually returns to the same denning area where she had her first successful litter, and it is thought that her female cubs use the same denning area as well.*

islands. In Greenland, an area of den concentration is found along the northeastern coast, a region that is deeply indented with fiords and has an abundant seal population. In Canada, which has the lion's share of the world's population of polar bears, there are major denning areas scattered throughout the Arctic. The largest Canadian denning area is the Owl River area southeast of Churchill, Manitoba, along the western coast of Hudson Bay. Here, approximately 100 to 150 female polar bears den each winter.

The bears in some of these core denning areas may overwinter very near to each other, a phenomenon that is extremely rare in any of the other species of bears. In the Canadian High Arctic, female polar bears have denned 25 metres (82 feet) apart. On Wrangel Island, Russian researchers found six dens in a 300-square-metre (359-square-yard) plot. The densest concentration of dens in the entire Arctic was found on Kong Karls Land in Svalbard, where there were 12 dens per square kilometre (31 per square mile) (Harington 1968; Uspenski and Kistchinski 1972; Larsen 1985).

With so much potential denning habitat to chose from, why do female polar bears den in concentrated groups? A number of explanations are possible. The need for seclusion and the pressure of human hunting may encourage bears to use a small number of areas that are free of disturbance. Female polar bears also show a high degree of fidelity to their maternity denning areas. Once a female successfully rears cubs in a denning area, she returns to the same general area for each subsequent litter, and it is likely that her female offspring use the same denning area as well.

Another factor that probably affects the location of denning areas is the proximity of a major polynya or lead system. Most, if not all, of the core denning areas are near an important area of open water or shifting pack ice where there are seals to hunt when the females leave their dens in March.

Ice Denning

In Alaska, the site where polar bears den is somewhat different. It is estimated that there are about two thousand polar bears in Alaska. Despite this high number, it was always a mystery where the female bears denned, since only a few dozen maternity dens had ever been located. Most researchers believed that the bears denned in either Siberia or Canada (Amstrup, Stirling and Lentfer 1986).

In 1974, the mystery was solved when Alaskan biologists documented the first polar bear maternity den located on drifting pack ice. The den was in drifted snow on the leeward side of a pressure ridge, 168 kilometres (104 miles) offshore from the coastal community of Point Barrow (Lentfer 1975). Since then, many dens have been located on the sea ice off the northern coast of Alaska, some as far offshore as 800 kilometres (497 miles) (Amstrup 1985).

Denning on the sea ice is rare in female polar bears from other populations. Why, then, is it so common in Alaskan bears? Veteran polar bear researcher Dr. Ian Stirling and his colleagues (1975) offered a plausible explanation:

It seems surprising that more maternal denning does not occur along the northern coast of Alaska and the Yukon. There is an abundance of suitable snowbanks and only short distances need to be crossed by females to hunt seals after leaving the den in the spring. However, the mainland coast area has been inhabited by whalers and Inuit supplied with firearms for over 80 years. It seems likely that adult female polar bears which utilized the mainland coast for denning were shot. Over the course of time they were simply eliminated when the use of firearms became widespread.

Today continued hunting pressure along the coast probably prevents the area from being re-established as a denning area.

Alaskan biologist Steve Amstrup has taken a special interest in ice denning. He has noted that female polar bears that den on the sea ice offshore from Alaska have small litters. The litters, in fact, are less than half the size of the litters produced by females in the neighbouring Beaufort Sea to the east, where most of the females are believed to den on land. Amstrup suspects that ice dens may put pregnant females into greater contact with other bears, and that the instability of the sea ice may subject cubs to greater risks.

The sea ice is not a static platform. It moves as much as 5 kilometres (3 miles) a day. From 1 November to 1 April, a hypothetical ice den could move 650 kilometres (404 miles). A drifting maternity den might transport a mother and her cubs to a poor feeding area, or worse, the den might be ferried into an area where the ice breaks up, prematurely subjecting the cubs to the full force of winter. These factors combined may explain the small litters observed in ice-denning polar bears, but further studies are being conducted to clarify the issue (Lentfer and Hensel 1980).

THE CHALLENGE OF LIFE ON THE ICE

Each year, when the sun sets on the North Pole on 21 September, it will not appear again for six months. Throughout the arctic realm of the polar bear, much of winter is a time of darkness. Still, there is often enough light for even a human to easily move about. In late December, at a latitude of 75° north, the southern horizon at noon is brightened by a narrow orange band of light that fades into the deep blue-purple of the upper sky, and by moonlight, there is enough brightness to discern the tracks of arctic hares (*Lepus articus*) and foxes and to follow them.

On a completely calm day, the average winter temperature in this high latitude is −35°C (−31°F). Add to that temperature the heat drain from an average wind speed of 25 km/h (15½ mph), and the conditions are equivalent to −57°C (−71°F). In such cold, even the rocks wince, and exposed skin freezes in seconds.

Polar bears are active at this latitude in winter. In fact, it is recorded that a family of bears travelled over the sea ice 1000 kilometres (621 miles) farther north than this latitude. On 20 December 1957, a female polar bear and her single cub became tangled in the wires of the runway lights of a drifting ice station positioned at 84° north latitude. The event was especially noteworthy since the bear broke the wire and turned off the runway lights just as an aircraft was about to land (Scott et al. 1959).

To survive under these conditions of darkness and extreme winter temperatures, the polar bear has evolved a number of adaptations in its eyes, feet and fur.

Vision in Polar Bears

The statement that bears have poor vision and are shortsighted has been repeated so often that it has attained a degree of authenticity. Bears probably see much better than we think, and polar bears, at least, are not nearsighted. For the moment, let's disregard all common knowledge and look at what actually is known about vision in bears, and in particular polar bears.

Surprisingly, I could find only one study that looked at the structure of a bear's retina. A Russian researcher (Andreev 1973) microscopically examined the retina of a polar bear. Retinas contain two types of light receptors, cones and rods. Cones are used for daylight colour vision and determine the acuteness of an animal's eyesight, whereas rods are used in night vision when light levels are very low. Based on the density and distribution of rods and cones that the researcher found in the retina of the polar bear, he concluded that the animal had reasonably sharp vision and also a fair sensitivity to low light levels.

The night vision of bears is further enhanced by a special reflective layer, called the tapetum lucidum, which lines the back of their eyeballs. The tapetum, which is present in many nocturnal animals, reflects light back through the retina, allowing the light a second chance to stimulate the rods. This increases the sensitivity of the eye to low light levels. The tapetum is responsible for the eyeshine you see when your car headlights or the beam of a flashlight illuminates an animal at night. These two features, the tapetum and the arrangement of rods in the retina, suggest that

BEAR MYTH

A myth that has followed polar bears for forty years is that they, like birds, have a transparent third eyelid, called a nictitating membrane, that they use like sunglasses to filter the damaging rays of the sun and to help them see underwater. I have examined the eyes of numerous adult polar bears. They indeed have a nictitating membrane, but it is opaque and often blotched with dark brown spots. A bear could not see through the membrane. The purpose of the membrane, however, remains a mystery.

To withstand the extreme winter temperatures of the Arctic, the polar bear has evolved adaptations in its eyes, feet and fur.

PREVIOUS PAGE: *The fur is thinnest on a polar bear's belly, and by stretching out on snow like this, the bear can cool off.*

bears are well adapted to see under dim light conditions and that the darkness of an arctic winter would not likely inhibit the movements of a polar bear (Ronald and Lee 1981).

One can determine whether a bear is nearsighted by examining the animal's eye. The ability to see objects near or far is largely determined by two factors, the curvature of the cornea, which is the clear window at the front of the eye, and the shape of the lens in the eye. When researchers (Sivak and Piggins 1975) examined the eye of a polar bear, they concluded that if anything, polar bears are slightly farsighted. In the same study, the researchers examined how well a polar bear sees underwater. It was decided that polar bears, like humans, are adapted for vision in air and that the bears

have none of the adaptations seen in more aquatic mammals such as seals.

Further studies on the retina of the polar bear are needed to determine whether the bears have colour vision. This aspect of vision has only been investigated in the American black bear. Humans are sensitive to three colour wavelengths—blue, red and green—and the three in combination endow us with our ability to perceive a wide range of colours and hues. Black bears were found to be sensitive to blue and green wavelengths, and possibly even red. Thus, black bears, at least, have substantial colour vision (Bacon and Burghardt 1976).

Colour vision would be advantageous for the black bear, which needs to locate foods that are many differ-

Bears have better vision than they are given credit for, and they probably see as well as many humans.

ent colours. The polar bear, however, lives mostly in a monochromatic world of white and gray, and colour vision would not be as essential. Nonetheless, the polar bear may perceive colours and only further reasearch will settle the issue.

As a former emergency physician, I am particularly interested in why polar bears don't suffer from snow blindness. In humans, the cornea is injured by excessive amounts of ultraviolet light. The bright snow fields in polar regions and at high altitudes present a special hazard. The snow reflects the harmful ultraviolet rays into our eyes and damages the cornea, producing the symptoms of snow blindness, which include severe pain, excessive tearing and extreme sensitivity to light. In humans, snow blindness can occur after only a few hours of exposure, and yet polar and alpine animals may spend months on snow, seemingly without any ill effects. When I searched the literature on snow blindness in wild animals, again, I found only one report.

In the study (Hemmingsen and Douglas 1970), Adelie penguins (*Pygoscelis adeliae*) and Antarctic skuas (*Catharacta skua*) were compared with domestic chickens, guinea pigs and California ground squirrels (*Citellus beecheyi*). Not surprisingly, the polar birds had greater resistance to corneal damage than did either of the two domestic animals. The surprise was the great resistance of the ground squirrel, which was two and a half times more tolerant of ultraviolet rays than even the penguin.

When the eyes of the ground squirrel were examined closely, a yellow pigment was found in the cornea. It was speculated that the pigment produced a "sunglass effect" that absorbed the ultraviolet rays and prevented damage to the cornea. Similar studies are needed in polar bears to determine whether they use the same tactic to prevent snow blindness.

Combatting the Cold

The most critical adaptations for a northern animal are

those that insulate it against the frigid temperatures. An arctic mammal's body temperature may differ from the air temperature by as much as 80°C (143°F). This is the same temperature difference that exists between room temperature and a cup of boiling water. Polar bears shield themselves from the heat-stealing northern climate with special adaptations in their feet and in their fur.

The bottoms of a polar bear's feet are heavily furred, insulating them from the ice and snow. This adaptation is also seen in the feet of the arctic fox. Hairy soles have evolved not only in polar animals but also in desert animals; two good examples are the sand cat (*Felis margarita*) and the fennec fox (*Fennecus zerda*). Desert animals have the reverse problem of the polar bear; they must shield their feet from the searing temperatures of hot desert sands, which can exceed 80°C (176°F).

Even if most of a polar bear's foot pads are covered by fur, it still has some furless areas that come into direct contact with the ground. Studies have shown that arctic mammals have specialized skin on their feet that can chill to 0°C (32°F) in temperature without becoming frostbitten or painful. In contrast, domestic dogs find it painful to stand on ice if they have been kept inside, and it takes them several weeks to become acclimated to cold winter temperatures. Human feet are the least adapted to survive in the Arctic. We experience intense pain if the skin on our feet drops much below 15°C (59°F) (Henshaw, Underwood and Casey 1972).

Not only are a polar bear's foot pads resistant to frostbite, but they are also roughened like coarse sandpaper to prevent slipping. When viewed under a microscope, the black skin of a polar bear's foot pads are covered with thousands of tiny bumps. This anti-skid feature might never have been examined in detail if it were not for a group of British researchers with the Ford Motor Company who were trying to develop slip-resistant footwear to reduce industrial accidents. The re-searchers decided to study the polar bear, since it is adapted to a slippery environment. Their findings led them to develop a soft shoe soling that was covered with small conical projections, similar to the pliable foot pads of a polar bear (Manning et al. 1985).

The dense, long fur of northern mammals is legendary, and it is the animals' principal defense against the cold. A thick coat of fur traps a layer of warm air next to the animal's skin, and it is this layer of air that insulates them from the cold.

The fur coat of a polar bear consists of an underwool of fine white hair that is penetrated by longer, coarse guard hairs lying on top of the underwool. The guard hairs, which are twice the length of the underwool hairs, are hollow. During the summer months in warm climates, polar bears in zoos occasionally look green. That is because algae may grow inside the hollow core of the hairs, giving the fur a greenish cast. The underwool hairs are not hollow, and they remain white (Lewin and Robinson 1979).

In late autumn, the number and the length of the underwool hairs increases so that the density of its pelt changes from 1000 hairs per square centimetre (6450 hairs per square inch) to 1500 hairs per square centimetre (9677 hairs per square inch), providing it with greater insulation (Frisch, Oritsland and Krog 1974).

Polar bears are well equipped for the cold with their denser winter coats, but what happens when the bears plunge into the water? Unlike most other aquatic mammals, such as muskrats, beavers and sea otters (*Enhydra lutris*), polar bears get soaked to the skin when they dive into the water. The other aquatic mammals retain a layer of air between their skin and the water because their pelts have a greater density than that of polar bears. The fur coat of a sea otter, for example, has 100,000 hairs per square centimetre (645,000 hairs per square inch), whereas the polar bear has a meagre 1500 hairs per square centimetre (9677 hairs per square inch). Obviously, the sea otter is much better equipped to keep water away from its skin.

Seals also get wet to the skin, and like seals, polar bears rely on their blubber layer to insulate them from the cold. Water conducts heat twenty-five times better than dry air, so the heat drain on an aquatic mammal is tremendous. Even with their layer of blubber, polar bears are not completely adapted to the water as seals are, and if they remain in cold water for a great length of time, they probably suffer heat loss (Oritsland 1970). In winter, most of the dips that polar bears take are relatively brief.

Since polar bears are best equipped to deal with cold when their pelts are dry, researchers wondered what would happen to them if their fur became soiled in an oil spill. When the thick coat of a polar bear becomes fouled with oil, it greatly reduces the insulative capacity of the animal's fur, and as a government study reported, "thermoregulatory and metabolic stresses develop which may cause serious disability if protracted in the wild" (Oritsland et al. 1981). Furthermore, since polar bears are clean animals, they lick the oil from their fur when they groom themselves. The ingested oil poisons the bears, producing intestinal ulcers and hemorrhage, collapse of lung segments, anemia, and kidney failure. The bears die within several weeks (Stirling 1990; St. Aubin 1990).

In the future, offshore drilling for oil in the Arctic will occur more and more. Large-scale spills and well blowouts, as well as considerable quantities of oil that are discharged through ballast water and the washing of ships, could affect many prime polar bear areas. The consequences for the bears, as well as the entire arctic marine ecosystem, could be disastrous.

Of the four species of northern bears, only the polar bear and the American black bear are holding their own and not declining in numbers. The causes of these declines are widespread deforestation, mineral and petroleum exploration and development, and human encroachment across the entire northern hemisphere. These activities will continue to threaten the existence of bears until we decide to adjust our priorities.

Bears keep me humble. They help me to keep the world in perspective and to understand where I fit on the spectrum of life. We need to preserve the wilderness and its monarchs for ourselves, and for the dreams of children. We should fight for these things as if our life depended upon it, because it does.

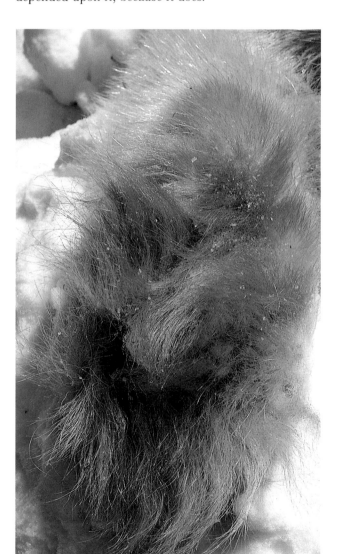

The hair on the bottom of a female polar bear's foot continues to grow during the five months that she dens. Later, when she travels on the sea ice, the hair will be worn down to a shorter length.

APPENDIX A

BEARS, CULTS and HUMAN MEDICINE

From the earliest times, in every part of the world, there has always been a predator that attracted special attention in the spiritual lives of the people. Invariably this animal was large, powerful and dangerous, and sometimes it preyed on humans. In the sweltering swamps of New Guinea and northern Australia this animal was the saltwater crocodile (*Crocodylus porosus*); in India and southeastern Asia it was the tiger; in the savannahs of tropical Africa it was the lion; in the forests of central Europe it was the wolf; and in the verdant rain forests of Central and South America it was *el tigre*, the jaguar (*Panthera onca*). In the tundra and northern coniferous forests of Eurasia and North America this special animal was the bear, the monarch of the northern wilderness. ¶ The bear has always figured prominently in the lives of northern people, and because of the animal's position of importance, elaborate customs and ceremonies evolved around it. Most of the customs involved the hunting of bears, the handling of the carcass and the disposal of the animals' bones. The ceremonies and formalities differed between geographical areas, but the common theme was an attitude of respect and reverence for the animal. ¶ Bears were most often hunted while the animals were in their winter dens. They were driven from their dens, sometimes with fire, and killed as they attempted to escape. Many times a hunter, clad only in skins and a mantle of bravery, would engage the bear in hand-to-claw combat as the aroused animal rushed from its refuge. In these classic contests, the men were mauled as often as the bears were killed. ¶ Before a hunt, or while the men surrounded the bear, one of the hunters would deliver a conciliatory speech to the animal explaining why the men were about to kill it, perhaps saying that they needed to feed their hungry children or to clothe themselves against the fury of winter. The spokesman would then apologize to the bear for the act the men were about to commit and implore the animal not to seek revenge on them in the afterlife in the "abode of the spirits."

The dried skull and front paw of an Asiatic black bear being sold at a farmer's market in Fengjie, China. Beneath the paw are dried bear gall bladders, and in the background there are various medicinal herbs.

After the bear was impaled on a spear or bludgeoned with an axe, the dead animal continued to be handled in a ceremonial fashion so as not to offend its spirit. Onlookers never pointed at the bear, and they never addressed the animal directly. When the people spoke about the dead bear, they used euphemisms of respect and endearment. They called the bear grandfather, or "old man with the fur garment." Taboos were associated with different parts of the bear's body. For example, in some cultures, the head and paws of a bear could not be eaten or even handled by women, and only men could eat the rump meat.

Additional customs dictated how a bear's remains were to be treated. Particular care was taken in disposing of the skull. Often it was placed in a tree in the forest or mounted on a special pole, sometimes at the site

where the bear was killed. The bear's other bones were treated with equal ceremony. Most often they were buried or wrapped in bark and hung in a tree along with the skull. It was an evil omen if the bear's bones happened to get chewed on by a hunter's dogs (Hallowell 1926; Ewers 1955; Shepard and Sanders 1985).

In these primitive human cultures, humans attributed virtually all living and nonliving things with life and intelligence, and frequently also with supernatural power. They believed that animals had the same capabilities as humans and thus animals could be beneficent and help humans in their pursuits, or be malevolent and heap misfortune on them.

The ancient ceremonialism associated with bears filled an important psychological need for primitive hunters. By placating the spirit of the bear with strict adherence to elaborate customs, the people hoped to ensure their future hunting success. As hunters, humans viewed wildlife as equal to themselves. This attitude towards wildlife, however, changed dramatically as the structure of society evolved from hunting to agriculture.

THE BIG BAD BEAR

Farmers and pastoralists recognized only two kinds of animals. There were "good" animals, such as goats, sheep and cattle, and then there were "bad" animals, in particular, predators like bears, that sometimes attacked the farmer's dull-witted livestock. The change in attitude towards wildlife fueled a campaign of destruction aimed at all predators.

Armed with moral righteousness and a sense of civil duty, we hounded bears with dogs, blasted them with bullets, destroyed their innards with poisons and mutilated them in traps. In the 1800s, the men who did the killing were celebrities, men like Ben Lilly, Holt Collier and Davy Crockett. Each of these bear hunters killed hundreds and sometimes thousands of bears, and their feats drew the awe and approval of royalty and presidents.

No tactic was too outrageous when ridding the land of bears. In the 1850s, Oliver Allen, the inventor of the whaling gun, used his deadly device to drive harpoons into grizzlies that roamed the wilds of California, and a hundred years later a World War II pilot was hired by the Alaskan government to "control" the brown bears of Kodiak Island. The pilot mounted a gun on his airplane and strafed and killed thirty-five bears from the air.

Humans were never content with just killing bears; we wanted to control them, so we imprisoned them in cages to gawk at and taunt, we muzzled them and forced them to dance, and sometimes we sentenced them to sanguineous spectacles. In Roman times, bears were commonly used in public shows. In one event during the reign of the Emperor Nero, four hundred bears and three hundred lions were slaughtered in the arena in contests with the cavalry (Matheson 1942).

Blood sports and bears did not disappear with the advance of civilization. In the mid-1800s, Californians loved to pit bears against bulls, and fights were staged in every settlement. A thick leather rope, 20 metres (65½ feet) long, was attached to the hind leg of a bear and the animal was dragged into an arena. The other end of the rope was tied to the front leg of a wild, brawny bull. If the combatants were reluctant to fight, they were jabbed with a nail fixed to the end of a stick. The animals had no recourse but to fight for their lives. Storer and Tevis (1955) vividly described a fight in their classic book *California Grizzly*:

The usual way by which the bear countered the bull was to crouch and, as the horns smashed against his own ribs, sink his teeth into the opponent's sensitive nose. More often than not the impact of the charge threw the grizzly onto his back. The bull, then suffering intense pain and bellowing horribly, could not gore him and would be forced to make frantic efforts to extricate itself. 'The noise was terrific and the dust rose in clouds, while the onlookers shouted as they saw that the fight was deadly and witnessed the flow of blood' [quote from a newspaper story].

After the grizzly dispatched the first bull, the event was not over, and the battered bruin was rarely pardoned or allowed to recover. Another fiery-tempered beast was led into the arena and the contest was repeated. Sometimes an exhausted grizzly would battle three bulls until a fourth animal gored it and ended the ordeal with bone-crushing finality.

CARRIER OF THE MEDICINE

In our battle with bears, we have always won, but still we have never broken the animal's spirit. Combine the bear's tenacious, defiant nature with a powerful, well-

◁ ◁
Native people in northern British Columbia call the bear "the carrier of the medicine" because of their belief in the animal's curative powers.

Even today, the polar bear is treated with reverence and respect by many native northern people.

armed body, and you have a creature guaranteed to inspire awe. Perhaps it is these qualities that have always endowed the bear with imagined curative and restorative powers, and since early times, bears have been considered powerful medicine.

The fat from a large black bear can yield 40 to 60 litres (10½ to 16 gallons) of oil (Hoyt 1934). For centuries, native Americans have prized bear oil as a liniment. Maggie Hodgson, a Carrier native from northern British Columbia, told me that her people rub bear oil on paralyzed and arthritic people. The bear is such an important animal for the Carrier people that they call it "the carrier of the medicine."

For over a thousand years, the bear has been an important part of traditional Oriental medicine as well. During the 1988 Summer Olympics in Seoul, Korea,

the Korean government imported thirty live Asiatic black bears from Thailand to feed to its country's athletes in the belief that the bear meat would enhance the athletes' performance.

Most people have heard about bear paw soup. Today a small bowl of the watery broth, which is reputed to confer health, costs wealthy Japanese and Korean diners eight hundred dollars a bowl.

In the Oriental medical pharmacopoeia, the most important part of a bear is the animal's gall bladder. A freshly removed gall bladder looks like a plastic bag, 10 to 12 centimetres (4 to 5 inches) long, filled with thick, greenish fluid. The gall bladder and its contents of bile are dried and then crushed. Once the powdered ingredients reach a consumer in the Orient, they may sell for $50 a gram ($1764 an ounce). The powdered gall bladders are prescribed to treat heart disease, headaches, abdominal pain and even hemorrhoids.

The traffic in bear parts is big business. In 1985, an Air India 747 jet from Canada exploded and crashed, killing 329 passengers. Among the cargo lost on the tragic flight were two suitcases, each weighing about 16 kilograms (35 pounds), filled with dried gall bladders from a thousand Canadian black bears. The Toronto writer who reported the story said that the shipment had probably cost the exporter over $120,000, with a street value in the Far East of a million dollars.

Today the principal consumers of bear parts are the Chinese, Koreans and Japanese. Recently, in Harbin, a city in northern China, the Chinese have started a number of bear farms where peasants raise Asiatic black bears in kennel fashion for export to rich Japanese and Korean buyers. The Chinese are also experimenting with techniques that will allow them to repeatedly drain a bear's gall bladder of its valuable bile through a permanent plastic tube. In this way, the bears do not need to be killed.

Whenever there is profit to be made, there are people to exploit the situation. The valuable market in bear parts has created a strong incentive for poachers. Some authorities believe that for every bear shot legally in North America, one or two others are killed illegally. A few years ago near my home in Alberta, wildlife officers found eight dead black bears in a small section of forest. The bears had been shot by poachers, and only their feet and gall bladders had been taken.

Today a poacher can sell a gall bladder for over four hundred dollars. Sometimes poachers try to foist off pig gall bladders as the real thing. Since it is often difficult for buyers to detect the fakes, they sometimes prefer to buy the entire bear. There are stories that dead bears are frozen and shipped in oil drums and even that live animals are drugged and air-freighted to the Far East.

No one doubts that millions of people believe that bear parts are powerful medicine, but what do western scientists think? An important lesson I learned while in medical school was to be wary about all claims made about any drug or medicine, so naturally I approached the matter of bear gall bladders with a healthy amount of skepticism. I was surprised by what I discovered.

The bile of bears was first mentioned in a pharmaceutical report written in China in the fifth century. By A.D. 1000 in China, the ingestion of bear bile was the treatment of choice for jaundice, abdominal pain and distention—all complications now known to be caused by liver and bile duct disease, and in particular, gallstones. It was not until the early decades of this century that western scientists finally investigated the composition of bear bile, and when they did they identified a new bile acid and coined the scientific name ursodeoxycholic acid (UDCA), the "urso" prefix in recognition of the origin of the compound.

In subsequent research, it was learned that administration of UDCA could dissolve gallstones in humans and thus alleviate the symptoms, namely, the pain, jaundice and abdominal distention, without producing any substantial side effects. Today, after extensive clinical testing, UDCA is the medical treatment of choice in many hospitals in North America for the dissolution of certain kinds of gallstones. It appears that the Chinese were right two thousand years ago (Bachrach and Hofmann 1982; Lindley and Carey 1987).

Bears have recently become the focus of other research that may also contribute to human medicine. Locked within the blood of bears are substances with enormous possibilities for saving lives. Bone specialists believe bears may hold a cure for osteoporosis. Cardiac surgeons hope that research on hibernating bears may increase the opportunities for additional heart transplants. And some researchers think bears have the "right stuff" to help astronauts endure lengthy flights in space.

Bears that enter their winter dens in October and November may stay curled up inside for five or six months. If you or I were confined to a bed for that length of time, our bones would begin to thin out and weaken within just a few weeks. Most people think that once we stop growing, our bones remain the same throughout our adult lives. Actually, many of the bones in our bodies, in particular, the vertebrae in our backs and the large bones in our arms and legs, are constantly being remodeled in response to the workload we impose upon them. If we increase the workload on our skeleton—for example, with heavy exercise—our body makes these bones stronger. In contrast, if we decrease the workload, our bones get thinner and weaken.

People who are paralyzed or bedridden, or astronauts who are weightless during space flight, put less weight on their bones, and as a result, their bones thin out and weaken. This bone-thinning disorder, called osteoporosis, not only affects the bedridden but will affect all of us at some point in our lives.

As people reach their late forties and fifties—especially women—osteoporosis begins to weaken their bones. As our bones weaken, the risk of fractures increases. In North America, one-third of all women and one-sixth of all men over the age of sixty-five will fracture a hip. Thirty years from now, as our population ages, there will be 60 million people in North America over the age of sixty-five. Unless osteoporosis is prevented, the annual cost in hospital and nursing home care from fractures and other complications may exceed $6 billion.

Dr. Timothy Floyd, an orthopedic surgeon from Sun Valley, Idaho, recalls the first day he thought about bears and bones. "I was lying in bed one night reading a book on grizzly bears when I should have been reading *The Journal of Bone and Joint Surgery.*" As he read, Dr. Floyd wondered whether bears develop osteoporosis when they are inactive in their dens the way humans do when they are bedridden. It was one of those strokes of serendipity that characterize many great scientific discoveries—the right person, at the right moment, with the right idea.

Floyd was soon collaborating with Dr. Ralph Nelson at the University of Illinois, who has studied bears and their relevance to human medicine for over twenty years. The men took bone samples from three denning black bears and discovered that the bones in these animals had *not* thinned out, even though the animals had been cramped inside a den without bearing weight for many months (Floyd, Nelson and Wynne 1990). Floyd explained: "My feeling is that bears probably produce a regulatory substance which is responsible for maintaining bone mass. We think this substance may be circulating in the blood." If he and Dr. Nelson isolate the bone-preserving substance, it may someday be used to prevent and treat osteoporosis in humans.

Just as exciting is another recent discovery. During hibernation, a bear's metabolism slows down by half, its heart rate drops from fifty beats per minute to ten beats per minute, and its body temperature drops by 3 to 7C° (5 to 9F°). These metabolic adjustments are less drastic than those that occur in deeper hibernators, such as ground squirrels, whose body temperature may drop below freezing and whose heart may beat only a few times a minute. Nonetheless, the substance that produces these metabolic changes, in both the hibernating bear and the hibernating ground squirrel, appears to be the same. Recent research findings suggest that this substance, dubbed Hibernation Induction Trigger (HIT), may have applications in human medicine—in particular, in the survival of organs for transplantation surgery.

Dr. Sufan Chien, an American cardiothoracic surgeon, was looking for a way to prolong the survival time of organs used in heart, lung and liver transplants. Normally, when an organ, such as a heart or liver, is removed from a donor, the organ deteriorates beyond usefulness within four to six hours. Dr. Chien had developed a method to increase the survival time of donor organs to sixteen hours, but when the donor organs were perfused with HIT, their survival time increased almost threefold to forty-three hours (Chien et al.

The grizzly bear is an essential ingedient of the natural heritage of all northern countries. If we lose this fascinating carnivore, we will have begun our own extinction.

1991). At present, 15 to 20 per cent of all human donor organs have to be discarded as a result of deterioration. Any method that prolongs organ survival means that more transplants can occur and more lives can be saved.

Relating to HIT again, research on bears and other hibernators may change the course of two other maladies, cancer and viral infections such as the common cold. Time and again, hibernators injected with pathological viruses have not become ill. And deadly tumour cells inoculated into hibernators have consistently failed to grow. Perhaps if hibernation could be induced in humans, these ailments might reverse their course, or at least be more susceptible to drug therapy.

Inducing hibernation in humans is not as far-fetched as it sounds. Consider this final bit of research conducted by Dr. Peter Oeltgen, a pathologist at the University of Kentucky. Oeltgen and his colleagues in-

jected HIT into a monkey, an animal that has never been known to hibernate. To the amazement of the researchers, the monkey fell asleep for six hours, its heart rate and body temperature dropped, and its appetite was depressed for over a week. This suggests that *all* mammals, possibly including humans, may be responsive to HIT. If humans respond to HIT as monkeys do, this hibernating substance may have applications in the treatment of insomnia, obesity and anorexia nervosa(Oeltgen et al. 1985).

We are just beginning to discover the complexity and richness of the biology of bears. But I think that bears serve a greater function than as test animals to remedy human ailments. Human health depends on more than a healthy body; it requires stimulation for the mind and fuel for the spirit and the imagination. Bears, in their wilderness haunts, provide these essential ingredients of human health.

APPENDIX B

T H E   T R O P I C A L   B E A R S

The tropical bears include the spectacled bear of South America, the sun bear of Southeast Asia, the giant panda of China and the sloth bear of India, Nepal and Sri Lanka. Taxonomists believe that the sun bear (*Ursus malayanus*) and the sloth bear (*Ursus ursinus*) are closely related to each other as well as to the four species of northern bears. As a result, these bears have been placed in the same genus, *Ursus*. In contrast, the spectacled bear (*Tremarctos ornatus*) and the giant panda (*Ailuropoda melanoleuca*) are believed to be distantly related to each other and to all of the other bears, so each has been assigned to its own separate genus.   ¶   From recent molecular studies, scientists have constructed a family tree for the eight species of bears alive today. The giant panda was the first bear to branch off from the family tree, about 18 to 25 million years ago. The spectacled bear was next, splitting away 13 to 16 million years ago. The remaining six bear species, including the sun bear, the sloth bear and the four northern bears, began to separate from each other about 7 to 10 million years ago (Nash and O'Brien 1987).

T H E   S P E C T A C L E D   B E A R

A few years ago, I tramped through a cloud forest on the slopes of the Andes in western Venezuela. The vegetation was thick and dripping, the shadows deep and the air heavy with moisture. Sunlight rarely reached the ground, so I often gazed up into the bright openings in the canopy. High overhead the tree branches were laden with greenery and covered with aerial gardens of orchids, ferns, vines and bromeliads. Occasionally birds whose names were as colourful as their plumage—sparkling violetear, bearded helmetcrest, sunangel and coppery-bellied puffleg—would fly by like flowers

The spectacled bear is one of the short-faced group of bears.

on the wing. These lofty, cloud-shrouded forests are home to the spectacled bear, the only bear that lives in South America and the only bear whose range spans the equator.

Origins of the Spectacled Bear

Today the spectacled bear is a little-known player in the world of bears, yet for a time during the Ice Age, the spectacled bear tribe was the dominant group of bears in the Americas. This tribe of bears included the Florida cave bear, *Tremarctos floridanus*, which was much larger than its living relative, the spectacled bear. The Florida cave bear disappeared at the end of the last glacial period, somewhere around ten thousand to twelve thousand years ago.

The most impressive of the spectacled bear's extinct relatives was the giant short-faced bear, *Arctodus simus*. This was possibly the largest bear that ever existed and the most powerful predator that lived during the Ice Age in North America. Large specimens of this bear would have dwarfed the modern brown bears of coastal Alaska.

The aspect of the giant short-faced bear that makes it most impressive is not its size but its predatory nature. The giant short-faced bear had exceptionally long legs adapted to swift pursuit. It had large carnassial teeth to easily shear flesh, and its snout was short, like that of the large predatory cats, enabling it to grab and hold prey with a powerful grip (Kurtén and Anderson 1980; Geist 1986). Imagine trekking across the open plains of Ice Age America, armed only with a spear and a stone axe, and encountering this bear, a rapacious predator that stood as tall as your shoulders, ran as fast as a horse and thrived on meat. The sight of the giant short-faced bear must have terrified early hunters.

Fossils of the giant short-faced bear, sometimes called the bulldog bear, have been found from Alaska to Central America. These bears disappeared around twelve thousand years ago, during the same sweep of extinction that claimed the mammoths, mastodons, ground sloths, sabre-toothed cats and dozens of other large mammals.

Some paleontologists have speculated that the giant short-faced bear may have prevented the grizzly from becoming widespread in North America after it migrated from Asia into Alaska. The oldest brown bear fossils outside of Alaska are about twelve thousand years old. Could it be that the giant short-faced bear included grizzlies in its diet? If so, the fearsome grizzly could not claim North America until the even more fearsome short-faced bear had become extinct.

The Spectacled Bear Today

The spectacled bear is the largest carnivore in South America and the second largest land mammal after the tapir (*Tapirus terrestris*). Male bears stand about 75 centimetres (30 inches) at the shoulder, and their average weight ranges between 100 and 120 kilograms (between 220 and 265 pounds), although there are records of males weighing as much as 225 kilograms (496 pounds). Usually female spectacled bears are two-thirds the size and weight of males (Nowak and Paradiso 1983; Peyton 1987).

Spectacled bears are covered with thick black fur. Typically, the bears have white or yellowish circles or semicircles around their eyes—hence the animals' common name. Frequently they also have light-coloured fur on their throats and muzzles. The appealing facial patterns vary from individual to individual and remain unchanged throughout the animal's life.

The spectacled bear occurs along the mountainous slopes of the Andes in Venezuela, Colombia, Ecuador, Peru and Bolivia, as shown in Figure B.1. A few bears may also live in southern Panama and northern Argentina. Within their range, spectacled bears use a variety of habitats, from low-elevation desert scrub to tropical alpine meadows, called the paramo. Between these two elevational extremes are the moist tropical forests, the habitat used most often by these bears (Brown and Rumiz 1988).

Figure B.1 *Estimated current distribution of the spectacled bear,* Tremarctos ornatus, *in South America. It is likely that the actual distribution is a chain of small, fragmented populations throughout the shaded area (Servheen 1990).*

The spectacled bear has been known to science since the mid-1800s, yet very little is known about the animal's ecology and behaviour in the wild. No biologist has ever put a radio collar on a spectacled bear, and for several very good reasons. Not only would the mountainous terrain swallow up any radio signals, but the heavy cloud cover in the region would make flying extremely dangerous. I learned about another deterrent to radio-telemetry when I chatted with biologist Bernie Peyton at a bear conference several years ago.

Peyton had studied spectacled bears in Peru. While struggling through the dense forests looking for the bears (he saw bears only eight times in four years), Peyton was captured and almost murdered by a group of guerrillas who were smuggling cocaine. Peyton (1980) later wrote about the incident:

Fortunately my backpack was stuffed with scats I had collected to analyze spectacled bear diet. After thoroughly searching my gear, my bewildered captors allowed me to explain that I was a bear scat collector, not a CIA agent. They let me leave with my clothes and a flashlight. I wondered what the coca mafia would have thought of a wandering Norte Americano with a radio and hand-held antenna. My suspicion was that no amount of bear scat would have saved me.

From the study of scats, biologists have learned that spectacled bears rely heavily on fruit, such as wild guava, avocados and grapes, and especially wild figs (*Ficus spp.*), for a major part of their diet. During months when fruits are not ripe, the bears feed on young bamboo stalks, palm shoots, orchid bulbs and in particular the succulent hearts of bromeliads (the pineapple is a familiar type of bromeliad).

The spectacled bear has a shorter muzzle than the four northern bears, and the design of its jaws enables the bear to eat tough, fibrous foods, which few other animals can eat. Occasionally, spectacled bears also eat insects and small rodents, but such animal foods make up less than 5 per cent of the bear's diet (Peyton

1980; Orejuela 1988; Goldstein 1988).

The spectacled bear will readily climb trees to reach the food it wants. To climb very large-diameter trees, the bears will sometimes climb vines on nearby trees or take advantage of the aerial roots that wrap around the tree trunks. The bears may forage as high as 15 metres (49 feet) off the ground. In Peru, Peyton (1980) found that many fig trees "had been climbed repeatedly over the years as indicated by the healed scars in the bark, suggesting that spectacled bears may define their home ranges around known groves of trees."

Many tropical trees produce fruit after the winter rains, which soak the mountain slopes from December to March. Scientists believe that spectacled bears have their cubs at the end of the winter rainy season. In this way the birthing and early nursing period coincides with the season of greatest fruit abundance. In captivity, spectacled bears have one to three cubs in a litter, but one or two cubs are probably more usual in the wild.

The Future of the Spectacled Bear

Many Andean peoples attribute magical and curative powers to the bear. In Venezuela, the fat is used for rheumatic problems, and the bones are ground up and mixed with milk and given to infants to strengthen them. Often when a bear is killed, its blood is immediately drunk as a sort of communion to help the hunter become more bearlike. In many regions, the baculum is also worn as an amulet for manhood, and the skin and paws are considered trophies and sold in rural markets. Even bear scats are believed to carry power, and peasants feed bear droppings to their cattle to make the animals stronger (Peyton 1987; Goldstein 1988).

The biggest threat to spectacled bears throughout their range is the loss of cloud forest habitat. When peasants move into these forest areas, the overall range of the bears becomes fragmented, and the animals' travel routes are disrupted. Furthermore, the people

The sun bear has small litters of cubs, usually only one or two.

clear the forest to plant corn and raise cattle. The corn and the cattle are naturally a temptation to the bears, and invariably crops are raided and livestock killed. In retaliation, the peasants shoot every spectacled bear they see.

Biologists don't know how many spectacled bears still survive in the wild, but their numbers are probably declining yearly. One population of spectacled bears that is likely to decline is the one that lives in the forested slopes that buttress the magnificent Inca citadel Machu Picchu in the Peruvian Andes. We pride ourselves on our regard and concern for things that are old, and we spend fortunes to restore, protect and preserve human antiquities such as Machu Picchu, which is a mere five hundred years old. The spectacled bear is millions of years old, and it seems to me that an enlightened society should feel the same responsibility for the bear's survival as it does for the survival of the stone and mortar of a lifeless piece of ancient human architecture.

THE SUN BEAR

The sun bear, *Ursus malayanus*, which is about half the size of the average American black bear, is the smallest of the eight living bear species and the least known of them all. As Mills (1991) accurately noted, "No one has studied it, and no one knows whether there are 50 or 50,000 of them left in the wild."

Figure B.2 shows the current distribution of the sun bear. Originally the sun bear inhabited the lowland forests of southeast Asia from Malaysia and Indonesia westward as far as India. The sun bear is now thought to have been extirpated from India, and it may have suffered a similar fate in Bangladesh; the last sun bear was sighted in Bangladesh in 1980. The situation is nearly as bleak in other parts of the sun bear's range, and in China, Burma and Vietnam the animal is seriously threatened.

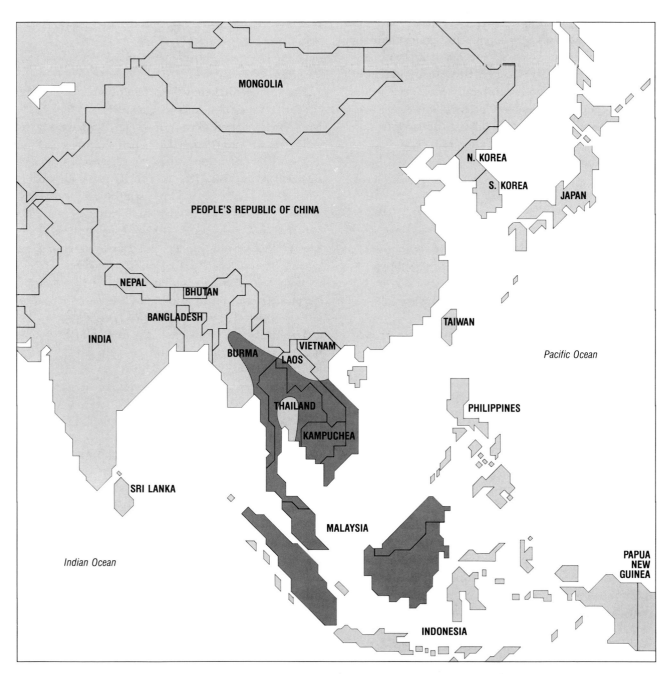

Figure B.2 *Estimated current distribution of the sun bear,* Ursus malayanus, *in Southeast Asia (Servheen 1990).*

The giant panda of China is likely the most endangered of the eight species of bears in the world today. It is thought that fewer than a thousand animals survive in the wild.

In Thailand, biologist Chris Servheen (1990) reported that "the sun bear is protected against hunting by legislation, but local people kill bears with impunity, usually for subsistence. Because 95 percent of the human population is rural and because rice fields, rubber plantations, and oil palm plantations cover most of the available lowland habitat, human intrusion into the range of the species is severe." Servheen also observed that

The illegal trade in wildlife in Thailand is another impact on both the sun bear and the Asiatic black bear. Bear parts, especially the gall bladders, are openly sold in Chinese medicine shops throughout Asia. Bears are preferred as a special meal to enhance health and vigor by Korean tourists who visit Bangkok to eat in special restaurants. These restaurants procure bears for such meals using the paws and meat and sometimes reportedly killing the bear in front of guests to assure them the meal is authentic and fresh. . . . Pet keeping also affects bears by creating a market for live bears, especially cubs, that are sold in local markets. Such animals usually are given away or sold to restaurants when they get older and less manageable.

In Malaysia, the sun bear population is under an equal amount of pressure. According to Servheen (1990), "Hunting of sun bears occurs throughout Malaysia for sale of their gall bladders, claws and hides. Bladders are used to heal bruises and broken bones because of the belief that the sun bear sometimes falls from high trees but suffers no ill effects."

The stronghold of the sun bear is on the Indonesian island of Borneo. Borneo has some of the largest tracts of tropical rain forest left in the world, but, predictably, these forests are being increasingly ravaged by timber companies, and the long-range prospects for the sun bear are not promising.

The sun bear is the runt of the bear clan. An adult bear is roughly the size of a large dog—100 to 140 centimetres (3¼ to 4½ feet) long and 70 centimetres (2¼ feet) tall, and weighing between 27 and 65 kilo-

grams (between 60 and 143 pounds). Sun bears exhibit very little sexual dimorphism, and female sun bears are only about 20 per cent smaller than males (Nowak and Paradiso 1983).

The sun bear has the shortest fur of any bear, giving the animal a stocky, muscular appearance. Sun bears have black fur, and most individuals also have a large yellowish-white or orange U-shaped chest blaze.

Most bears can climb trees, but the sun bear is particularly adept at it. The soles of its paws are naked, ensuring a good grip on tree trunks, and its ivory-coloured claws are sharp and strongly curved. Whereas the American and Asiatic black bears and the spectacled bear may inadvertently build nests in trees when the animals are feeding on fruit, flowers or leaves, the sun bear regularly builds tree nests in which to sleep. The small sun bear may feel more secure resting aloft in a tree (Lekagul and McNeely 1977).

The sun bear is primarily nocturnal and sleeps during the day. At night it forages for fruit, small rodents and birds. Using its long claws, it tears apart logs for insects and excavates ant colonies. Locally, the sun bear is also known as the honey bear because it climbs trees to ravage the nests of wild bees.

Like all of the tropical bears, the sun bear is active year round and never hibernates. In captivity, sun bears have small litters of one or two cubs. In the wild, they likely breed throughout the year, and the cubs stay with their mothers until they are nearly full grown.

The sun bear is the least known of the bears. With the current rate of tropical deforestation, the animal may disappear before anything is known about it.

THE GIANT PANDA

Hidden within the forests and bamboo jungles of the hinterlands of central China there is an entire menagerie of wildlife unfamiliar to most westerners: the goat-like serow (*Capricornis sumatrensis*); the takin (*Budorcas taxicolor*), a peculiar oxlike animal reminis-

cent of the muskox; the exquisite golden monkey (*Pygathrix roxellanae*); the elusive snow leopard (*Panthera uncia*); Temminck's tragopan (*Tragopan temminckii*), a flamboyantly feathered pheasant; the muntjac (*Muntiacus spp.*), a tiny barking deer with 7-centimetre (2¾-inch) tusks; and the famous giant panda (Guangmei, Huadong and Jialin 1990).

Giant pandas were mentioned in Chinese literature as early as two thousand years ago. The prized black and white bruins were kept as pets by emperors and even entombed with their owners in royal mausoleums.

The first panda was introduced to the West in 1869, when a French missionary, Père Armand David, shipped a skin to the Museum of Natural History in Paris. David wrote about the animal in his diary:

My Christian hunters return today after a ten-day absence. They bring me a young white bear, which they took alive but unfortunately killed so it could be carried more easily. The young white bear, which they sell to me very dearly, is all white except for the legs, ears, and around the eyes, which are deep black. This must be a new species of Ursus, very remarkable not only because of its color, but also for its paws, which are hairy underneath, and for other characters. [Schaller et al 1985]

At the time of its discovery by Père David, the giant panda was given the scientific name *Ursus melanoleuca*, meaning black and white bear, launching a century of controversy over the animal's classification. In the last hundred years, the giant panda has been called a bear, it has been called a raccoon, and for a while it was even thought to belong to its own animal group, quite separate from either the raccoons or the bears. Scientists used the panda's behaviour, its resemblance to other animals and its unique colouration and anatomy to defend their individual positions and discredit the arguments of their opponents. Recent molecular methods have determined that the giant panda is a bear that branched off from the main line of ursid evolution 18 to 25 million years ago. Today the giant panda's official

scientific name is *Ailuropoda melanoleuca*.

Giant pandas have roughly the same measurements as the average American or Asiatic black bear, and they weigh between 80 and 125 kilograms (between 176 and 276 pounds). Male pandas are only 10 to 20 per cent larger than females.

The fur of the giant panda is thick and woolly and slightly oily to the touch. The climate where the panda lives is often cool and damp, and the nature of its fur shields it from the chilling effects of the elements. The most striking aspect of the giant panda's fur coat is, of course, the distinctive black and white pattern. Surely such a conspicuous pelt evolved for a purpose, and biologists have proposed a number of explanations.

Contrasting black and white fur is not unique to the giant panda. More than a dozen species of skunks sport similarly conspicuous fur coats. The black and white pattern in skunks warns predators that the animals are armed with noxious scent glands. Some scientists have suggested that the panda's pelt similarly advertises the animals' weaponry—its strong jaws. Adult pandas have few enemies, so protection from predators is probably not the reason they are black and white (Morris and Morris 1982).

The eminent American field biologist Dr. George Schaller has offered the most likely explanation for the pelt pattern of the giant panda: "Striking colors send complex signals to other members of a species, and it is in this context that the adaptive value of the pelage must lie. Pandas generally avoid contact, they are silent, their habitat is dense, and their vision is not acute. In such a situation a conspicuous coat may help prevent too close an encounter" (Schaller et al. 1985).

Originally, the giant panda was widespread throughout China, and fossils have been found in Burma as well. Today the panda is restricted to a belt of bamboo forest that runs along the edge of the Tibetan Plateau in central China. Pandas are not found everywhere in this belt of forest but are limited to six small regions, as seen in Figure B.3. Even within

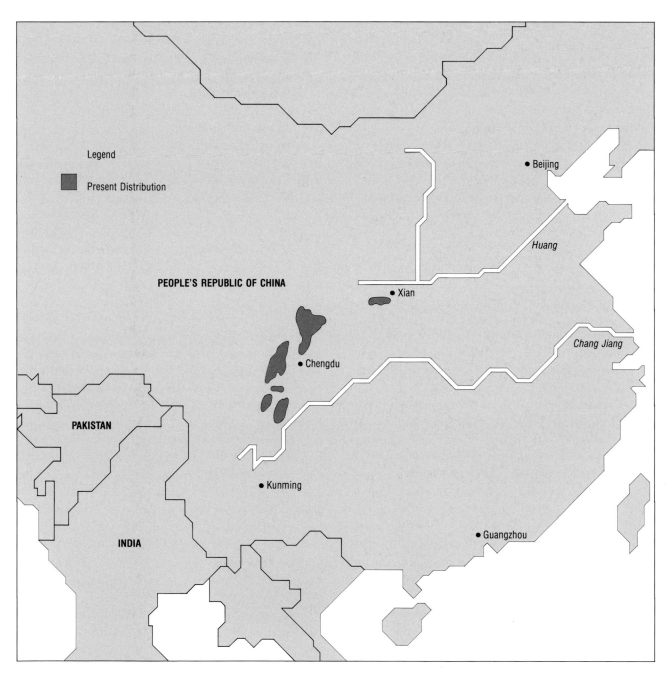

Figure B.3 **The location of the six remnant populations of the giant panda,** Ailuropoda melanoleuca, *in central China (Schaller et al. 1985).*

these six small blocks of habitat, not all of the land can be used by the pandas. In most of the areas, peasants farm in the valley bottoms, and in many places they cultivate the lower slopes as well, so the pandas are restricted to mid and upper elevations. Often the bears are confined to narrow belts of bamboo forest no more than 1000 to 1200 metres (approximately 3300 to 4000 feet) wide. Not all of the habitat may be usable; in many regions, including those within the dozen or so Panda Reserves, the pandas must eke out an existence using a meagre 15 to 35 per cent of the land area (Schaller et al. 1985).

Adapting to a Bamboo Diet

Although giant pandas eat several dozen types of plants, over 99 per cent of their diet consists of the leaves, stems and shoots of bamboo. Evolution has honed the giant panda into a highly specialized bamboo-eating bear, and in the process the panda has acquired a number of important adaptations, most notably those in its front paws, its teeth, its jaws and its upper intestinal tract.

On each front paw, the panda has an elongated wrist bone (a radial sesamoid), which is covered with a tough, fleshy pad. The elongated wrist bone functions like an opposable thumb and enables the panda to grasp the stems of bamboo with great precision and dexterity. This modified wrist bone is unique among the bears, but it is present in the red panda (*Ailurus fulgens*), a small carnivore that lives in China and throughout the Himalayas. Because both the giant panda and the red panda have elongated wrist bones and both animals eat bamboo, the two pandas were thought for a time to be more closely related than they actually are. The red panda is now considered a member of the raccoon family (Roberts and Gittleman 1984; Johnson, Schaller and Jinchu 1988a).

To pulverize tough, fibrous bamboo leaves and stems, the giant panda has large cheek teeth and powerful jaw muscles. It also has a prominent bony crest on the top of its skull and enlarged cheekbones, allowing the attachment of powerful muscles of mastication. The bulky muscles, in turn, give the panda its endearing round facial contours.

The final two adaptations to a steady diet of bamboo involve the panda's esophagus and its stomach. The panda's esophagus has a horny lining to protect it against injury when the animal swallows sharp splinters, and its stomach is exceptionally muscular, almost gizzardlike, enabling it to churn up the bamboo and speedily digest it (Chorn and Hoffman 1978).

After outfitting the giant panda with so many adaptations to a diet of bamboo, evolution didn't quite finish the job. The giant panda has the short intestine typical of all bears. As described in Chapter 2, most plant-eating mammals have a long intestinal tract to give their body ample time to extract the maximum amount of nutrients from their food, and this is especially important when the animal is eating vegetation such as bamboo that is fibrous and difficult to break down. Having a short intestine, the giant panda can extract only a portion of the nutrients available in the bamboo, so it must eat great quantities of bamboo to compensate, and it must also pass the vegetation through its intestine rapidly. As a result, an adult panda may forage for fifteen hours a day, eat 10 to 18 kilograms (22 to 40 pounds) of bamboo leaves and stems, and produce more than one hundred droppings. When a panda eats newly emerging bamboo shoots, it may consume up to 38 kilograms (84 pounds) in a single day—half its body weight (Schaller et al. 1985; Dierenfeld et al. 1982).

Mating and Hibernation

The mating season for giant pandas occurs in April and May. Like all female bears, the female panda is only in heat for a short time, typically two to seven days. Unlike other male bears, the male panda may advertise his presence to females by calling loudly. Sometimes a male will climb into a tree to call. From such a lofty perch, its call can carry over a distance of a kilometre (½ mile).

The pregnant panda chooses a hollow tree or rock cavity in which to deliver her one or two cubs, which are born in August or September. Implantation is delayed in the giant panda, as it is in the other bears, so the unborn panda cubs grow for less than two months before they are born. As a result of such a short developmental period, newborn pandas are the size of a rat and weigh a mere 90 to 130 grams (3 to 4½ ounces), 1/900 the weight of their mother. The young pandas are sparsely covered with fine white hair at birth, but they acquire the characteristic black legs, ears and eyes by the time they are a month old.

Female pandas stay at their maternity den until their cubs are four to seven weeks old. During this time, the mother panda may regularly leave her youngsters alone in the den for two or three hours while she goes off to feed on bamboo nearby. Young panda cubs begin to eat bamboo when they are five or six months old, and they are fully weaned by the age of nine months. The panda family finally breaks up at the start of a new breeding season, when the young are a year and a half old.

Of the eight species of bears in the world, only half of them hibernate. The giant panda is one of those that does not, and there are two good reasons why. First, the panda already eats as much bamboo as it can just to meet its daily energy requirements. The animal could not eat enough additional bamboo to accumulate the necessary fat reserves it would need to enable it to fast during hibernation. Second, vegetation of equal nutritional value is available year round where the panda lives, so there is no necessity for the animal to become dormant to avoid a time of food scarcity.

Threats to the Panda's Survival

Scientists estimate that there are approximately a thousand pandas still alive in the wild. The greatest threat to their survival is the loss of bamboo forest habitat, the fragmentation of their remaining habitat into isolated islands of forest, and poaching.

Bamboo belongs to the grass family, but unlike most grasses, bamboo does not flower every year. Most bamboo species that grow in temperate latitudes flower at intervals of 10 to 150 years. Of the bamboo species eaten by giant pandas, most flower at intervals between 30 and 50 years. When bamboo plants flower, they do so in unison over wide areas, and then all of the plants in the area die immediately afterwards.

In former times, pandas responded to these periodic bamboo die-offs by moving to unaffected areas. Today pandas cannot move readily from one mountain area to another, because their traditional travel routes are blocked by people and their farms. In addition, there are fewer alternative sites for the pandas to move to when the bamboo dies off in an area. As a consequence, bamboo die-offs can have a devastating effect on a panda population (MacKinnon and Minjang 1986).

In the mid-1970s, three species of bamboo died in the Min Mountains. As a result, at least 138 pandas starved to death. In the early eighties, in the Wolong Reserve, the largest of China's Panda Reserves, there was a substantial bamboo die-off, and plant coverage dropped from 55 per cent to 13 per cent. In response, the pandas moved to lower elevations. Although no pandas starved as a result of the bamboo die-off, a third of them died from natural mortalities and poaching as a result of the move to lower elevations (Johnson, Schaller and Jinchu 1988b).

In some areas, pandas are intentionally trapped or accidentally caught in snares set for musk deer. In either case, the pandas end up dead. A black market exists in Hong Kong and Macao, where a panda pelt may be sold for twenty thousand dollars. In the late 1980s, Chinese authorities revealed that in recent years they had apprehended hundreds of poachers and confiscated 146 panda pelts. Two poachers were sentenced to death, some received life imprisonment, and others were fined heavily.

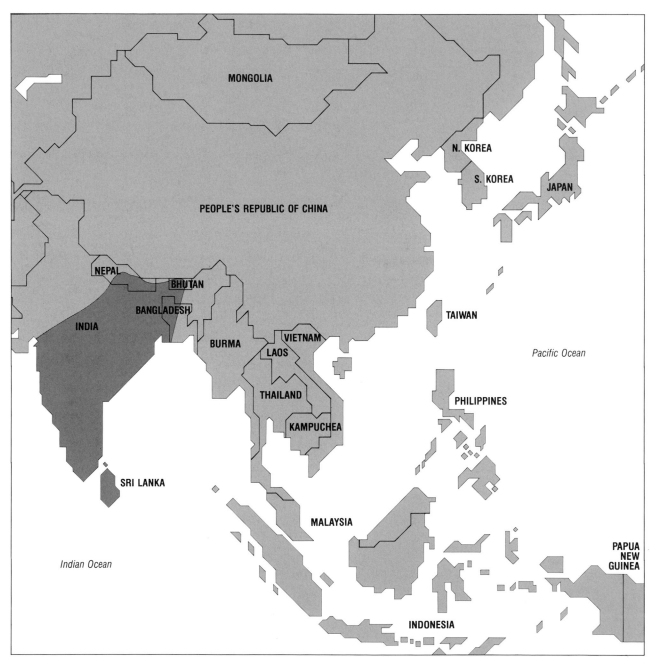

Figure B.4 Estimated current distribution of the sloth bear, Ursus ursinus, on the Indian subcontinent (Servheen 1990).

In 1961, the World Wildlife Fund adopted the giant panda as its mascot, and this attractive black and white bear has come to symbolize the conservation movement. Should the giant panda disappear, global conservation would suffer a blow far beyond the borders of China.

THE SLOTH BEAR

The sloth bear is found in Nepal, Bhutan, Bangladesh and Sri Lanka, but it is most widespread in the dry deciduous forests of India (Figure B.4). Within its range, the sloth bear has some interesting neighbours, sharing its habitat with tigers and leopards, striped hyenas (*Hyaena hyaena*), Asiatic wild dogs (*Cuon alpinus*), elephants (*Elaphas maximus*), rhinos (*Rhinoceros unicornis*), pythons (*Python spp.*), peacocks (*Pavo cristatus*) and a dozen venomous snakes, including cobras (*Naja naja*), vipers (*Vipera spp.*) and kraits (*Bungarus caeruleus*).

There are possibly fewer than ten thousand sloth bears remaining in the wild, but no one knows for certain. With more than 800 million people living in India alone, it will take a concerted effort to preserve the few remaining tracts of wilderness forest where the sloth bear is found.

The sloth bear is a medium-sized bear, 140 to 170 centimetres (4½ to 5½ feet) long from its nose to the tip of its tail. It stands 85 centimetres (2¾ feet) tall at the shoulder, and adult males weigh between 127 and 145 kilograms (between 280 and 320 pounds). Female sloth bears are slightly smaller than males (Prater 1971).

When I saw my first sloth bears in a zoo—which is no place for any species of bear—my first impression was how shaggy and unkempt they looked. Their fur, especially around the head and neck, seemed to stick up in all directions, and it surprised me that a tropical bear would have fur that was so long and thick.

Sloth bears have deep black fur, sometimes mixed with grey and brown. Rarely, cinnamon-coloured sloth bears have been seen. Most sloth bears have a white or yellow V-shaped mark on their lower neck and chest, and all have a sparsely furred greyish-white muzzle.

Not much is known about the biology of sloth bears, but in 1990 researcher Anup Joshi radio-collared eight sloth bears in Royal Chitwan National Park in Nepal, the first study of its kind ever conducted on this animal. Joshi has found that the bears in Nepal breed in June and July during the monsoon season and then give birth to one or two cubs in late December, at the beginning of the dry season. As in many species of bears, young sloth bears travel with their mothers until they are about a year and a half old, when they then become independent.

What is most fascinating and unusual about the sloth bear is its diet, the adaptations it has evolved to cope with its diet, and the influence that its diet has had on how young bears travel with their mothers.

Although sloth bears eat many kinds of fruits and will climb trees to tear apart the nests of wild bees to lap up the honey, they eat termites more often than anything else. In Joshi's study in Nepal, *all* of the scats collected in the first year of field work contained termite remains.

In Nepal, termite nests may either be totally subterranean or be large, visible pillars, up to 2 metres (6½ feet) tall. The bears attack the tall pillars by digging a hole into the base of the pillar to reach the insects inside. The underground colonies are probably located by smell, which is how other ant and termite predators find these insects. Once the bear sniffs out one of these hidden underground colonies, it digs straight down into the ground to reach the termites. Joshi has seen some excavations that were 2 metres (6½ feet) deep. In such a deep hole, the digging sloth bear would have been completely lost from sight.

All bears have an acute sense of smell, so it is not surprising that a sloth bear can locate termites with its nose. In fact, I have watched an American black bear locate an underground bumblebee nest in a similar way. If the sloth bear's keen sense of smell is not one of its adaptations to a termite diet, what, then, *are* its adaptations?

The sloth bear has large, floppy lips, a mobile snout covered with very little hair, nostrils that can be closed, absent upper incisor teeth, creating a gap at the front of its mouth, and a high, arched palate. These adaptations help the sloth bear in the following way. The bear's floppy lips make it easier for the animal to capture fleeing termites. Its lightly furred snout is less likely to become gummed up with the defensive secretions sprayed by angry termites. Its closed nostrils prevent soldier termites from launching a counterattack, and its missing teeth and high palate enable it to create a vacuum and an orifice through which it can suck up the tasty termites. Sloth bears also have very long front claws, up to 7 centimetres (2¾ inches) long, that enable the bear to tunnel through the sun-baked soil that encases many termite colonies (Nowak and Paradiso 1983).

For centuries, hunters have located sloth bears by the loud huffing and puffing noises the bears make while they are vacuuming up termites. The noise can be heard several hundred metres away. Scientists have speculated that the conspicuous feeding noises may alert other bears and keep the animals spaced apart. As attractive and plausible as this hypothesis is, it has still to be proven.

The most intriguing behavioural trait shown by sloth bears is the way young bears ride on their mothers' backs. On rare occasions, mother bears of other species let their cubs ride on them, but in the sloth bear it is a regular mode of family travel. A young sloth bear up to a third the size of its mother will ride on her back positioned crosswise or with its head forward. The cub will even stay mounted while its mother vigorously digs for termites. At these times, the young bear may get showered with dirt, jostled around and sometimes even bucked off by its distracted mother (Laurie and Seidensticker 1977).

Why would a bear that eats termites also carry its young on its back? At first glance you would probably conclude, as I did, that the two behaviours are completely unrelated. Surprisingly, when you look at the behaviour of other mammals that specialize in eating termites and ants, you discover that many of them also carry their young around with them in this way. This is true of the giant anteater (*Myrmecophaga tridactyla*) of the South American grasslands, and of the six or seven species of scaly pangolins (*Manis spp.*) found in Africa and southern Asia. It is more than coincidence, then, that all of these termite and anteaters, including the sloth bear, carry their young with them on their backs.

Scientists have tried to explain the association by suggesting that young termite eaters travel with their mothers because termite colonies are often widely spaced, and a mother must hunt over a relatively large area, making it hard for her to continually return to a den to attend to her young. Another explanation is that the behaviour evolved as an anti-predator strategy. This explanation seems to fit for the sloth bear. Young sloth bears may be preyed upon by leopards and tigers, and the youngsters offer a less vulnerable target when they are clinging to their mothers' backs. In addition, sloth bears frequently dig for termites in open grasslands, where there are no trees to provide an escape from danger. Clinging to mother may be the best option in this circumstance. No explanation is totally satisfactory in explaining the riding behaviour of any of the termite eaters, including the sloth bear. The current research on sloth bears in Nepal may help to explain the mystery (Laurie and Seidensticker 1977; McNab 1984).

One final intriguing tidbit of biology concerns the long fur coat of the sloth bear. In the sweltering heat of the tropics, you would think that the bear would become overheated and that such a thick pelt would be maladaptive. Recently, researcher Dr. Brian McNab (1991) discovered that the sloth bear has a metabolic rate much lower than that of either the brown bear or the polar bear. McNab suggests that ants and termites are usually considered low-energy food sources, and it follows that such a low-energy diet could only sustain an animal with a low rate of metabolism.

The low metabolic rate of the sloth bear also means that the animal produces less internal heat. Since it generates less internal heat, the bear must reduce the heat it loses to the air or else its body temperature will drop. It does this by insulating itself inside a thick fur coat. The giant anteater of tropical South America also has a low metabolic rate, and McNab (1984) believes that it, like the sloth bear, relies on its long, shaggy coat to maintain its body temperature. Thus, the thick fur coat of the tropical sloth bear, instead of being an evolutionary mistake, turns out to be an ingenious adaptation to a low-energy diet. Nature always seems to get it right.

THE FUTURE OF TROPICAL BEARS

Humans and their activities have severely affected all of the tropical bears. Dr. Chris Servheen, in his report on the status of the bears of the world (1990), wrote that throughout the tropics bear habitat is being degraded by agriculture, timber operations, and mineral and petroleum exploration and development. In many areas, bears are also killed for food or to protect crops. Servheen warned that "a serious threat to bears in Asia and South America is the killing and capture of bears for the use of their parts in primitive medicine, aphrodisiacs, or as pets. The selling of bears and bear parts is a lucrative business in Asia that has the potential to extirpate the Asian species we know the least about."

Servheen concluded his authoritative report with this dire prediction: "The fate of bears in many areas of the world will be decided in the next 10-20 years. The future of several species is in serious doubt. The elimination of bears from 50-75 percent of their historic range has already occurred and the remaining range will decrease unless serious efforts are focused on bear conservation."

BIBLIOGRAPHY

Alt, G. L. 1978. 14½ miles of bear tracks. *Pennsylvania Game News* 49(6):24–29.

———. 1980. Rate of growth and size of Pennsylvania black bears. *Pennsylvania Game News* 51(12):7–17.

———. 1981. Color phases of the black bear. *Pennsylvania Game News* 52(9):13–15.

———. 1983. Bear dens under interstate highway. *Pennsylvania Game News* 54(8):9–10.

———. 1984a. Cub adoption in the black bear. *J. Mamm.* 65(3):511–12.

———. 1984b. Black bear cub mortality due to flooding of natal dens. *J. Wildl. Manage.* 48(4):1432–34.

———. 1989. Reproductive biology of female black bears and early growth and development of cubs in northeastern Pennsylvania. Ph.D. diss., West Virginia University, Morgantown, West Virginia.

Alt, G. L., G. J. Matula, F. W. Alt and J. S. Lindzey. 1977. Movements of translocated nuisance black bears of northeastern Pennsylvania. *Transactions Northeast Section, The Wildlife Society, Fish and Wildlife Conference* 34:119–26.

———. 1980. Dynamics of home range and movements of adult black bears in northeastern Pennsylvania. *Int. Conf. Bear Res. and Manage.* 4:131–36.

Alt, G. L., and J. J. Beecham. 1984. Reintroduction of orphaned black bear cubs into the wild. *Wildl. Soc. Bull.* 12:169–74.

Amstrup, S. C. 1986. Research on polar bears in Alaska, 1983–1985. In *Proc. 9th Meeting of IUCN/SSC Polar Bear Specialist Group*, 85–112. Gland, Switz.: IUCN.

———. 1988. Polar bear—*Ursus maritimus*. In *Selected Marine Mammals of Alaska—Species Accounts and Management Recommendations*, ed. J. W. Lentfer, 39–56. Washington, D.C.: Marine Mammal Commission.

Amstrup, S. C., I. Stirling and J. W. Lentfer. 1986. Past and present status of polar bears in Alaska. *Wildl. Soc. Bull.* 14(3):241–54.

Andreev, F. V. 1973. On the structure of the polar bear eye. In *Ekologiia I Morfologiia Beloogo Medvedia*, ed. V. E. Sokolov. Moscow: Izdatel. Cited in Ronald, K., and J. Lee. 1981. Spectral sensitivity of a polar bear. *Comp. Biochem. Physiol.* 70A:595–98.

Andriashek, D., H. P. L. Kiliaan and M. K. Taylor. 1985. Observations on foxes, *Alopex lagopus* and *Vulpes vulpes*, and wolves, *Canis lupus*, on the off-shore sea ice of northern Labrador. *Can. Field-Nat.* 99(1):86–89.

Applegate, R. D., L. L. Rogers, D. A. Casteel and J. M. Novak. 1979. Germination of cow parsnip seeds from grizzly bear feces. *J. Mamm.* 60(3):655.

Atwell, G., D. L. Boone, J. Gustafson and V. D. Berns. 1980. Brown bear summer use of alpine habitat on the Kodiak National Wildlife Refuge. *Int. Conf. Bear Res. and Manage.* 4:297–305.

Bachrach, W. H., and A. F. Hofmann. 1982. Ursodeoxycholic acid in the treatment of cholesterol cholelithiasis—Part II. *Digestive Diseases and Sciences* 27(9):833–46.

Bacon, E. S. 1980. Curiosity in the American black bear. *Int. Conf. Bear Res. and Manage.* 4:153–57.

Bacon, E. S., and G. M. Burghardt. 1976. Learning and color discrimination in the American black bear. *Int. Conf. Bear Res. and Manage.* 3:27–36.

Bailey, E. P., and N. H. Faust. 1984. Distribution and abundance of marine birds breeding between Amber and Kamishak Bays, Alaska, with notes on interactions with bears. *Western Birds* 15:161–74.

Ballard, W. B. 1980. Brown bear kills gray wolf. *Can. Field Nat.* 94(1):91.

———. 1982. Grey wolf-brown bear relationships in the Nelchina Basin of South-Central Alaska. In *Wolves of the World: Perspectives of Behavior, Ecology, and Conservation*, 71–80. Park Ridge, N. J.: Noyes Publications.

Ballard, W. B., T. H. Spraker and K. P. Taylor. 1981. Causes of neonatal moose calf mortality in south central Alaska. *J. Wildl. Manage.* 45(2):335–42.

Banci, V. 1991. *The status of the grizzly bear in Canada in 1990*. Cosewic Status Report.

Barber, K. M., and F. G. Lindzey. 1986. Breeding behavior of black bears. *Int. Conf. Bear Res. and Manage.* 6:129–36.

Barnes, B. M. 1989. Freeze avoidance in a mammal: body temperatures below 0°C in an arctic hibernator. *Science* 244:1593–95.

Barnes, V. G., and O. E. Bray. 1966. Black bears use drainage culverts for winter dens. *J. Mamm.* 47(4):712–13.

Barry, T. W. 1968. Observations on natural mortality and native use of eider ducks along the Beaufort Sea coast. *Can. Field Nat.* 82:140–44.

Bassett, C. A. 1965. Electrical effects in bone. *Sci. Am.*, October:18–25.

Beecham, J. J., D. G. Reynolds and M. G. Hornocker. 1983. Black bear denning activities and characteristics in west-central Idaho. *Int. Conf. Bear Res. and Manage.* 5:79–86.

Beeman, L. E., and M. R. Pelton. 1980. Seasonal foods and feeding ecology of black bears in the Smoky Mountains. *Int. Conf. Bear Res. and Manage.* 4:141–47.

Behrend, D. F., and R. W. Sage, Jr. 1974. Unusual feeding behavior by black bears. *J. Wildl. Manage.* 38(3):570.

Bennett, L. J., P. F. English and R. L. Watts. 1943. The food habits of the black bear in Pennsylvania. *J. Mamm.* 24(1):25–31.

Berducou, C., L. Faliu and J. Barrat. 1983. The food habits of the brown bear in the national park of the western Pyrenees (France) as revealed by faeces analysis. *Acta. Zool. Fennica.* 174:153–56.

Berns, V. D., G. C. Atwell and D. L. Boone. 1980. Brown bear movements and habitat use at Karluk Lake, Kodiak Island. *Int. Conf. Bear Res. and Manage.* 4:293–96.

Best, R. C. 1977. Ecological aspects of polar bear nutrition. In *Proceedings of the 1975 Predator Symposium*, ed. Phillips, R. L., and C. Jonkel, 203–11. Missoula: University of Montana Press.

———. 1982. Thermoregulation in resting and active polar bears. *J. Comp. Physiol.* 146:63–73.

———. 1984. Digestibility of ringed seals by the polar bear. *Can. J. Zool.* 63:1033–36.

Blanchard B. M. 1983. Grizzly bear—habitat relationships in the Yellowstone area. *Int. Conf. Bear Res. and Manage.* 5:118–23.

———. 1987. Size and growth patterns of the Yellowstone grizzly bear. *Int. Conf. Bear Res. and Manage.* 7:99–107.

Bledsoe, T. 1987. *Brown Bear Summer—Life among Alaska's Giants*. New York: E. P. Dutton.

Blix, A. S., and J. W. Lentfer. 1979. Modes of thermal protection in polar bear cubs—at birth and on emergence from the den. *Am. J. Physiol.* 236(1):R67–74.

Bowen, W. D., O. T. Oftedal and D. J. Boness. 1985. Birth to weaning in 4 days: Remarkable growth in the hooded seal, *Cystophora cristata*. *Can. J. Zool.* 63:2841–46.

Brody, A. J., and M. R. Pelton. 1988. Seasonal changes in digestion in black bears. *Can. J. Zool.* 66:1482–84.

Bromlei, F. G. 1965. Bears of the south far-eastern U.S.S.R. Translated from Russian in 1973 and published for the U.S. Dept. of the Interior, Washington, D.C.

Brown, A. D., and D. I. Rumiz. 1988. Habitat and distribution of the spectacled bear (*Tremarctos ornatus*) in the southern limit of its range. In *Proceedings of the First International Symposium on the Spectacled Bear*, ed. Rosenthal, M., 93–103. Chicago: Lincoln Park Zoological Gardens.

Brown, D. E. 1985. *The Grizzly in the Southwest*. Norman: University of Oklahoma Press.

Brown, L. 1976. *Eagles of the World*, London: David & Charles.

Bunnell, F. L., and D. E. N. Tait. 1985. Mortality rates of North American bears. *Arctic* 38(4):316–23.

Burghardt, G. M., R. O. Hietala and M. R. Pelton. 1972. Knowledge and attitudes concerning black bears by users of The Great Smoky Mountains National Park. *Int. Conf. Bear Res. and Manage.* 2:255–73.

Burst, T. L. 1979. An analysis of trees marked by black bears in the Great Smoky Mountains National Park. Master's thesis, University of Tennessee, Knoxville.

Burst, T. L., and M. R. Pelton. 1983. Black bear mark trees in the Smoky Mountains. *Int. Conf. Bear Res. and Manage.* 5:45–53.

Burt, W. H. 1943. Territory and home range concepts as applied to mammals. *J. Mamm.* 24:346–52.

Calvert, W., and I. Stirling. 1990. Interactions between polar bears and overwintering walruses in the Central Canadian High Arctic. *Int. Conf. Bear Res. and Manage.* 8:351–56.

Chapman, J. A. 1955. Ladybird beetles and army cutworm adults as food for grizzly bears in Montana. *Ecology* 36(1):156–58.

Chien, S., P. R. Oeltgen, J. N. Diana, X. Shi, S. P.

Nilekani and R. Salley. 1991. Two-day preservation of major organs with autoperfusion multiorgan preparation and hibernation induction trigger. *J. Thorac. Cardiovasc. Surg.* 102:224–34.

Chorn, J., and R. S. Hoffman 1978 *Ailuropoda melanoleuca.* Mammalian Species No. 110. Provo, Utah: American Society of Mammalogists.

Clarke, S. H., J. O'Pezio and C. Hackford. 1980. Fostering black bears cubs in the wild. *Int. Conf. Bear Res. and Manage.* 4:163–66.

Clarkson, P., and I. Liepins. 1989. *Inuvialiut wildlife studies, grizzly bear research progress report, 1988–1989.* Technical Report No. 8. Wildlife Management Advisory Council, Dept. of Renewable Resources, Government of N.W.T., Inuvik.

Clevenger, A. P., F. J. Purroy and M. R. Pelton. 1990. Movement and activity patterns of a European brown bear in the Cantabrian Mountains, Spain. *Int. Conf. Bear Res. and Manage.* 8:205–11.

Cowan, I. McT. 1938. Geographic distribution of colour phases of the red fox and black bear in the Pacific Northwest. *J. Mamm.* 19:202–6.

Craighead, F. C., and J. J. Craighead. 1972. *Grizzly bear prehibernation and denning activities as determined by radiotracking.* Wildl. Monographs No. 32.

Craighead, J. J., F. C. Craighead and J. Sumner. 1976. Reproductive cycles and rates in the grizzly bear, *Ursus arctos horribilis,* of the Yellowstone ecosystem. *Int. Bear Res. and Manage.* 3:337–56.

Craighead, J. J., and J. A. Mitchell. 1982. Grizzly bear, *Ursus arctos.* In *Wild Mammals of North America— Biology, Management, and Economics,* ed. Chapman, J. A., and G. A. Feldhamer, 515–56. Baltimore: Johns Hopkins University Press.

Daniel, J. C. 1974. Conditions associated with embryonic diapause during reproduction in the black bear. *East. Workshop Black Bear Manage. and Res.* 2:103–7.

Danvir, R., F. Lindzey and G. Chapman. 1983. The black bear in Utah—1983: A survey. Utah Cooperative Wildlife Research Unit, Logan. Unpublished.

Darling, L. M. 1987. Habitat use by grizzly bear family groups in interior Alaska. *Int. Conf. Bear Res. and Manage.* 7:169–78.

Dawkins, R. 1989. *The Selfish Gene.* 2d. ed. New York, Oxford University Press.

Dean, F. C., L. M. Darling and A. G. Lierhaus. 1986. Observations of intraspecific killing by brown bears, *Ursus arctos. Can. Field Nat.* 100(2):208–11.

DeMaster, D. P., and I. Stirling. 1981. *Ursus maritimus.* Mammalian Species No. 145. American Society of Mammalogists.

Derocher, A. E. 1990. Supernumerary mammae and nipples in the polar bear (*Ursus maritimus*). *J. Mamm.* 71(2):236–37.

Derocher, A. E., R. A. Nelson, I. Stirling and M. A. Ramsay. 1990. Effects of fasting and feeding on serum urea and serum creatinine levels in polar bears. *Marine Mammal Science* 6(3):196–203.

Derocher, A. E., and I. Stirling. 1990a. Distribution of polar bears (*Ursus maritimus*) during the ice-free period in western Hudson Bay. *Can. J. Zool.* 68:1395–1403.

————. 1990b. Observations of aggregating behaviour in adult male polar bears (*Ursus maritimus*). *Can. J. Zool.* 68:1390–94.

Diamond, M. 1970. Intromission pattern and species vaginal code in relation to induction of pseudopregnancy. *Science* 169:995–97.

Dierenfeld, E. S., H. F. Hintz, J. B. Robertson, P. J. Van Soest and O. T. Oftedal. 1982. Utilization of bamboo by the giant panda. *J. Nutr.* 112:636–41.

Egbert, A. L., and A. W. Stokes. 1974. The social behaviour of brown bears on an Alaskan salmon stream. *Int. Conf. Bear Res. and Manage.* 3:41–56.

Eley, T. J. 1978. An analysis of polar bear predation on ice pinniped populations of Alaska. Unpublished report, Alaska Department of Fish and Game, Fairbanks.

Elgmork, K. 1982. Caching behavior of brown bears (*Ursus arctos*). *J. Mamm.* 63(4):607–12.

Elowe, K. D. 1987. Factors affecting black bear reproductive success and cub survival in Massachusetts. Ph.D. diss., University of Massachusetts.

Elton, C. S. 1954. Further evidence about the barren-ground grizzly bear in northeast Labrador and Quebec. *J. Mamm.* 35(3):345–56.

Erickson, A. W. 1959. The age of self-sufficiency in the black bear. *J. Wildl. Manage.* 23(4):401–5.

Ewer, R. F. 1973. *The Carnivores.* London: Weidenfeld and Nicolson. Ewers, J. C. 1955. The bear cult among the Assiniboin and their neighbours of the northern plains. *Southwestern Journal of Anthropology* 11(1):1–13.

Fagen, R., and J. Fagan. 1990. Play behavior of brown bears (*Ursus arctos*) and human presence at Pack Creek, Admiralty Island, Alaska. *Int. Conf. Bear Res. and Manage.* 8:315–19.

Fair, J. S. 1978. Unusual dispersal of black bears in Utah. *J. Wildl. Manage.* 42(3):642–44.

Fay, F. H. 1982. *Ecology and biology of the Pacific walrus, Odobenus rosmarus divergens.* North American Fauna, No. 74. Washington, D.C.: U.S. Department of the Interior.

Feltz, E. T., and F. H. Fay. 1966. Thermal requirements of *in vitro* epidermal cells from seals. *Cryobiology* 3(3):261–64.

Finley, K. J. 1979. Haul-out behaviour and densities of ringed seals (*Phoca hispida*) in the Barrow Strait area, N.W.T. *Can. J. Zool.* 57:1985–97.

Floyd, T., R. A. Nelson and G. F. Wynne. 1990. Calcium and bone metabolic homeostasis in active and denning black bears (*Ursus americanus*). *Clinical Orthopedics and Related Research* 255:301–9.

Folk, G. E. 1967. Physiological observations of subarctic bears under winter den conditions. In *Mammalian Hibernation III,* 75–86. New York: American Elsevier.

Frame, G. W. 1974. Black bear predation on salmon at Olsen Creek, Alaska. *Z. Tierpsychol.* 35:23–38.

Franzmann, A. W., C. C. Schwartz and R. O. Peterson. 1980. Moose calf mortality in summer on the Kenai Peninsula, Alaska. *J. Wildl. Manage.* 44(3):764–68.

Freeman, M. M. R. 1973. Polar bear predation on beluga in the Canadian Arctic. *Arctic* 26:162–63.

French, A. R. 1988. The patterns of mammalian hibernation. *American Scientist* 76:569–75.

French, S. P., and M. G. French. 1990. Predatory behavior of grizzly bears feeding on elk calves in Yellowstone National Park, 1986–1988. *Int. Conf. Bear Res. and Manage.* 8:335–41.

Frisch, J., N. A. Oritsland and J. Krog. 1974. Insulation of furs in water. *Biochem. Physiol.* 47A:403–7.

Furnell, D. J., and D. Oolooyuk. 1980. Polar bear predation on ringed seals in ice-free water. *Can. Field Nat.* 94:88–89.

Garner, N. P., and M. R. Vaughan. 1987. Black bears' use of abandoned homesites in Shenandoah National Park. *Int. Conf. Bear Res. and Manage.* 7:151–57.

Garshelis, D. L., and M. R. Pelton. 1980. Activity of black bears in the Great Smoky Mountains National Park. *J. Mamm.* 61(1):8–19.

Gebhard, J. G. 1982. Annual activities and behavior of a grizzly bear (*Ursus arctos*) family in northern Alaska. Master's thesis. University of Alaska, Fairbanks.

Geist, V. 1986. Did large predators keep humans out of North America? World Archeological Congress, Southampton, England. Unpublished.

Gittleman, J. L., and O. T. Oftedal. 1987. Comparative growth and lactation energetics in carnivores. *Symp. Zool. Soc. London* 57:41–77.

Glenn, L. P. 1980. Morphometric characteristics of brown bears on the central Alaska Peninsula. *Int. Conf. Bear Res. and Manage.* 4:313–19.

Glenn, L. P., J. W. Lentfer, J. B. Faro and L. H. Miller. 1976. Reproductive biology of female brown bears (*Ursus arctos*), McNeil River, Alaska. *Int. Conf. Bear Res. and Manage.* 3:381–90.

Goldman, D., P. R. Giri and S. J. O'Brien. 1989. Molecular genetic-distance estimates among the Ursidae as indicated by one- and two-dimensional protein electrophoresis. *Evolution* 43(2):282–95.

Goldstein, I. 1988. Distribution, habitat use, and diet of spectacled bears (*Tremarctos ornatus*) in Venezuela. In *Proceedings of the First International Symposium on the Spectacled Bear,* ed. Rosenthal, M., 2–16. Chicago: Lincoln Park Zoological Gardens.

Gorman, M. L., and B. J. Trowbridge. 1989. The role of odours in the social lives of carnivores. In *Carnivore Behavior, Ecology, and Evolution,* ed. Gittleman, J. L., 57–88 Ithaca: Cornell University Press.

Grenfell, W. E., and A. J. Brody. 1983. Seasonal foods of black bears in Tahoe National Forest, California. *Calif. Fish and Game* 69(3):132–50.

Griffin, D. R. 1984. *Animal Thinking.* Cambridge, Mass.: Harvard University Press.

Guangmei, Z., W. Huadong and X. Jialin. 1990. *The Natural History of China*. Toronto: McGraw-Hill Ryerson.

Hallowell, A. I. 1926. Bear ceremonialism in the northern hemisphere. *American Antiquity* 28(1):1–175.

Hamer, D., and S. Herrero. 1990. Courtship and use of mating areas by grizzly bears in the Front Ranges of Banff National Park, Alberta. *Can. J. Zool.* 68:2695–97.

Hamilton, R. J., and R. L. Marchinton. 1980. Denning and related activities of black bears in the coastal plain of North Carolina. *Int. Conf. Bear Res. and Manage.* 4:121–26.

Hansson, R., and J. Thomassen. 1983. Behavior of polar bears with cubs in the denning area. *Int. Conf. Bear Res. and Manage.* 5:246–54.

Harding, L. E. 1976. Den-site characteristics of arctic coastal grizzly bears (*Ursus arctos*) on Richards Island, Northwest Territories, Canada. *Can. J. Zool.* 54:1357–63.

Harington, C. R. 1968. *Denning habits of the polar bear (Ursus maritimus)*. Report Series No. 5. Ottawa: Canadian Wildlife Service.

Hatler, D. F. 1972. Food habits of black bears in Interior Alaska. *Can. Field Nat.* 86:17–31.

Hausfater, G., and S. Blaffer Hrdy. 1984. *Infanticide—Comparative and Evolutionary Perspectives*. New York: Aldine.

Hellgren, E. C., M. R. Vaughan, F. C. Gwazdauskas and B. Williams, and P. F. Scanlon and R. L. Kirkpatrick. 1990. Endocrine and electrophoretic profiles during pregnancy and nonpregnancy in captive female black bears. *Can. J. Zool.* 69:892–98.

Hemmingsen, E. A., and E. L. Douglas. 1970. Ultraviolet radiation thresholds for corneal injury in Antarctic and temperate-zone animals. *Comp. Biochem. Physiol.* 32:593–600.

Henry, J. D., and S. M. Herrero. 1974. Social play in the American black bear: Its similarities to canid social play and an examination of its identifying characteristics. *Amer. Zool.* 14:371–89.

Henshaw, R. E., L. S. Underwood and T. M. Casey. 1972. Peripheral thermoregulation: Foot temperature in two arctic canines. *Science* 175:988–90.

Herrero, S. 1972. Aspects of evolution and adaptation in American black bears (*Ursus americanus* Pallas) and brown and grizzly bears (*U. arctos* Linné.) of North America. *Int. Conf. Bear Res. and Manage.* 2:221–31.

———. 1983. Social behaviour of black bears at a garbage dump in Jasper National Park. *Int. Conf. Bear Res. and Manage.* 5:54–70.

Heyland, J. D., and K. Hay. 1976. An attack by a polar bear on a juvenile beluga. *Arctic* 29(1):56–57.

Horejsi, B. L., G. E. Hornbeck and R. M. Raine. 1984. Wolves, *Canis lupus*, kill female black bear, *Ursus americanus*, in Alberta. *Can. Field Nat.* 98(3):368–69.

Horner, R. A. 1976. Sea ice organisms. *Oceangr. Mar. Biol. Ann. Rev.* 14:167–82.

Houston, D. B. 1978. Elk as winter-spring food for carnivores in northern Yellowstone National Park. *J. Appl. Ecol.* 15:653–61.

Hoyt, L. F. 1934. Bear grease. *Oil and Soap* 11:85–86.

Hrdy, S. F. 1979. Infanticide among animals: A review, classification, and examination of the implications for the reproductive strategies of females. *Ethology and Sociobiology* 1:13–40.

Huber, D., and H. U. Roth. 1989. Home ranges and movements of brown bears in Croatia, Yugoslavia. *Abstract, 8th Int. Conf. Bear Res. and Manage.*

Jenness, R., A. W. Erickson and J. J. Craighead. 1972. Some comparative aspects of milk from four species of bears. *J. Mamm.* 53(1):34–47.

Johnson, G. J., and M. R. Pelton. 1981. Selection and availability of dens for black bears in Tennessee. *J. Wildl. Manage.* 45(1):111–19.

Johnson, K. G., D. O. Johnson and M. R. Pelton. 1978. Simulation of winter heat loss for a black bear in a closed tree den. *Proc. Eastern Black Bear Workshop* 4:155–66.

Johnson, K. G., and M. R. Pelton. 1980. Environmental relationships and the denning period of black bears in Tennessee. *J. Mamm.* 61(4):653–60.

Johnson, K. G., G. B. Schaller and H. Jinchu. 1988a. Comparative behavior of red and giant pandas in the Wolong Reserve, China. *J. Mamm.* 69(3):552–64.

———. 1988b. Responses of giant pandas to a bamboo die-off. *National Geographic Research* 4(2):161–77.

Jonkel, C. J., G. B. Kolenosky, R. J. Robertson and R. H. Russell. 1972. Further notes on polar bear denning habits. *Int. Conf. Bear Res. and Manage.* 2:142–58.

Jonkel, C. J., and I. McT. Cowan. 1971. *The black bear in the spruce-fir forest*. Wildl. Monogr. No. 27.

Jonkel, J., and F. L. Miller. 1970. Recent record of black bears (*Ursus americanus*) on the barren grounds of Canada. *J. Mamm.* 51(4):826–28.

Jordan, R. H. 1976. Threat behavior of the black bear (*Ursus americanus*). *Int. Conf. Bear Res. and Manage.* 3:57–63.

Judd, S. L., R. R. Knight and B. M. Blanchard. 1986. Denning of grizzly bears in the Yellowstone National Park area. *Int. Conf. Bear Res. and Manage.* 6:111–17.

Kansas, J. L., R. M. Raine and M. L. Gibeau. 1989. Ecological studies of the black bear in Banff National Park, Alberta, 1986–1988. Unpublished report, Canadian Parks Service.

Kendall, K. C. 1983. Use of pine nuts by grizzly bears and black bears in the Yellowstone area. *Int. Conf. Bear Res. and Manage.* 5:166–73.

Kendall, K. C., and S. F. Arno. 1990. Whitebark pine—an important but endangered wildlife resource. In *Proceedings—Symposium on Whitebark Pine Ecosystems: Ecology and Management of a High-Mountain Resource*, 264–73. Ogden, Utah: Intermountain Research Station, U.S. Dept. Agriculture.

Kiliaan, H. P. L., I. Stirling and C. J. Jonkel. 1978. *Polar bears in the area of Jones Sound and Norwegian Bay*. Canadian Wildlife Service, Progress Notes No. 88.

Knudsen, B. 1978. Time budgets of polar bears (*Ursus maritimus*) on North Twin Island, James Bay, during summer. *Can. J. Zool.* 56:1627–28.

Kolenosky, G. B., and J. P. Prevett. 1983. Productivity and maternity denning of polar bears in Ontario. *Int. Conf. Bear Res. and Manage.* 5:238–45.

Kolenosky, G. B., and S. M. Strathearn. 1987. Winter denning of black bears in east-central Ontario. *Int. Conf. Bear Res. and Manage.* 7:305–16.

Kordek, W. S., and J. S. Lindzey. 1980. Preliminary analysis of female reproductive tracts from Pennsylvania black bears. *Int. Conf. Bear Res. and Manage.* 4:159–61.

Kurtén, B. 1964. The evolution of the polar bear *Ursus maritimus* Phipps. *Acta Zoologica Fennica* 108:2–30.

———. (1976) *The Cave Bear Story—Life and Death of a Vanished Animal*. New York: Columbia University Press.

Kurtén, B., and E. Anderson. 1980. *Pleistocene Mammals of North America*. New York: Columbia University Press.

Landers, J. L., R. J. Hamilton, A. S. Johnston and R. L. Marchinton. 1979. Foods and habitats of black bears in southeastern North Carolina. *J. Wildl. Manage.* 43(1):143–53.

Larsen, T. 1985. Polar bear denning and cub production in Svalbard, Norway. *J. Wildl. Manage.* 49(2):320–26.

———. 1986. Population biology of the polar bear (*Ursus maritimus*) in the Svalbard area. *Skrifter* Nr.184. Norsk Polarinstitutt.

Latour, P. B. 1981a. Spatial relationships and behavior of polar bears (*Ursus maritimus* Phipps) concentrated on land during the ice-free season of Hudson Bay. *Can. J. Zool.* 59:1763–74.

———. 1981b. Interactions between free-ranging, adult male polar bears (*Ursus maritimus* Phipps): A case of adult social play. *Can. J. Zool.* 59:1775–83.

Laurie, A., and J. Seidensticker. 1977. Behavioural ecology of the sloth bear (*Melursus ursinus*). *J. Zool. Lond.* 182:187–204.

LeCount, A. L. 1987. Causes of black bear cub mortality. *Int. Conf. Bear Res. and Manage.* 7:75–82.

Lekagul, B., and J. A. McNeely. 1977. *Mammals of Thailand*. Bangkok: Sahakarnbhat.

Lentfer, J. W. 1975. Polar bear denning on drifting sea ice. *J. Mamm.* 56(3):716–18.

Lentfer, J. W., and R. J. Hensel. 1980. Alaskan polar bear denning. *Int. Conf. Bear Res. and Manage.* 4:101–8.

Lentz, W. M., R. L. Marchinton and R. E. Smith. 1983. Thermodynamic analysis of northeastern Georgia black bear dens. *J. Wildl. Manage.* 47(2):545–50.

Lewin, R. A., and P. T. Robinson. 1979. The greening of polar bears in zoos. *Nature* 278:445–47.

Lindley, P. F., and M. C. Carey. 1987. Molecular packing of bile acids: Structure of ursodeoxycholic acid. *J. Crystallographic and Spectroscopic Research* 17(2):231–49.

Lindzey, F. G., and E. C. Meslow. 1976a. Winter dormancy in black bears on southwestern Washington.

J. Wildl. Manage. 40(3):408–15.

——. 1976b. Characteristics of black bear dens on Long Island, Washington. *Northwest Sci.* 50:236–42.

Lono, O. 1970. The polar bear (*Ursus maritimus* Phipps) in the Svalbard area. Norsk Polarinstitutt Skrifter Nr. 149. 102 pp.

Lowry, L. F., J. J. Burns and R. R. Nelson. 1987. Polar bear, *Ursus maritimus*, predation on belugas, *Delphinapterus leucas*, in the Bering and Chukchi seas. *Can. Field Nat.* 101(2):141–46.

Luque, M. H., and A. W. Allen. 1976. Fishing behaviour of Alaska brown bear. *Int. Conf. Bear Res. and Manage.* 3:71–78.

Lyman, C. P., J. S. Willis, A. Malan and L. C. H. Wang. 1982. *Hibernation and Torpor in Mammals and Birds.* New York: Academic Press.

Macdonald, D. 1984. *The Encyclopedia of Mammals.* New York: Facts on File.

McKelvey, R. W., and D. W. Smith. 1979. A black bear in a bald eagle nest. *Murrelet* 106–7.

MacKinnon, J., and Q. Minjang. 1986. Masterplan for saving the giant panda and its habitat. Unpublished. Joint Report, Chinese Ministry of Forestry and World Wildlife Fund.

McNab, B. K. 1984. Physiological convergence amongst ant-eating and termite eating mammals. *J. Zool. Lond.* 203:485–510.

——. 1991. Rate of metabolism in the termite-eating sloth bear (*Ursus ursinus*). *J. Mamm.* In Press.

Maehr, D. S. 1984. The black bear as a seed disperser in Florida. *Florida Field Naturalist* 12:40–42.

Magoun, A. J. 1979. Summer scavenging activity in northeastern Alaska. *National Park Service Trans. Proc. Ser.* 5:335–40.

Manning, D. P., J. E. Cooper, I. Stirling, C. M. Jones, M. Bruce and P. C. McCausland. 1985. Studies on the footpads of the polar bear (*Ursus maritimus*) and their possible relevance to accident prevention. *J. Hand Surg.* 10B(3):303–7.

Matheson, C. 1942. Man and bear in Europe. *Antiquity* 16:151–59.

Mathews, N. E., and W. F. Porter. 1988. Black bear predation of white-tailed deer neonates in the central Adirondacks. *Can. J. Zool.* 66:1241–42.

Matjushkin, E. N., V. I. Zhivotchenko and E. N. Smirnov. 1980. *The Amur tiger in the U.S.S.R.* Central Laboratory on Nature Conservation of the U.S.S.R., Sikhote-Alin State Reserve. Translated from Russian by the IUCN, Gland, Switzerland.

Matson, J. R. 1954. Observations on the dormant phase of a female black bear. *J. Mamm.* 35:28–35.

Mattson, D. J., and C. Jonkel. 1990. Stone pines and bears. In *Proceedings—Symposium on Whitebark Pine Ecosystems: Ecology and Management of a High-Mountain Resource*, 223–26. Ogden, Utah: Intermountain Research Station, U.S. Dept. Agriculture.

Mead, R. A. 1989. The physiology and evolution of

delayed implantation in carnivores. In *Carnivore Behavior, Ecology and Evolution*, ed. Gittleman, J. L., 437–64. Ithaca: Cornell University Press.

Mealey, S. P. 1980. The natural food habits of grizzly bears in Yellowstone National Park. *Int. Conf. Bear Res. and Manage.* 4:281–92.

Merriam, C. H. 1918. *Review of the grizzly and big brown bears of North America (genus Ursus) with a description of a new genus, Velularctos.* North American Fauna No. 41. Washington, D.C.: U.S. Dept. Agr. Bureau of Biological Survey, Government Printing Office.

Miller, S. J., N. Barichello and D. Tait. 1982. *The grizzly bears of the Mackenzie Mountains, Northwest Territories.* Completion Report No. 3. Yellowknife: N.W.T. Wildlife Service.

Mills, J. 1991. I want to eat sun bear. *International Wildlife* January/February: 39–43.

Morris, R., and D. Morris. Revised by J. Barzdo. 1982. *The Giant Panda.* New York: Penguin Books.

Murie, A. 1937. Some food habits of the black bear. *J. Mamm.* 18(2):238–40.

——. 1981. *The grizzlies of Mount McKinley.* Seattle: University of Washington Press. Originally published as Scientific Monograph Series No. 14. National Parks Service, U.S. Dept. of the Interior.

Nagy, J. A., R. H. Russell, A. M. Pearson, M. C. S. Kingsley and C. B. Larsen. 1983. A study of grizzly bears on the barren-grounds of Tuktoyaktuk Peninsula and Richards Island, Northwest Territories, 1974–1978. Canadian Wildlife Service. Unpublished.

Nash, W. G., and S. J. O'Brien. 1987. A comparative chromosome banding analysis of the Ursidae and their relationship to other carnivores. *Cytogenet. Cell Genet.* 45:206–12.

Nelson, J. N. 1957. Bear cub taken by an eagle. *Victoria Naturalist* 14(5):62–63.

Nelson, R. A. 1987. Black bears and polar bears—still metabolic marvels. *Mayo Clin. Proc.* 62:850–53.

Nelson, R. A., and T. D. I. Beck. 1984. Hibernation adaptation in the black bear: Implications for management. *Proc. East. Workshop Black Bear Manage. and Res.* 7:48–53.

Nelson, R. A., G. E. Folk, E. W. Pfeiffer, J. J. Craighead, C. J. Jonkel and D. L. Steiger. 1983. Behavior, biochemistry, and hibernation in black, grizzly, and polar bears. *Int. Conf. Bear Res. and Manage.* 5:284–90.

Nelson, R. A., H. W. Wahner, J. D. Jones, R. D. Ellefson and P. E. Zollman. 1973. Metabolism of bears before, during, and after winter sleep. *Am. J. Physiol.* 224:491–96.

Northcott, T. M., and F. E. Elsey. 1971. Fluctuations in black bear populations and their relationship to climate. *Can. Field Nat.* 85:123–28.

Nowak, R. M., and J. L. Paradiso. 1983. *Walker's Mammals of the World*, Vols. I & II. 4th ed. Baltimore: Johns Hopkins University Press.

Nozaki, E., S. Azuma, T. Aoi, H. Torii, T. Ito and K.

Maeda. 1983. Food habits of the Japanese black bear. *Int. Conf. Bear Res. and Manage.* 5:106–9.

Oeltgen, P. R., R. A. Blouin, W. A. Spurrier and R. D. Myers. 1985. Hibernation "trigger" alters renal function in the primate. *Physiology and Behavior* 34:79–81.

Oftedal, O. T., and J. L. Gittleman. 1989. Patterns of energy output during reproduction in carnivores. In *Carnivore Behavior, Ecology, and Evolution*, ed. Gittleman, J. L., 355–78. Ithaca: Cornell University Press.

Orejuela, J. E. 1988. La Planada Nature Reserve and the conservation of spectacled bears in Columbia. In *Proceedings of the First International Symposium on the Spectacled Bear*, ed. Rosenthal, M., 60–73. Chicago: Lincoln Park Zoological Gardens.

Oritsland, N. A. 1970. Temperature regulation of the polar bear (*Thalarctos maritimus*). *Comp. Biochem. Physiol.* 37:225–33.

Oritsland, N. A., F. R. Engelhardt, F. A. Juck, R. J. Hurst and P. D. Watts. 1981. *Effect of crude oil on polar bears.* Environmental Studies No. 24. Ottawa: Northern Affairs Program, Indian and Northern Affairs Canada.

Palmer, R. S., ed. 1988a. *Handbook of North American Birds*, Vol. 4, *Diurnal Raptors—Part 1.* New Haven: Yale University Press.

——. 1988b. *Handbook of North American Birds*, Vol. 5, *Diurnal Raptors—Part 2.* New Haven: Yale University Press.

Paquet, P. C., and L. N. Carbyn. 1986. Wolves, *Canis lupus*, killing denning black bears, *Ursus americanus*, in the Riding Mountain National Park Area. *Can. Field Nat.* 100(3):371–72.

Pearson, A. M. 1975. *The northern interior grizzly bear Ursus arctos.* Report Series No. 34. Canadian Wildlife Service.

Pelton, M. R. 1982. Black bear, *Ursus americanus*. In *Wild Mammals of North America—Biology, Management, and Economics*, ed. Chapman, J. A., and G. A. Feldhamer, 504–14. Baltimore: Johns Hopkins University Press.

Pelton, M. R., L. E. Beeman and D. C. Eager. 1980. Den selection by black bears in the Great Smoky Mountains National Park. *Int. Conf. Bear Res. and Manage.* 4:149–51.

Percy, J. 1989. Piranhas of the frozen seas. *Nature Canada.* Winter: 8–9.

Peterson, R. O., J. D. Woolington and T. N. Bailey. 1984. *Wolves of the Kenai Peninsula, Alaska.* Wildl. Monographs No. 88.

Peyton, B. 1980. Ecology, distribution, and food habits of spectacled bears, *Tremarctos ornatus*, in Peru. *J. Mamm.* 61(4):639–52.

——. 1987. Bear in the eyebrow of the jungle. *Animal Kingdom*, March/April: 38–45.

Poelker, R. J., and H. D. Hartwell. 1973. *Black bear of Washington.* Biological Bulletin No. 14. Washington State Game Dept.

Popov, L. A. 1976. Cited in Quakenbush, L. T. 1988.

Spotted seal. In *Selected Marine Mammals of Alaska: Species Accounts with Research and Management Recommendations*. Washington, D.C.: Marine Mammal Commission.

Prater, S. H. 1971. *The Book of Indian Animals*. 3d ed. Bombay: Bombay Natural History Society.

Pruitt, C. H. 1976. Play and agonistic behavior in young captive black bears. *Int. Conf. Bear Res. and Manage.* 3:79–86.

Pulliainen, E. 1972. Distribution and population structure of the bear (*Ursus arctos*) in Finland. *Ann. Zool. Fennici* 9:199–207.

Radman, M. A. 1969. Chemical composition of the sapwood of four tree species in relation to feeding by the black bear. *Forest Science* 15(1):11–15.

Raine, R. M., and J. L. Kansas. 1990. Black bear food habits and distribution by elevation in Banff National Park, Alberta. *Int. Conf. Bear Res. and Manage.* 8:297–304.

Ramsay, M. A., and D. S. Andriashek. 1986. Long distance route orientation of female polar bears (*Ursus maritimus*) in spring. *J. Zool. Lond.* (A) 208:63–72.

Ramsay, M. A., and R. L. Dunbrack. 1986. Physiological constraints on life history phenomena: The example of small bear cubs at birth. *American Naturalist* 127(6):735–43.

Ramsay, M. A., and I. Stirling. 1986. On the mating system of polar bears. *Can. J. Zool.* 64:2142–51.

———. 1988. Reproductive biology and ecology of female polar bears (*Ursus maritimus*). *J. Zool. Lond.* 214:601–34.

Reynolds, H. V., J. A. Curatolo and R. Quimby. 1976. Denning ecology of grizzly bears in northeastern Alaska. *Int. Conf. Bear Res. and Manage.* 3:403–9.

Reynolds, H. V., and J. Hechtel. 1979. Structure, status, reproductive biology, movement, distribution and habitat utilization of a grizzly bear population. Vol. 1, *North Slope Grizzly Bear Studies, July 1978–June 1979*. Juneau: Alaska Dept. of Fish and Game.

Reynolds, D. G., and J. J. Beecham. 1980. Home range activities and reproduction of black bears in west-central Idaho. *Int. Conf. Bear Res. and Manage.* 4:181–90.

Reynolds, H. V., and G. W. Garner. 1987. Patterns of grizzly bear predation on caribou in northern Alaska. *Int. Conf. Bear Res. and Manage.* 7:59–67.

Richie, D. 1988. The great Montana bear binge. *National Wildlife*, April/May: 28.

Roberts, M. S., and J. L. Gittleman. 1984. *Ailurus fulgens*. Mammalian Species No. 222. Provo, Utah: American Society of Mammalogists.

Rogers, L. L. 1974. Shedding of foot pads by black bears during denning. *J. Mamm.* 55(3):672–74.

———. 1978. Effects of food supply, predation, cannibalism, parasites, and other health problems on black bear populations. *Symposium on Natural Regulation of Wildlife Populations*: 194–211.

———. 1980. Inheritance of coat colour and changes in pelage coloration in black bears in northeastern Minnesota. *J. Mamm.* 61(2):324–26.

———. 1981. A bear in its lair. *Natural History* 90(10):64–70.

———. 1987. *Effects of food supply and kinship on social behavior, movements, and population growth of black bears in northeastern Minnesota*. Wildl. Monographs No. 97.

Rogers, L. L., and L. D. Mech. 1981. Interactions of wolves and black bears in northeastern Minnesota. *J. Mamm.* 62(2):434–36.

Rogers, L. L., and R. D. Applegate. 1983. Dispersal of fruit seeds by black bears. *J. Mamm.* 64(2):310–11.

Rogers, L. L., and S. C. Durst. 1987. Evidence that black bears reduce peripheral blood flow during hibernation. *J. Mamm.* 68(4):876–78.

Rogers, L. L., and G. W. Wilker. 1990. How to obtain behavioral and ecological data from free-ranging, researcher-habituated black bears. *Int. Conf. Bear Res. and Manage.* 8:321–27.

Ronald, K., and J. Lee. 1981. Spectral sensitivity of a polar bear. *Comp. Biochem. Physiol.* 70A:595–98. Ross, P. I., G. E. Hornbeck and B. L. Horejsi. 1988. Late denning black bears killed by grizzly bear. *J. Mamm.* 69(4):818–20.

Roth, H. U. 1983. Diel activity of a remnant population of European brown bears. *Int. Conf. Bear Res. and Manage.* 5:223–29.

Rounds, R. C. 1987. Distribution and analysis of colourmorphs of the black bear (*Ursus americanus*). *Journal of Biogeography* 14:521–38.

Rowan, W. 1947. A case of six cubs in the common black bear. *J. Mamm.* 28(4):404–5.

Russell, R. H. 1975. The food habits of polar bears of James Bay and southwest Hudson Bay in summer and autumn. *Arctic* 28:117–29.

Russell, R. H., J. W. Nolan, N. A. Woody and G. Anderson. 1979. *A study of the grizzly bear* (Ursus arctos) *in Jasper National Park, 1975–1979*. Final Report. Ottawa: Canadian Wildlife Service.

Savage, R. J. G. 1977. Evolution in carnivorous mammals. *Palaeontology* 20(2):237–71.

Schaller, G. B., H. Jinchu, P. Wenshi and Z. Jing. 1985. *The Giant Pandas of Wolong*. Chicago: University of Chicago Press.

Schaller, G. B., T. Qitao, K. G. Johnson, W. Xiaoming, S. Heming and H. Jinchu. 1989. The feeding ecology of giant pandas and Asiatic black bears in the Tiangjiahe Reserve, China. In *Carnivore Behavior, Ecology, and Evolution*, ed. Gittleman, J. L., 212–41. Ithaca: Cornell University Press.

Schlegel, M. W. 1976. Factors affecting calf elk survival in north-central Idaho: A progress report. *Annu. Conf. West Assoc. State Game and Fish Comm.* 56:342–55.

Schoen, J. W., L. R. Beier, J. W. Lentfer and L. J. Johnson. 1987. Denning ecology of brown bears on Admiralty and Chichagof Islands. *Int. Conf. Bear Res.*

and Manage. 7:293–304.

Schwartz, C. C., S. D. Miller and A. W. Franzmann. 1987. Denning ecology of three black bear populations in Alaska. *Int. Conf. Bear Res. and Manage.* 7:281–91.

Schweinsburg, R. E. 1979. Summer snow dens used by polar bears in the Canadian High Arctic. *Arctic* 32(2):165–69.

Schweinsburg, R. E., W. Spencer and D. Williams. 1984. Polar bear denning area at Gateshead Island, Northwest Territories. *Arctic* 37(2):169–71.

Scott, R. F., K. W. Kenyon, J. L. Buckley and S. T. Olson. 1959. Status and management of the polar bear and Pacific walrus. *North American Wildl. Conf.* 24:366–74.

Servheen, C. 1990. *The Status and Conservation of the Bears of the World*. Int. Conf. Bear Res. and Manage. Monogr. Series No. 2.

Servheen, C., and R. Klaver. 1983. Grizzly bear dens and denning activity in the Mission and Rattlesnake mountains, Montana. *Int. Conf. Bear Res. and Manage.* 5:201–7.

Sharafutdinov, I. Y., and A. M. Korotkov. 1976. On the ecology of the brown bear in the southern Urals. *Int. Conf. Bear Res. and Manage.* 3:309–11.

Shepard, P., and B. Sanders. 1985. *The Sacred Paw—The Bear in Nature, Myth and Literature*. New York: Viking.

Sivak, J. G., and D. J. Piggins. 1975. Refractive state of the eye of the polar bear (*Thalarctos maritimus*). *Norwegian J. Zool.* 23(1):89–91.

Slobodyan, A. A. 1976. The European brown bear in the Carpathians. *Int. Conf. Bear Res. and Manage.* 3:313–19.

Smith, T. G. 1980. Polar bear predation of ringed and bearded seals in the land-fast sea ice habitat. *Can. J. Zool.* 58:2201–9.

Smith, T. G., and M. O. Hammill. 1981. Ecology of the ringed seal, *Phoca hispida*, in its fast ice breeding habitat. *Can. J. Zool.* 59:966–81.

Smith, T. G., and B. Sjare. 1990. Predation of belugas and narwhals by polar bears in nearshore areas of the Canadian High Arctic. *Arctic* 43(2):99–102.

Smith, T. G., and I. Stirling. 1975. The breeding habitat of the ringed seal (*Phoca hispica*). The birth lair and associated structures. *Can. J. Zool.* 53:1297–1305.

Sorensen, O. J. 1989. Norwegian Institute of Nature Research, Personal Communication.

Stalmaster, M. V. 1987. *The Bald Eagle*. New York: Universe Books.

St. Aubin, D. J. 1990. Physiologic and toxic effects on polar bears. In *Sea Mammals and Oil: Confronting the Risks*, ed. Geraci, J. R., and D. J. St. Aubin, 235–39. New York: Academic Press.

Stirling, I. 1974. Midsummer observations on the behavior of wild polar bears, *Ursus maritimus. Can. J. Zool.* 52:1191–98.

———. 1980. The biological importance of polynyas in the Canadian Arctic. *Arctic* 33(2):303–15.

———. 1984. A group threat display given by walruses to a

polar bear. *J. Mamm.* 65(2):352–53.

——. 1990. Polar bears and oil: Ecological perspectives. In *Sea Mammals and Oil: Confronting the Risks*, ed. Geraci, J. R., and D. J. St. Aubin, 223–34. New York: Academic Press.

Stirling, I., D. Andriashek, P. Latour and W. Calvert. 1975. *The distribution and abundance of polar bears in the eastern Beaufort Sea.* Beaufort Sea Technical Report No. 2. Victoria, B.C.: Beaufort Sea Project, Dept. of the Environment.

Stirling, I., and W. R. Archibald. 1977. Aspects of predation of seals by polar bears. *J. Fish. Res. Board Can.* 34:1126–29.

Stirling, I., W. Calvert and D. Andriashek. 1980. *Population ecology studies of the polar bear in the area of south-eastern Baffin Island.* Occasional Paper No. 44. Ottawa: Canadian Wildlife Service.

——. 1984. Polar bear (*Ursus maritimus*) ecology and environmental considerations in the Canadian High Arctic. In *Northern Ecology and Resource Management*, ed. Olson, R. et al., 201–21. Edmonton: University of Alberta Press.

Stirling, I., and H. Cleator, eds. 1981. *Polynyas in the Canadian Arctic.* Occasional Paper No. 45. Ottawa: Canadian Wildlife Service.

Stirling, I., and A. E. Derocher. 1990. Factors affecting the evolution and behavioral ecology of the modern bears. *Int. Conf. Bear Res. and Manage.* 8:189–204.

Stirling, I., and D. Guravich. 1988. *Polar Bears.* Ann Arbor: University of Michigan Press.

Stirling, I., C. Jonkel, P. Smith, R. Robertson and D. Cross. 1977. *The ecology of the polar bear* (Ursus maritimus) *along the western coast of Hudson Bay.* Occasional Paper No. 33. Ottawa: Canadian Wildlife Service.

Stirling, I., and P. B. Latour. 1978. Comparative hunting abilitites of polar bear cubs of different ages. *Can. J. Zool.* 56:1768–72.

Stirling, I., and E. H. McEwan. 1975. The caloric value of whole ringed seals (*Phoca hispida*) in relation to polar bear (*Ursus maritimus*) ecology and hunting behavior. *Can. J. Zool.* 53:1021–27.

Stonorov, D., and A. W. Stokes. 1972. Social behavior of the Alaska brown bear. *Int. Conf. Bear Res. and Manage.* 2:232–42.

Storer, T. I., and L. P. Tevis Jr. 1955. *California Grizzly.* Berkeley: University of California Press.

Stroganov, S. U. 1962. *Carnivorous Mammals of Siberia.* Academy of Science of the U.S.S.R., Siberian Branch. Translated from Russian by Israel Program for Scientific Translations, Jerusalem, 1969.

Tait, D. E. N. 1980. Abandonment as a reproductive tactic—the example of grizzly bears. *American Naturalist* 115(6):800–808.

Tate, J., and M. R. Pelton. 1983. Human-bear interactions in Great Smoky Mountains National Park. *Int. Conf. Bear Res. and Manage.* 5:312–21.

Taylor, M., L. Larsen and R. E. Schweinsburg. 1985. Observations of intraspecific aggression and cannibalism in polar bears (*Ursus maritimus*). *Arctic* 38(4):303–9.

Taylor-Ide, D. 1984. New bear found in Nepal. International Association for Bear Research and Management, Newsletter Vol 84., Nos. 2–3. Unpublished.

Thing, H., P. Henrichsen and P. Lassen. 1984. *Status of the muskox in Greenland.* Biol. Pap. Univ. Alaska Spec. Rep. No. 4:1–6.

Tietje, W. D., B. O. Pelchat and R. L. Ruff. 1986. Cannibalism of denned black bears. *J. Mamm.* 67(4):762–66.

Troyer, W. A., and R. J. Hensel. 1962. Cannibalism in brown bear. *Animal Behavior* 10:231.

——. 1969. The brown bear of Kodiak Island. Kodiak, Alaska: U.S. Dept. Interior, Bureau of Sport Fisheries and Wildlife, Branch of Wildlife Refuges, Kodiak National Wildlife Refuge. Unpublished.

Uspenski, S. M. 1977. *The polar bear.* Moscow: Nauka. Translated by the Canadian Wildlife Service, Ottawa, 1978.

Uspenski, S. M., and S. E. Belikov. 1980. Data on the winter ecology of the polar bear in Wrangel Island. *Int. Conf. Bear Res. and Manage.* 4:119.

Uspenski, S. M., and A. A. Kistchinski. 1972. New data on the winter ecology of the polar bear (*Ursus maritimus*) on Wrangel Island. *Int. Conf. Bear Res. and Manage.* 2:181–97.

Van Daele, L. J., V. G. Barnes, Jr. and R. S. Smith. 1990. Denning characteristics of brown bears on Kodiak Island, Alaska. *Int. Conf. Bear Res. and Manage.* 8:257–67.

Van de Velde, F. 1957. Nanuk—king of the arctic beasts. *Eskimo* 45:4–18.

Vroom, G. W., S. Herrero and R. T. Ogilvie. 1980. The ecology of winter den sites of grizzly bears in Banff National Park, Alberta. *Int. Conf. Bear Res. and Manage.* 4:321–30.

Waddell, T. E., and D. E. Brown. 1984. Weights and color of black bears in the Pinaleño Mountains, Arizona. *J. Mamm.* 65(2):350–514.

Watanabe, H. 1977. Damage to conifers by Japanese black bears. *Int. Conf. Bear Res. and Manage.* 4:67–70.

Wathen, W. G., K. G. Johnson and M. R. Pelton. 1986. Characteristics of black bear dens in the southern Appalachian region. *Int. Conf. Bear Res. and Manage.* 6:119–27.

Watts, P. D. 1983. Ecological energetics of denning polar bears and related species. Ph.D. diss. Faculty of Mathematics and Natural Sciences, University of Oslo, Oslo, Norway.

Watts, P. D., N. A. Oritsland, C. Jonkel and K. Ronald. 1981. Mammalian hibernation and the oxygen consumption of a denning black bear (*Ursus americanus*). *Comp. Biochem. Physiol.* 69A:121–23.

Watts, P. D., and C. Jonkel. 1988. Energetic cost of winter

dormancy in the grizzly bear. *J. Wildl. Manage.* 52(4):654–56.

Wemmer, C., M. Von Ebers and K. Scow. 1976. An analysis of the chuffing vocalization of the polar bear (*Ursus maritimus*). *J. Zool. Lond.* 180:425–39.

Wilk, R. J., J. W. Solberg, V. D. Berns and R. A. Sellers. 1988. Brown bear, *Ursus arctos*, with six young. *Can. Field Nat.* 102(3):541–43.

Wilton, M. L. 1983. Black bear predation on young cervids—a summary. *Alces—19th North American Moose Conf. and Workshop*: 136–46.

Zunino, F., and S. Herrero. 1972. The status of the brown bear (*Ursus arctos*) in Abruzzo National Park, Italy, 1971. *Biological Conservation* 4(4):263–71.

INDEX